WORKING PAPERS
Volume I / Chapters 1-13
to accompany

ACCOUNTING
PRINCIPLES
7th Edition

JERRY J. WEYGANDT Ph.D., C.P.A.
Arthur Andersen Alumni Professor of Accounting
University of Wisconsin
Madison, Wisconsin

DONALD E. KIESO Ph.D., C.P.A.
KPMG Peat Marwick Emeritus Professor of Accountancy
Northern Illinois University
DeKalb, Illinois

PAUL D. KIMMEL Ph.D., C.P.A.
Associate Professor of Accounting
University of Wisconsin - Milwaukee
Milwaukee, Wisconsin

Prepared by
DICK D. WASSON M.B.A., C.P.A.
Southwestern College
San Diego State University
University of Phoenix

WILEY

JOHN WILEY & SONS, INC.

COVER PHOTO © Pete Turner/The Image Bank/Getty Images.

To order books or for customer service call 1-800-CALL-WILEY (225-5945).

ISBN 0-471-47726-5

Printed in the United States of America

10 9 8 7 6 5 4 3 2 1

Printed and bound by Courier Kendallville, Inc.

CONTENTS

#1		Assets	Liabilities	Owner's Equity	
1	(a)	$ 90 000	$ 50 000		1
2					2
3	(b)		45 000	70 000	3
4					4
5	(c)	94 000		65 000	5

	#2		
6	#2		6
7	(a)		7
8	(b)		8
9	(c)		9
10			10

	#3		
11	#3		11
12	(a)		12
13			13
14	(b)		14
15			15
16	(c)		16
17			17

#4		Assets	Liabilities	Owner's Equity	
18					18
19	(a)				19
20					20
21	(b)				21
22					22
23	(c)				23

#5		Assets	Liabilities	Owner's Equity	
24					24
25	(a)				25
26					26
27	(b)				27
28					28
29	(c)				29
30					30

	#6			
31	#6			31
32	(a)	(e)		32
33	(b)	(f)		33
34	(c)	(g)		34
35	(d)			35

	#7		
36	#7		36
37	(a)		37
38	(b)		38
39	(c)		39
40			40

#8		
Gomez Company		
Balance Sheet		
December 31, 2005		
Assets		
Liabilities and Owner's Equity		

#9

(a)

(b)

(c)

(d)

(e)

(f)

#10

(a)

(b)

(c)

(d)

(e)

		Asset	Liability	Owner's Equity	
#1					

#2

1.
2.
3.
4.
5.
6.
7.
8.
9.

#3

1.
2.
3.
4.
5.
6.
7.
8.

1	(a)	1
2	1.	2
3	2.	3
4		4
5	3.	5
6	4.	6
7		7
8	5.	8
9	6.	9
10	7.	10
11	8.	11
12	9.	12
13	10.	13
14		14
15		15
16		16
17		17
18		18
19		19
20		20
21	(b)	21
22		22
23		23
24		24
25		25
26		26
27		27
28		28
29		29
30		30
31	(c)	31
32		32
33		33
34		34
35		35
36		36
37		37
38		38
39		39
40		40

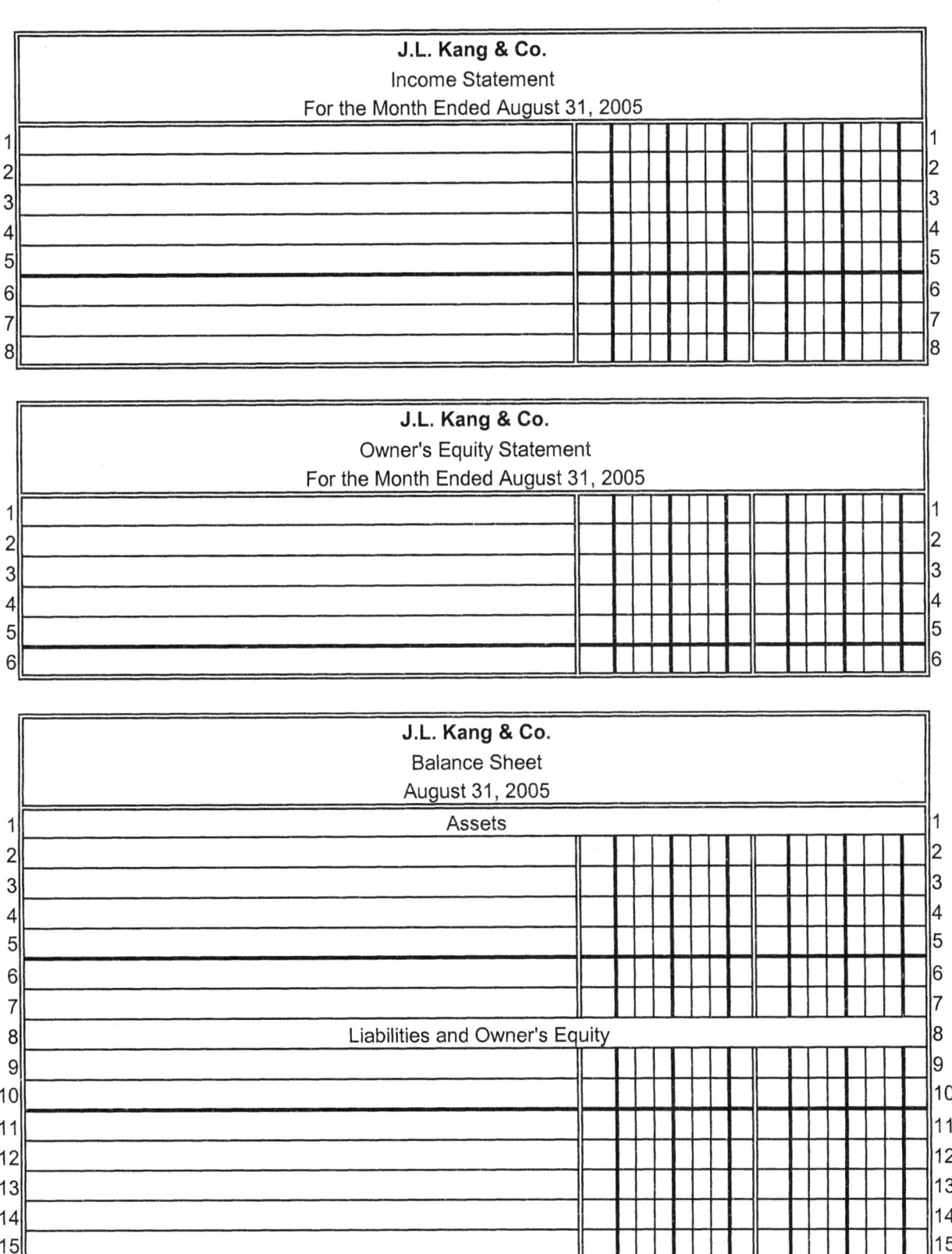

J.L. Kang & Co.
Income Statement
For the Month Ended August 31, 2005

J.L. Kang & Co.
Owner's Equity Statement
For the Month Ended August 31, 2005

J.L. Kang & Co.
Balance Sheet
August 31, 2005

Assets

Liabilities and Owner's Equity

	(a)									
1										1
2										2
3										3
4										4
5										5
6										6
7										7
8										8
9										9
10										10
11	(b)									11
12										12
13										13
14										14
15										15
16										16
17										17
18										18
19										19
20										20
21	(c)									21
22										22
23										23
24										24
25										25
26										26
27										27
28										28
29										29
30										30
31										31
32										32
33										33
34										34
35										35
36										36
37										37
38										38
39										39
40										40

Craig Stevens & Holly Enterprises

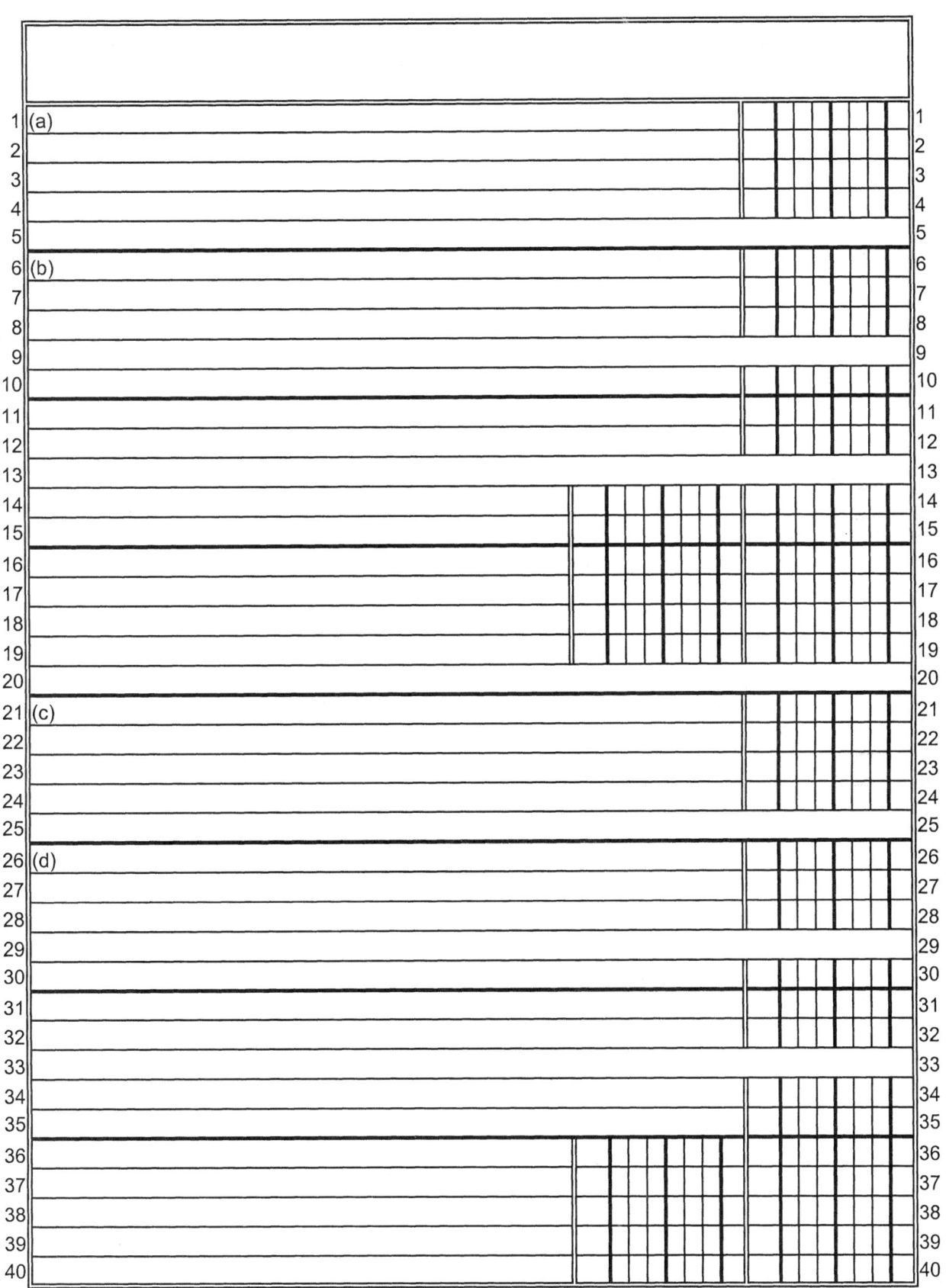

Karin Weigel Co.
Income Statement
For the Year Ended December 31, 2005

1			
2			
3			
4			
5			
6			
7			
8			
9			
10			

Karin Weigel Co.
Owner's Equity Statement
For the Year Ended December 31, 2005

1	
2	
3	
4	
5	
6	
7	
8	
9	
10	

#9

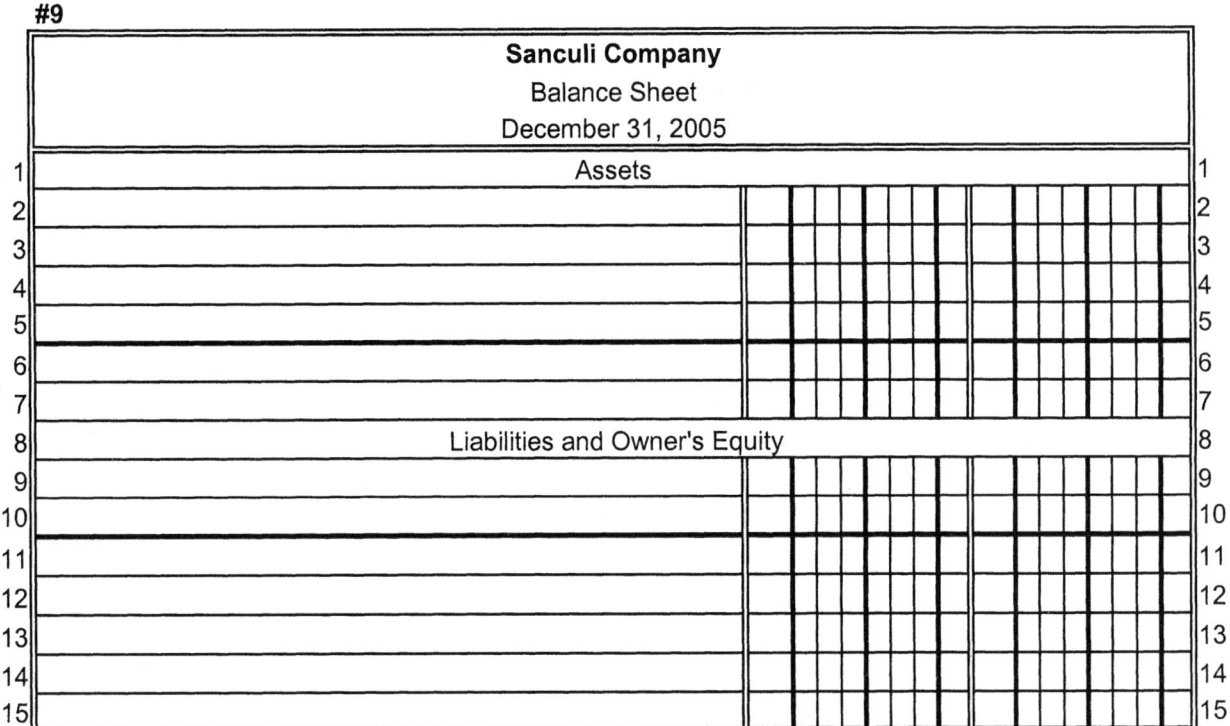

Sanculi Company
Balance Sheet
December 31, 2005

Assets

Liabilities and Owner's Equity

#11

Debra-Joan Cruise Company
Income Statement
For the Year Ended December 31, 2005

(a)

(b)

Bear Park

Balance Sheet

December 31, 2005

Assets

Liabilities and Owner's Equity

Douglas William, Attorney
Owner's Equity Statement
For the Year Ended December 31, 2005

1	
2	
3	
4	
5	
6	
7	
8	
9	
10 Supporting Computations	
11	
12	
13	
14	
15	
16	
17	
18	
19	
20	
21	
22	
23	
24	
25	
26	
27	
28	
29	
30	
31	
32	
33	
34	
35	
36	
37	
38	
39	
40	

(a)

Matrix Travel Agency

Trans-actions	Assets				Liabilities	Owner's Equity
	Cash	+ Accounts Receivable	+ Supplies	+ Office Equip-ment	= Accounts Payable	+ Holly Palmer, Capital
1.						
2.						
3.						
4.						
5.						
6.						
7.						
8.						
9.						
10						

(b)

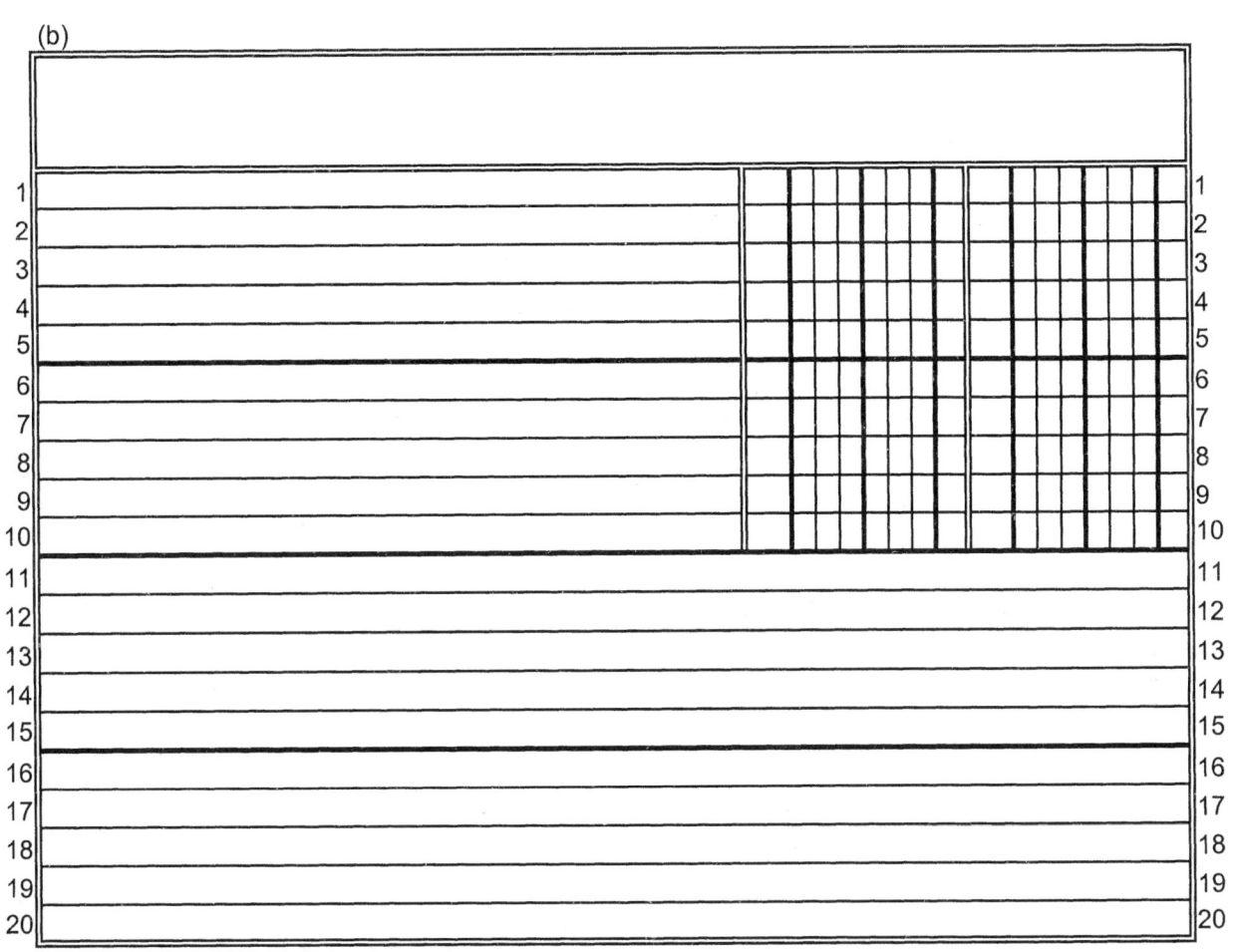

(a)

Mandy Arnold, Attorney at Law

Trans-actions	Assets				Liabilities		Owner's Equity
	Cash	Accounts Receivable	Supplies	Office Equip-ment	Notes Payable	Accounts Payable	Mandy Arnold, Capital
Bal.	$ 4000	$ 1500	$ 500	$ 5000		$ 4200	$ 6800
1.							
2.							
3.							
4.							
5.							
6.							
7.							
8.							

(b)

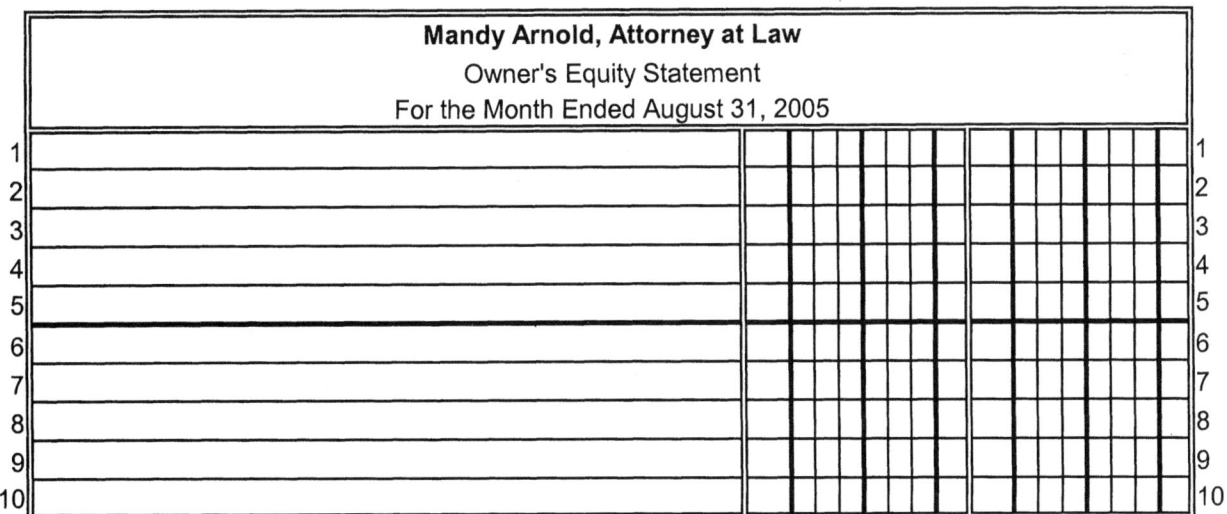

Mandy Arnold, Attorney at Law

Income Statement

For the Month Ended August 31, 2005

	Revenues		
1			
2			
3			
4			
5	Expenses		
6			
7			
8			
9			
10			
11			
12			
13			
14	Net Income (Loss)		
15			
16			
17			
18			
19			
20			

Mandy Arnold, Attorney at Law

Owner's Equity Statement

For the Month Ended August 31, 2005

1			
2			
3			
4			
5			
6			
7			
8			
9			
10			

(b) (Continued)

	Mandy Arnold, Attorney at Law		
	Balance Sheet		
	August 31, 2005		
1	Assets		1
2			2
3			3
4			4
5			5
6			6
7			7
8			8
9			9
10			10
11	Liabilities and Owner's Equity		11
12			12
13			13
14			14
15			15
16			16
17			17
18			18
19			19
20			20
21			21
22			22
23			23
24			24
25			25
26			26
27			27
28			28
29			29
30			30

(a)

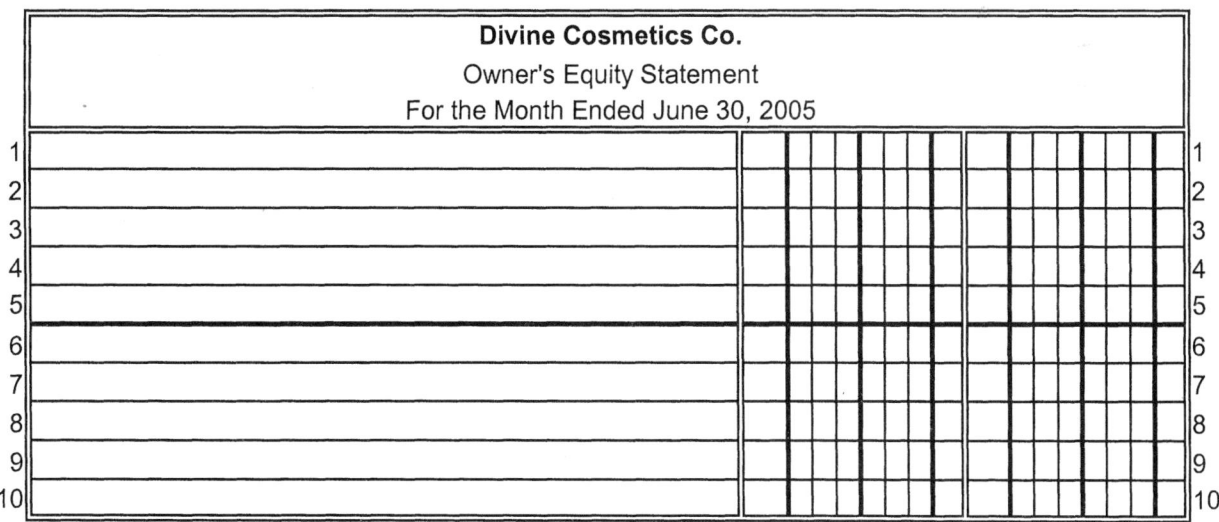

Divine Cosmetics Co.
Income Statement
For the Month Ended June 30, 2005

1	Revenues
2	
3	
4	
5	Expenses
6	
7	
8	
9	
10	
11	
12	
13	
14	Net Income (Loss)
15	
16	
17	
18	
19	
20	

Divine Cosmetics Co.
Owner's Equity Statement
For the Month Ended June 30, 2005

(a) Continued

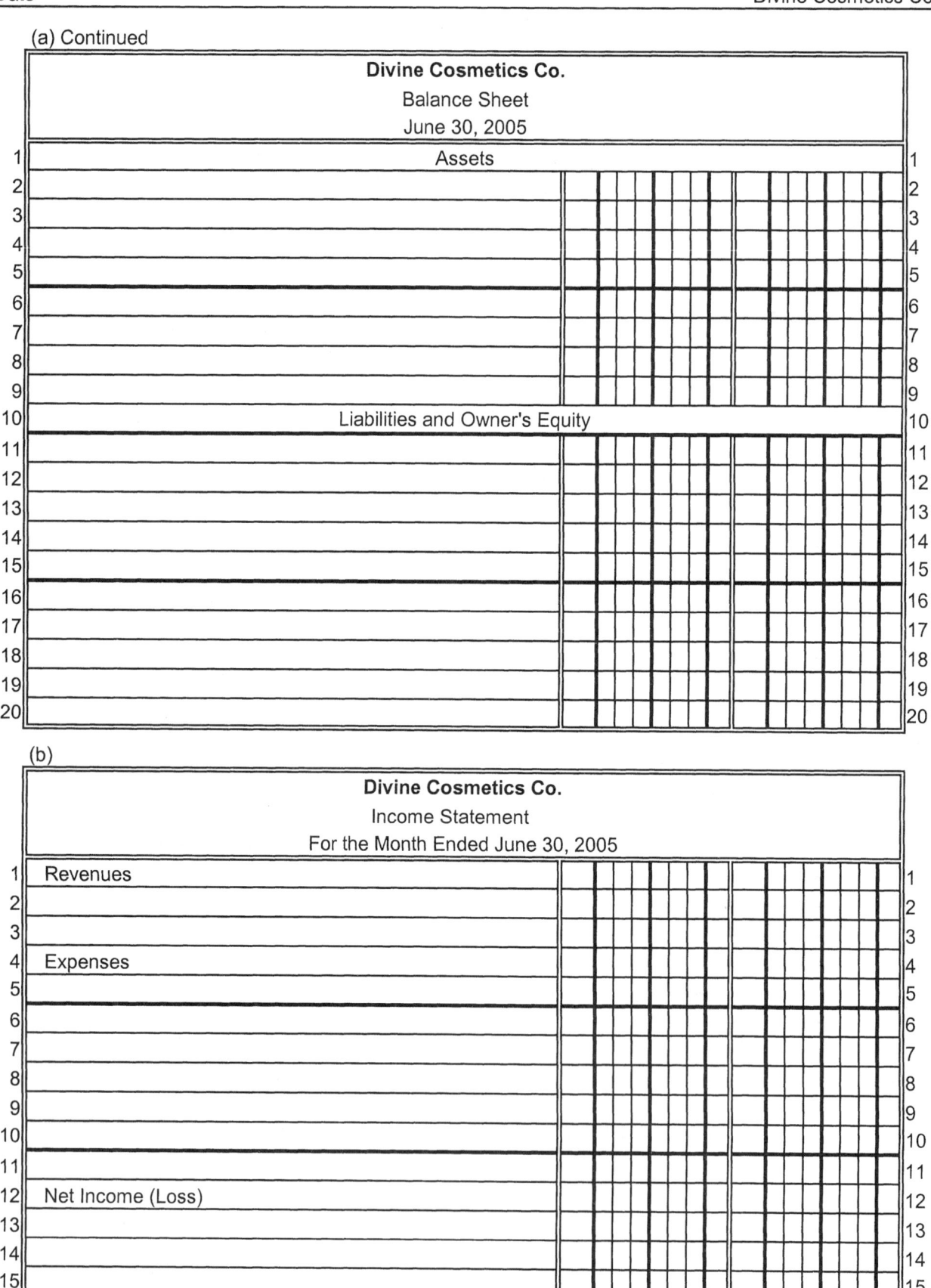

Divine Cosmetics Co.

Balance Sheet

June 30, 2005

	Assets	
1		
	Liabilities and Owner's Equity	

(b)

Divine Cosmetics Co.

Income Statement

For the Month Ended June 30, 2005

1	Revenues	
4	Expenses	
12	Net Income (Loss)	

(b) Concluded

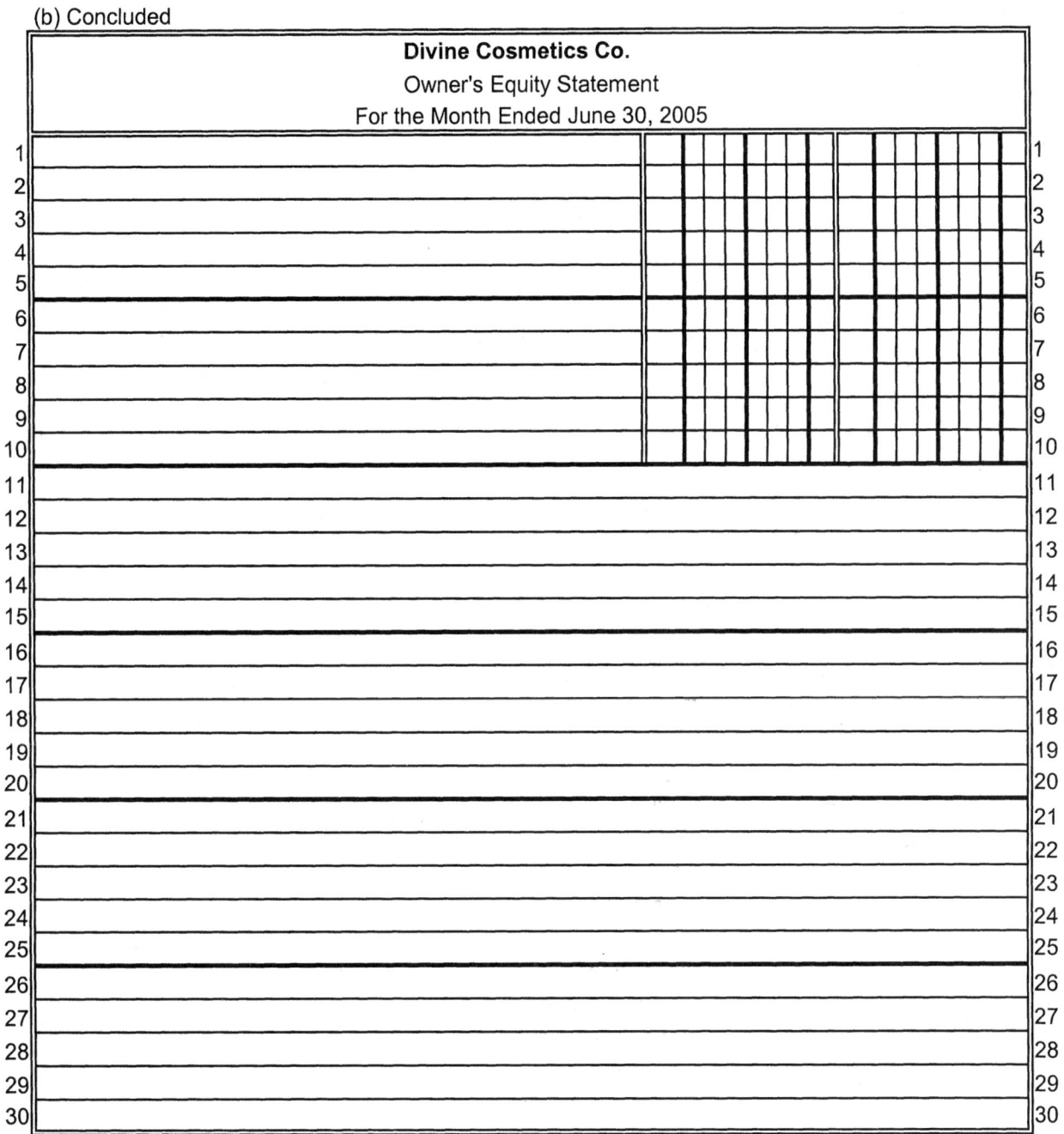

Divine Cosmetics Co.
Owner's Equity Statement
For the Month Ended June 30, 2005

(a)

Stiner Consulting

	Assets				Liabilities		Owner's Equity
Date	Cash	Accounts Receivable	Supplies	Office Equip- ment	Notes Payable	Accounts Payable	L. Stiner, Capital
1 May 1							
2							
3							
4							
5							
6							
7							
8							
9							
10							
11 12							
12							
13 15							
14							
15 17							
16							
17 20							
18							
19 23							
20							
21 26							
22							
23 29							
24							
25 30							

(b)

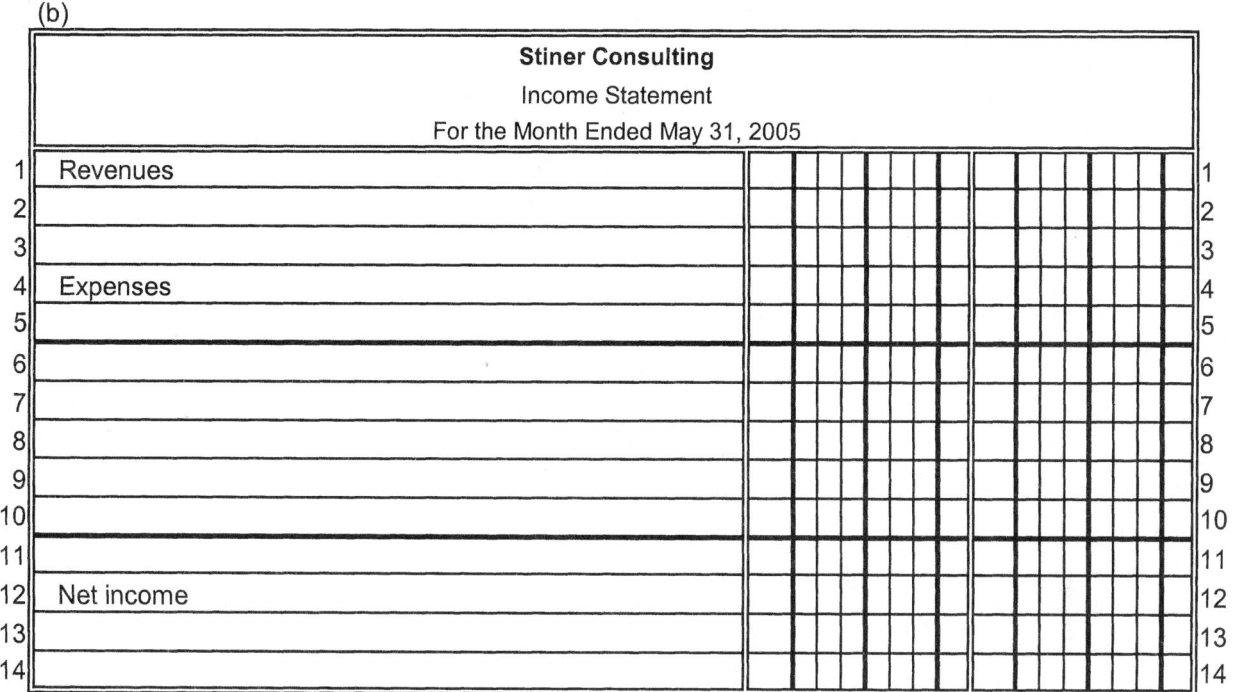

Stiner Consulting

Income Statement

For the Month Ended May 31, 2005

1	Revenues			
2				
3				
4	Expenses			
5				
6				
7				
8				
9				
10				
11				
12	Net income			
13				
14				

(c)

Stiner Consulting

Balance Sheet

May 31, 2005

1	Assets			
2				
3				
4				
5				
6				
7				
8	Liabilities and Owner's Equity			
9				
10				
11				
12				
13				
14				
15				
16				
17				
18				

(a)

		Winger Company	Selara Company	Delta Company	Hindi Company	
1	January 1, 2005					1
2	Assets	$ 75000	$ 90000	$	$ 150000	2
3	Liabilities	50000		75000		3
4	Owner's Equity		50000	54000	100000	4
5	December 31, 2005					5
6	Assets		117000	180000		6
7	Liabilities	55000	62000		80000	7
8	Owner's Equity	40000		100000	140000	8
9	Owner's equity					9
10	changes in year					10
11	Additional investment		8000	10000	15000	11
12	Drawings	10000		12000	10000	12
13	Total revenues	350000	400000		500000	13
14	Total expenses	335000	385000	360000		14
15						15

(b)

Winger Company
Owner's Equity Statement
For the Year Ended December 31, 2005

1		
2		
3		
4		
5		
6		
7		
8		
9		
10		

(c)

11	
12	
13	
14	
15	
16	
17	
18	
19	
20	

(a)

McInnes's Repair Shop

Trans-actions	Assets				=	Liabilities	+	Owner's Equity
	Cash	+	Accounts Receivable	+	Supplies	+	Office Equip-ment	=	Accounts Payable	+	J. McInnes, Capital
1.								
2.								
3.								
4.								
5.								
6.								
7.								
8.								
9.								
10.								
11.								

(b)

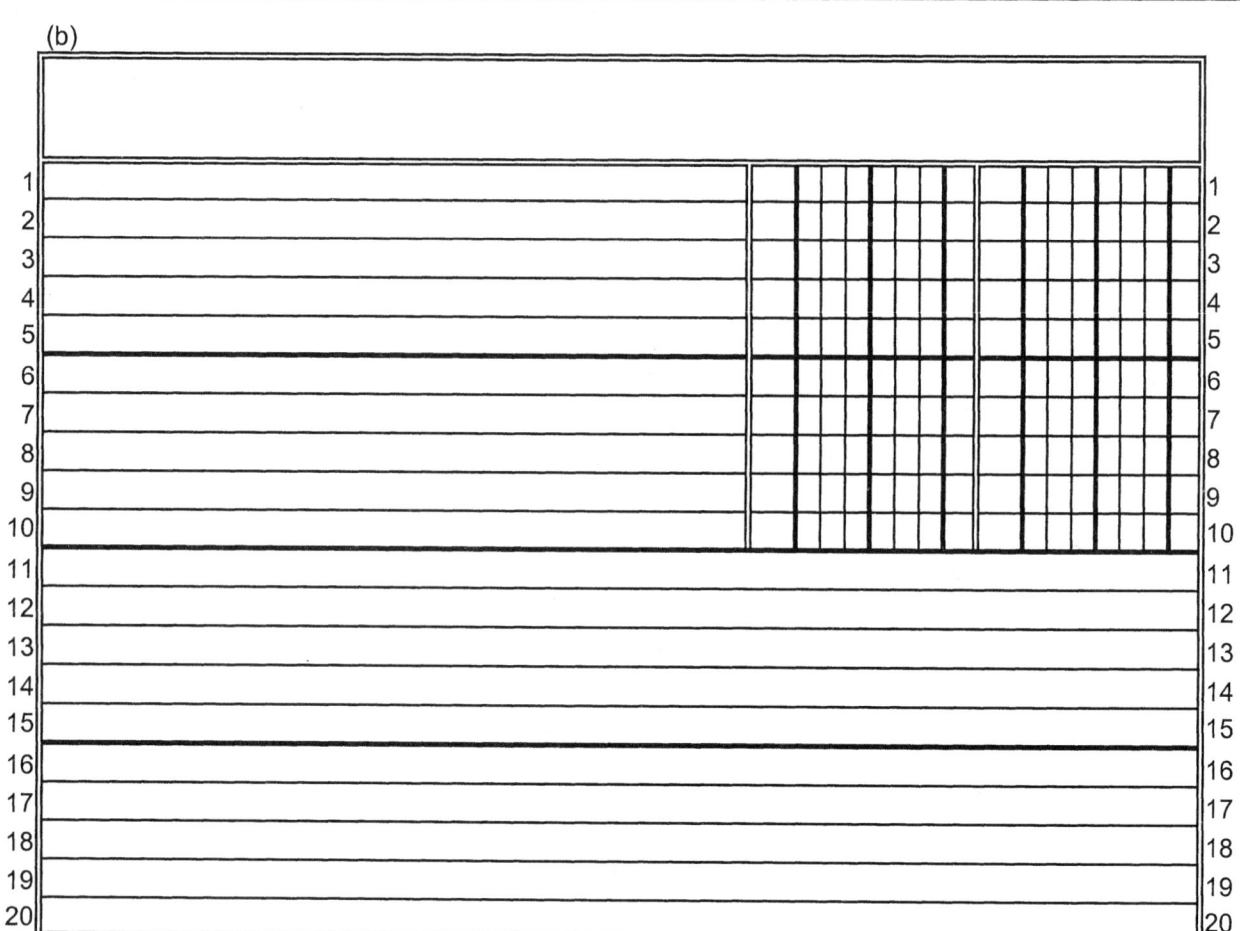

(a)

Patericia Perez, Verterinarian

Trans-actions	Assets					Liabilities		Owner's Equity
	Cash	Accounts Receivable	Supplies	Office Equip-ment		Notes Payable	Accounts Payable	P. Perez, Capital
	+	+	+	=	=	+	+	+
Bal.	$ 9000	$ 1700	$ 600	$ 6000			$ 3600	$ 13700
1.								
2.								
3.								
4.								
5.								
6.								
7.								
8.								

(b)

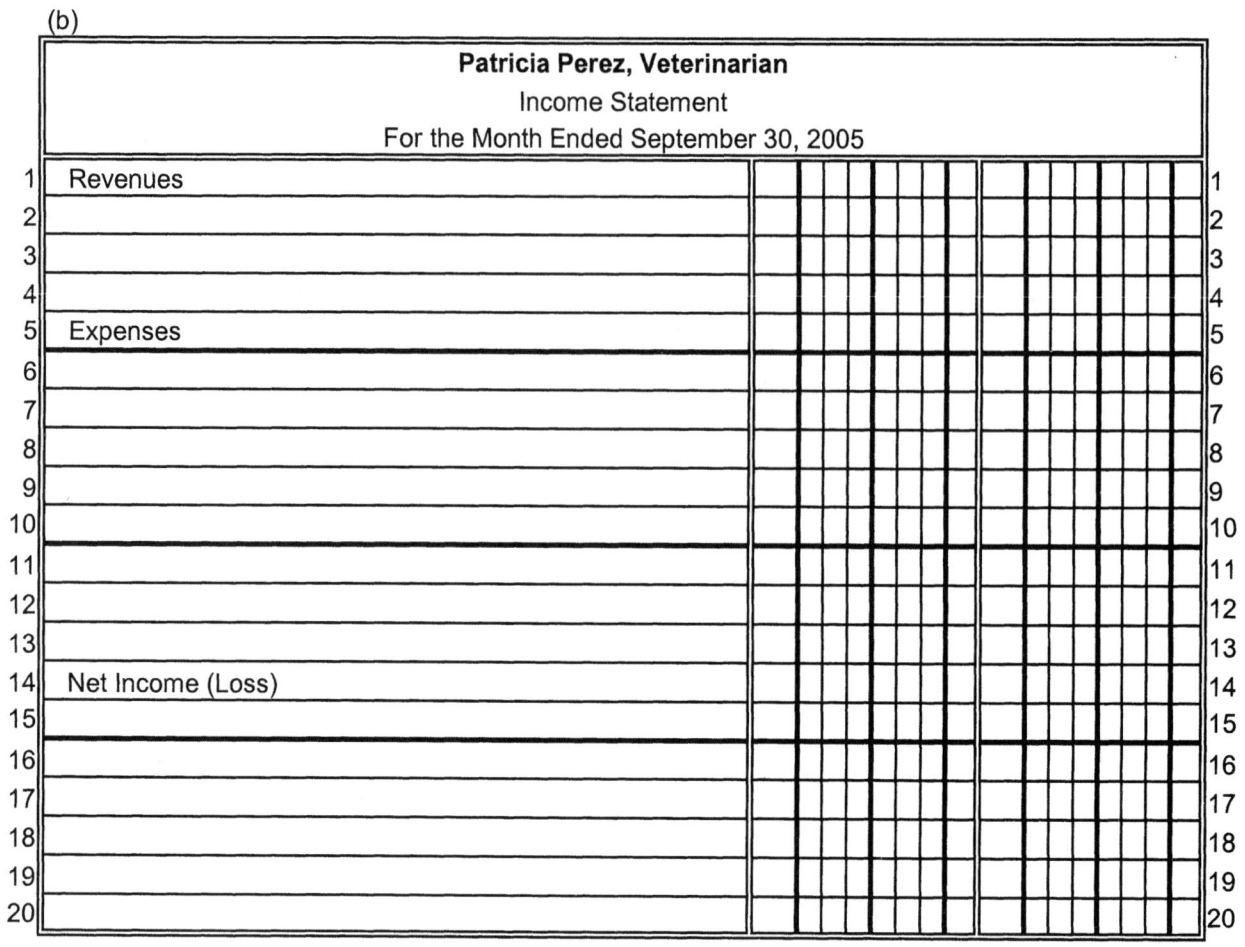

Patricia Perez, Veterinarian		
Income Statement		
For the Month Ended September 30, 2005		
Revenues		
Expenses		
Net Income (Loss)		

Patricia Perez, Veterinarian	
Owner's Equity Statement	
For the Month Ended September 30, 2005	

(b) (Continued)

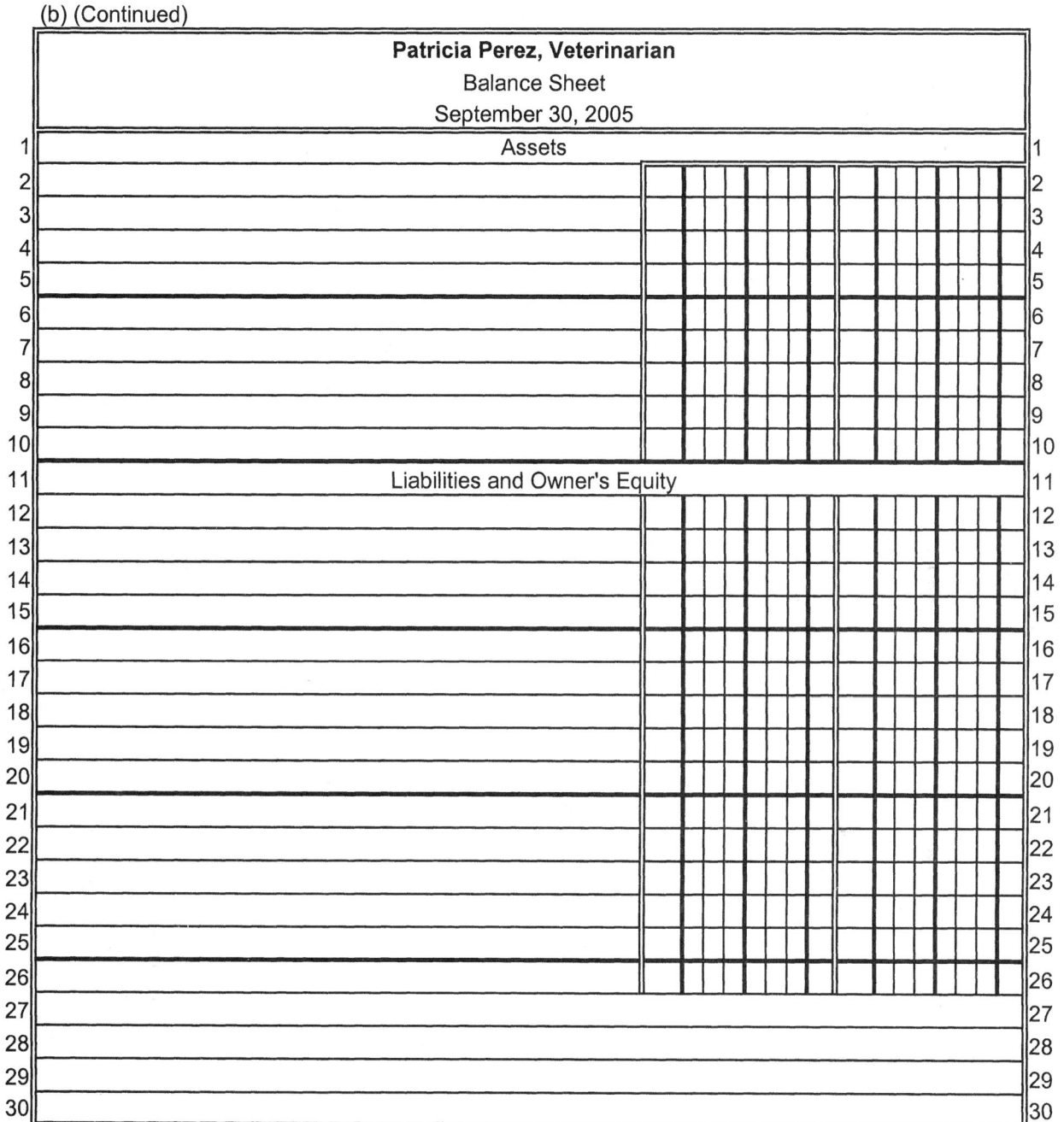

Patricia Perez, Veterinarian
Balance Sheet
September 30, 2005

Assets

Liabilities and Owner's Equity

(a)

Skyward Flying School					
Income Statement					
For the Month Ended May 31, 2005					
1	Revenues				1
2					2
3					3
4					4
5	Expenses				5
6					6
7					7
8					8
9					9
10					10
11					11
12					12
13					13
14	Net Income (Loss)				14
15					15
16					16
17					17
18					18
19					19
20					20

Skyward Flying School					
Owner's Equity Statement					
For the Month Ended May 31, 2005					
1					1
2					2
3					3
4					4
5					5
6					6
7					7
8					8
9					9
10					10

(a) Continued

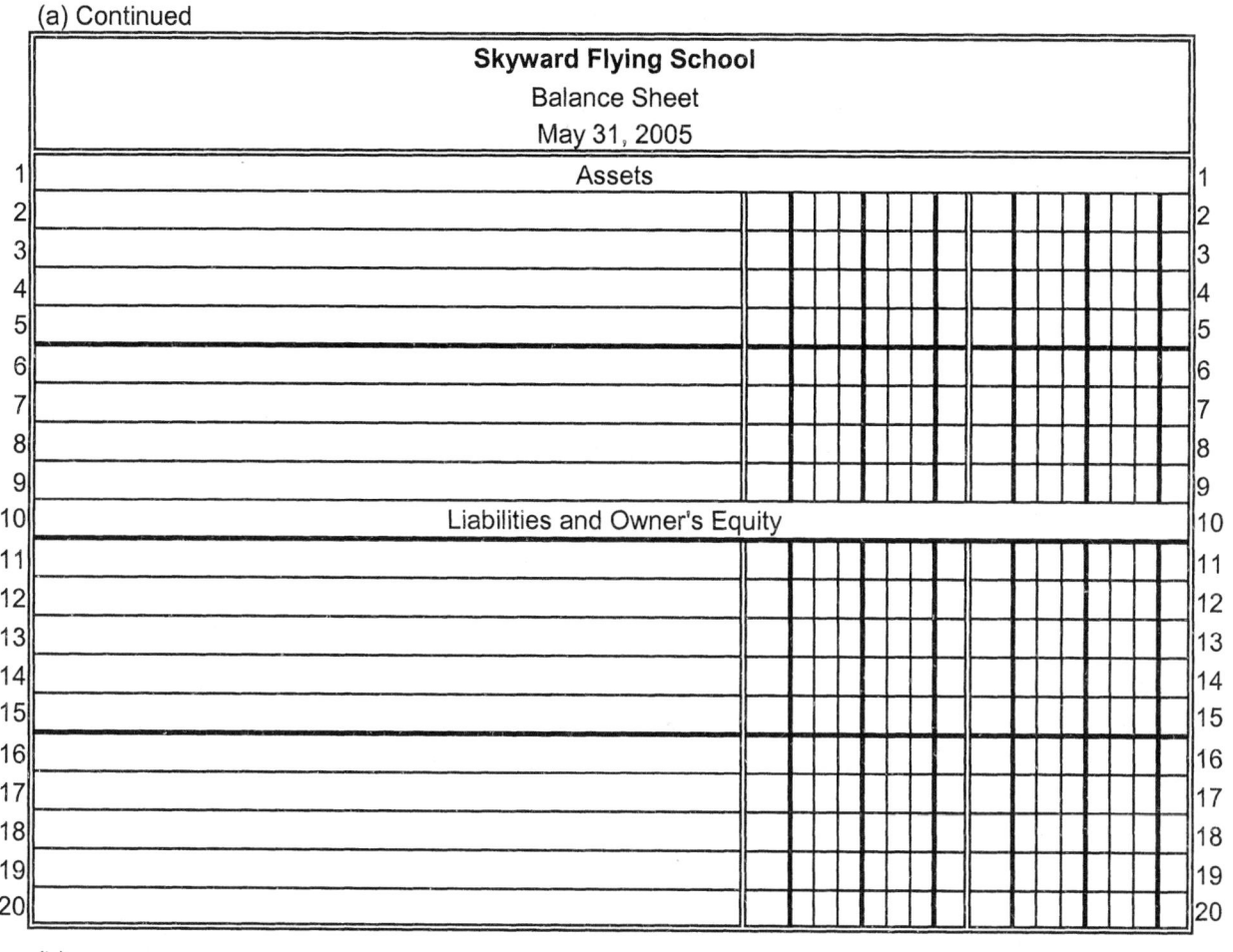

Skyward Flying School
Balance Sheet
May 31, 2005

Assets

Liabilities and Owner's Equity

(b)

Skyward Flying School
Income Statement
For the Month Ended May 31, 2005

Revenues

Expenses

Net Income (Loss)

(b) Concluded

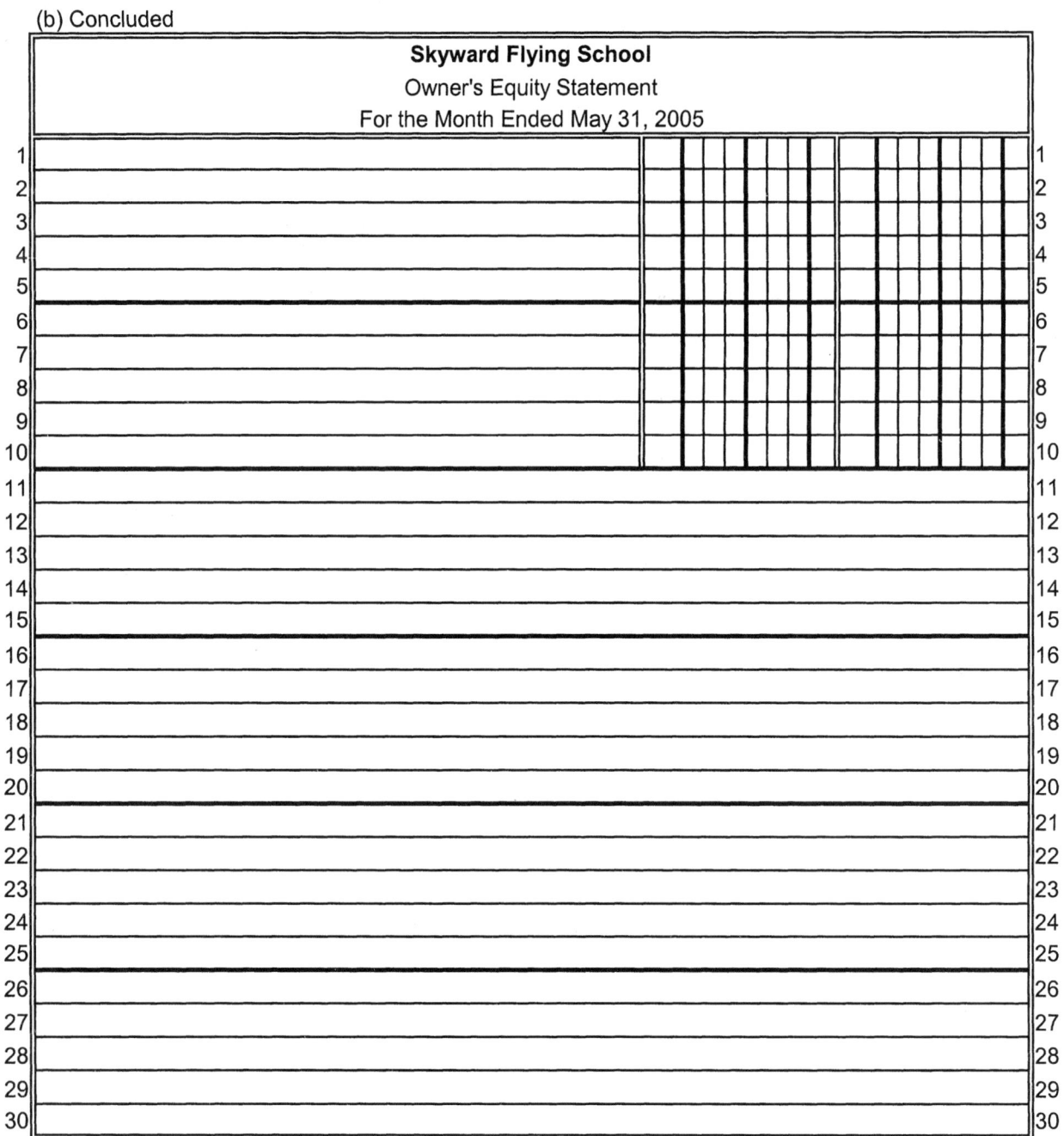

Skyward Flying School
Owner's Equity Statement
For the Month Ended May 31, 2005

(a)

Donohue Deliveries

Date	Assets				Liabilities		Owner's Equity
	Cash	+	Accounts Receivable	+	Supplies	+	Delivery Van	=	Notes Payable	+	Accounts Payable	+	P. Donohue, Capital

	Date
1	June 1
2	2
3	
4	3
5	
6	5
7	
8	9
9	
10	
11	12
12	
13	15
14	
15	17
16	
17	20
18	
19	23
20	
21	26
22	
23	29
24	
25	30

(b)

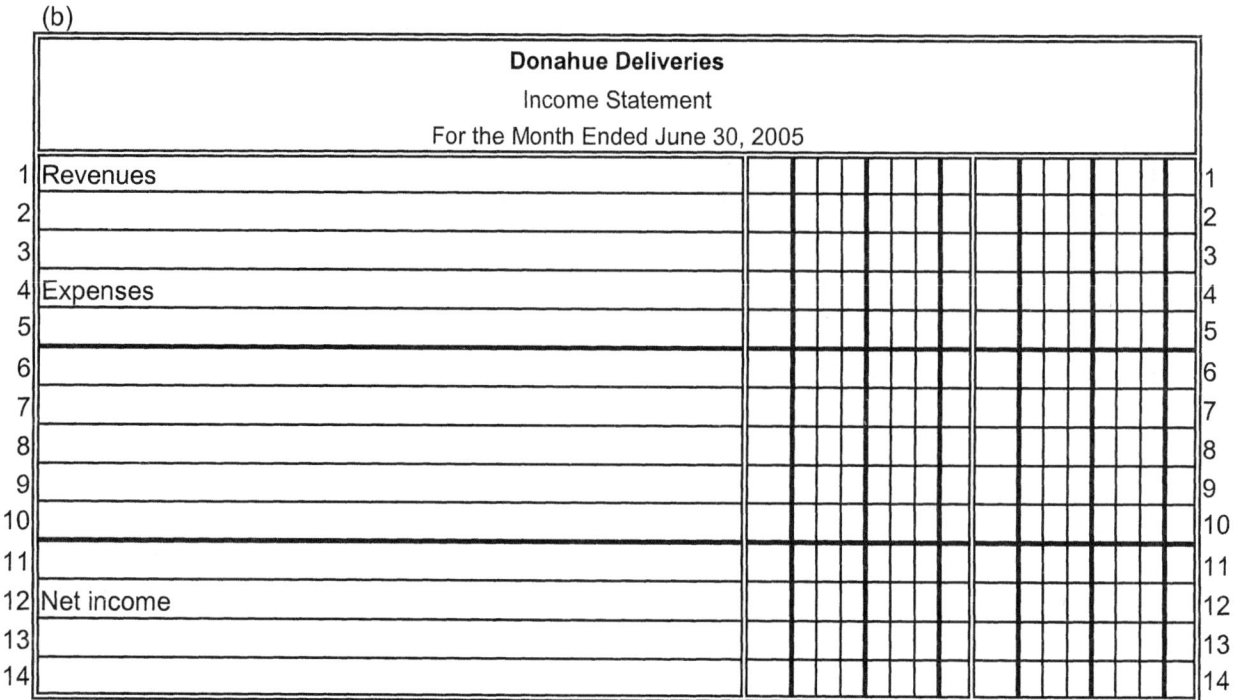

Donahue Deliveries

Income Statement

For the Month Ended June 30, 2005

	Revenues		
1	Revenues		
2			
3			
4	Expenses		
5			
6			
7			
8			
9			
10			
11			
12	Net income		
13			
14			

Donahue Deliveries

Balance Sheet

June 30, 2005

	Assets		
1	Assets		
2			
3			
4			
5			
6			
7			
8	Liabilities and Owner's Equity		
9			
10			
11			
12			
13			
14			
15			
16			
17			
18			

(a)

	Karma Company	Molly Company	McCain Company	Bodie Company	
1	January 1, 2005				1
2	Assets	$ 89 000	$ 110 000	$	$ 170 000	2
3	Liabilities	50 000		75 000		3
4	Owner's Equity		60 000	40 000	90 000	4
5	December 31, 2005					5
6	Assets		147 000	200 000		6
7	Liabilities	55 000	75 000		80 000	7
8	Owner's Equity	60 000		130 000	160 000	8
9	Owner's equity					9
10	changes in year					10
11	Additional investment		15 000	10 000	15 000	11
12	Drawings	25 000		14 000	20 000	12
13	Total revenues	350 000	420 000		520 000	13
14	Total expenses	320 000	385 000	342 000		14
15						15

(b)

Molly Company
Owner's Equity Statement
For the Year Ended December 31, 2005

1				1
2				2
3				3
4				4
5				5
6				6
7				7
8				8
9				9
10				10

(c)

11		11
12		12
13		13
14		14
15		15
16		16
17		17
18		18
19		19
20		20

(a)

(b)

(c)

(d) Net sales - 2000:

      2001:

      2002:

(e)

		PepsiCo	Coca-Cola	
1	(a) (in millions)			1
2				2
3	1. Total assets			3
4				4
5	2. Accounts receivable(net)			5
6				6
7	3. Net sales			7
8				8
9	4. Net income			9
10				10
11				11
12				12
13				13
14	(b)			14
15				15
16				16
17				17
18				18
19				19
20				20
21				21
22				22
23				23
24				24
25				25
26				26
27				27
28				28
29				29
30				30
31				31
32				32
33				33
34				34
35				35
36				36
37				37
38				38
39				39
40				40

(a)

(b)

(c)

			Financial	Management	
		Auditing	and Tax	Accounting	
1	(a)				1
2					2
3					3
4					4
5	(b)				5
6					6
7					7
8					8
9	(c)				9
10					10
11					11
12					12
13					13
14					14
15					15
16					16
17					17
18					18
19					19
20					20
21	(d)				21
22					22
23					23
24					24
25					25
26					26
27					27
28					28
29					29
30					30
31					31
32					32
33					33
34					34
35					35
36					36
37					37
38					38
39					39
40					40

(d) (Continued)

1		1
2		2
3		3
4		4
5		5
6		6
7		7
8		8
9		9
10		10
11		11
12		12
13		13
14		14
15		15
16		16
17		17
18		18
19		19
20		20
21		21
22		22
23		23
24		24
25		25
26		26
27		27
28		28
29		29
30		30
31		31
32		32
33		33
34		34
35		35
36		36
37		37
38		38
39	(e)	39
40		40

(a)

1		1
2		2
3		3
4		4
5		5

(b)

Chip-Shot Driving Range
Balance Sheet
March 31, 2005

	Assets	
1	Assets	1
2		2
3		3
4		4
5		5
6		6
7		7
8		8
9		9
10		10
11	Liabilities and Owner's Equity	11
12		12
13		13
14		14
15		15
16		16
17		17
18		18
19		19
20		20
21		21
22		22
23		23
24		24
25		25
26		26
27		27
28		28
29		29
30		30

(c)

(d)

Name

Section

Date

1	1
2	2
3	3
4	4
5	5
6	6
7	7
8	8
9	9
10	10
11	11
12	12
13	13
14	14
15	15
16	16
17	17
18	18
19	19
20	20
21	21
22	22
23	23
24	24
25	25
26	26
27	27
28	28
29	29
30	30
31	31
32	32
33	33
34	34
35	35
36	36
37	37
38	38
39	39
40	40

New York Company
Balance Sheet
December 31, 2005

Assets

Liabilities and Owner's Equity

1	(a)
2	
3	
4	
5	
6	
7	
8	
9	
10	
11	(b)
12	
13	
14	
15	
16	
17	
18	
19	
20	
21	
22	
23	
24	
25	
26	
27	
28	
29	(c)
30	
31	
32	
33	
34	
35	
36	
37	
38	
39	

#1		(a) Debit Effect	(b) Credit Effect	(c) Normal Balance	
1	1. Accounts Payable				1
2	2. Advertising Expense				2
3	3. Service Revenue				3
4	4. Accounts Receivable				4
5	5. B.C. King, Capital				5
6	6. B.C. King, Drawing				6
7					7

#2		Accounted Debited	Account Credited	
8				8
9	June 1			9
10	2			10
11	3			11
12	12			12

#3

	Date	Account Titles	Debit	Credit	
13					13
14					14
15	June 1				15
16					16
17					17
18	2				18
19					19
20					20
21	3				21
22					22
23					23
24	12				24
25					25

#4

26		26
27		27
28		28
29		29
30		30
31		31
32		32
33		33
34		34
35		35
36		36
37		37
38		38
39		39
40		40

#5

		(a) Effect on Accounting Equation	(b) Debit - Credit Analysis	
	Date			
1	Aug. 1			1
2				2
3				3
4				4
5				5
6	4			6
7				7
8				8
9				9
10				10
11	16			11
12				12
13				13
14				14
15				15
16	27			16
17				17
18				18
19				19

#6

	Date	Account Titles	Debit	Credit	
20					20
21	Date	Account Titles	Debit	Credit	21
22	Aug. 1				22
23					23
24					24
25	4				25
26					26
27					27
28	16				28
29					29
30					30
31	27				31
32					32
33					33
34					34
35					35

#7

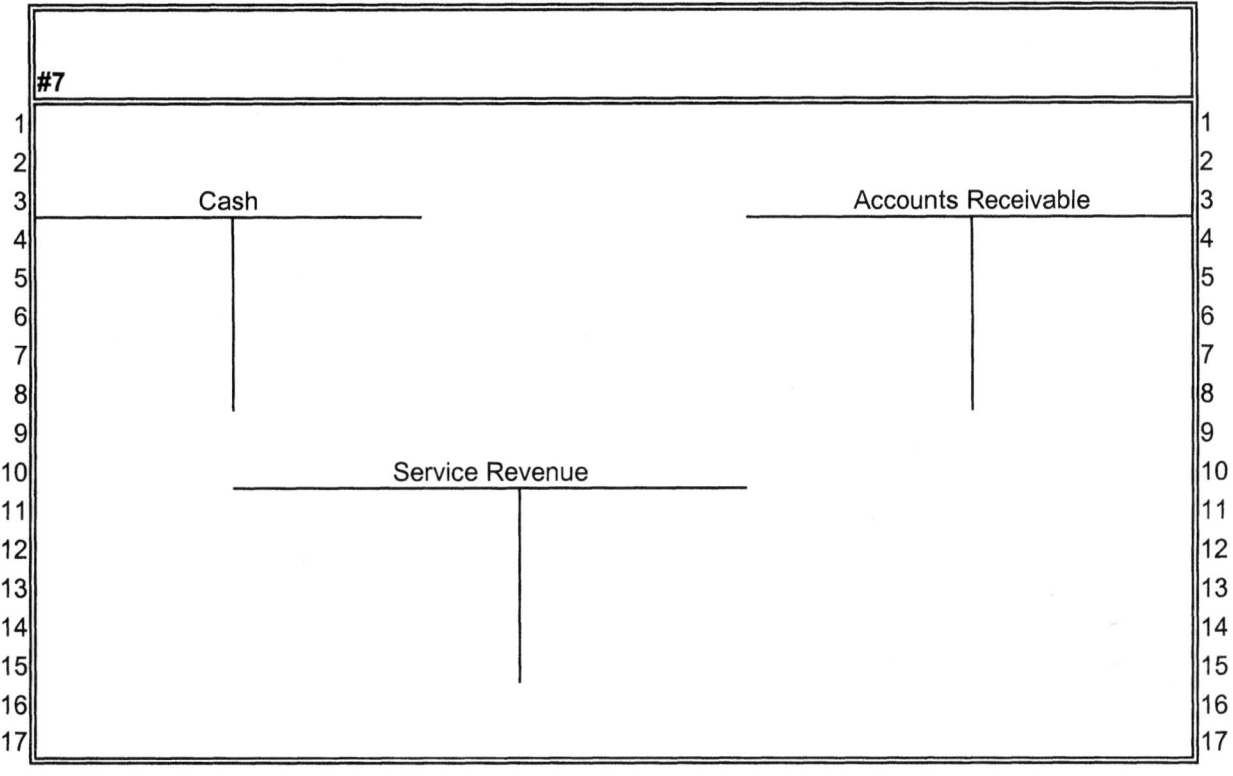

| Cash | Accounts Receivable | Service Revenue |

#8

Cash

Date	Explanation	Debit	Credit	Balance

Accounts Receivable

Date	Explanation	Debit	Credit	Balance

Service Revenue

Date	Explanation	Debit	Credit	Balance

#9

P.J. Farve Company		
Trial Balance		
June 30, 2005		
	Debit	Credit
1		
2		
3		
4		
5		
6		
7		
8		
9		
10		
11		
12		

#10

Cheng Company		
Trial Balance		
December 31, 2005		
	Debit	Credit
1		
2		
3		
4		
5		
6		
7		
8		
9		
10		
11		

Exercise 2-1

H. Burns

Trans-action No.	Account Debited (a) Basic Type	(b) Specific Account	(c) Effect	(d) Normal Balance	Account Credited (a) Basic Type	(b) Specific Account	(c) Effect	(d) Normal Balance
Jan. 2	Asset	Cash	Increase	Debit	Owner's Equity	H. Burns, Capital	Increase	Credit
3								
9								
11								
16								
20								
23								
28								

General Journal   J1

	Date	Account Titles and Explanation	Ref.	Debit	Credit	
1	Jan. 2					1
2						2
3						3
4	3					4
5						5
6						6
7	9					7
8						8
9						9
10	11					10
11						11
12						12
13	16					13
14						14
15						15
16	20					16
17						17
18						18
19	23					19
20						20
21						21
22	28					22
23						23
24						24
25						25
26						26
27						27
28						28
29						29
30						30
31						31
32						32
33						33
34						34
35						35
36						36
37						37
38						38
39						39
40						40

#3

	Date	
1	Oct. 1	
2		
3		
4		
5	2	
6		
7	3	
8		
9		
10	6	
11		
12		
13	27	
14		
15		
16	30	
17		
18		

#4

	Date	Account Titles and Explanation	Ref.	Debit	Credit
1	Oct. 1				
2					
3					
4	2				
5					
6	3				
7					
8					
9	6				
10					
11					
12	27				
13					
14					
15	30				
16					
17					

(a)

CASH	NOTES PAYABLE
ACCOUNTS RECEIVABLE	ROBERTA MENDEZ, CAPITAL
OFFICE EQUIPMENT	SERVICE REVENUE

(b)

Roberta Mendez, Investment Broker

Trial Balance

August 31, 2005

	Debit	Credit
1		
2		
3		
4		
5		
6		
7		
8		
9		
10		

(a)

General Journal

	Date	Account Titles and Explanation	Ref.	Debit	Credit	
1	Apr. 1					1
2						2
3						3
4						4
5	12					5
6						6
7						7
8						8
9	15					9
10						10
11						11
12						12
13	25					13
14						14
15						15
16						16
17	29					17
18						18
19						19
20						20
21	30					21
22						22
23						23
24						24
25						25
26						26

(b)

Padre Landscaping Company

Trial Balance

April 30, 2005

		Debit	Credit	
1				1
2				2
3				3
4				4
5				5
6				6
7				7
8				8
9				9

(a)

General Journal

	Date	Account Titles and Explanation	Ref.	Debit	Credit	
1	Oct. 1					1
2						2
3						3
4						4
5	10					5
6						6
7						7
8						8
9	10					9
10						10
11						11
12						12
13	20					13
14						14
15						15
16						16
17	20					17
18						18
19						19
20						20
21						21
22						22
23						23

(b)

Maxim Company
Trial Balance
October 31, 2005

		Debit	Credit	
1				1
2				2
3				3
4				4
5				5
6				6
7				7
8				8
9				9
10				10
11				11
12				12
13				13

(a)

General Journal   J1

	Date	Account Titles and Explanation	Ref.	Debit	Credit	
1	Sept. 1					1
2						2
3						3
4	5					4
5						5
6						6
7						7
8	25					8
9						9
10						10
11	30					11
12						12

(b)

Cash   No. 101

Date	Explanation	Ref.	Debit	Credit	Balance

Equipment   No. 157

Date	Explanation	Ref.	Debit	Credit	Balance

Accounts Payable   No. 201

Date	Explanation	Ref.	Debit	Credit	Balance

Neve Campbell, Capital   No. 301

Date	Explanation	Ref.	Debit	Credit	Balance

Neve Campbell, Drawing   No. 306

Date	Explanation	Ref.	Debit	Credit	Balance

 # 9

	Error	(a) In Balance	(b) Difference	(c) Larger Column	
1	1. Credit posting of $400 to Accounts				1
2	Receivable was omitted	No	$400	Debit	2
3					3
4	2.				4
5					5
6					6
7	3.				7
8					8
9					9
10	4.				10
11					11
12					12
13	5.				13
14					14
15					15
16	6.				16
17					17
18					18

#10

		Debit	Credit	
	Speedy Delivery Service Trial Balance July 31, 2005			
1				1
2				2
3				3
4				4
5				5
6				6
7				7
8				8
9				9
10				10
11				11
12				12
13				13
14				14
15				15
16				16
17				17

Surepar Miniature Golf and Driving Range

General Journal

J1

	Date	Account Titles and Explanation	Ref.	Debit	Credit	
1	Mar. 1					1
2						2
3						3
4	3					4
5						5
6						6
7						7
8						8
9	5					9
10						10
11						11
12	6					12
13						13
14						14
15	10					15
16						16
17						17
18	18					18
19						19
20						20
21	19					21
22						22
23						23
24	25					24
25						25
26						26
27	30					27
28						28
29						29
30	30					30
31						31
32						32
33	31					33
34						34
35						35
36						36
37						37
38						38
39						39
40						40

(a)

	General Journal					J1
	Date	Account Titles and Explanation	Ref.	Debit	Credit	
1	Apr. 1					1
2						2
3						3
4	1					4
5						5
6						6
7	2					7
8						8
9						9
10	3					10
11						11
12						12
13	10					13
14						14
15						15
16	11					16
17						17
18						18
19	20					19
20						20
21						21
22	30					22
23						23
24						24
25	30					25
26						26
27						27
28						28
29						29
30						30
31						31
32						32
33						33
34						34
35						35
36						36
37						37
38						38
39						39
40						40

(b)

Cash   No. 101

Date	Explanation	Ref.	Debit	Credit	Balance

Accounts Receivable   No. 112

Date	Explanation	Ref.	Debit	Credit	Balance

Supplies   No. 126

Date	Explanation	Ref.	Debit	Credit	Balance

Accounts Payable   No. 201

Date	Explanation	Ref.	Debit	Credit	Balance

Unearned Revenue   No. 205

Date	Explanation	Ref.	Debit	Credit	Balance

Judi Dench, Capital   No. 301

Date	Explanation	Ref.	Debit	Credit	Balance

(b) (Continued)

Service Revenue   No. 400

Date	Explanation	Ref.	Debit	Credit	Balance

Salaries Expense   No. 726

Date	Explanation	Ref.	Debit	Credit	Balance

Rent Expense   No. 729

Date	Explanation	Ref.	Debit	Credit	Balance

(c)

Judi Dench, Architect
Trial Balance
April 30, 2005

		Debit	Credit	
1	Cash			1
2	Accounts Receivable			2
3	Supplies			3
4	Accounts Payable			4
5	Unearned Revenue			5
6	Judi Dench, Capital			6
7	Service Revenue			7
8	Salaries Expense			8
9	Rent Expense			9
10				10
11				11

(a)

General Journal

	Trans.	Account Titles and Explanation	Ref.	Debit	Credit	
1	1.					1
2						2
3						3
4	2.					4
5						5
6						6
7	3.					7
8						8
9						9
10	4.					10
11						11
12						12
13	5.					13
14						14
15						15
16	6.					16
17						17
18						18
19	7.					19
20						20
21						21
22	8.					22
23						23
24						24
25	9.					25
26						26
27						27
28	10.					28
29						29
30						30
31	11.					31
32						32
33						33
34	12.					34
35						35
36						36
37						37
38						38
39						39
40						40

(b)

Cash				Accounts Payable	

Accounts Receivable		Dennis Chambers, Capital	

Office Supplies		Brokerage Revenue	

Prepaid Insurance		Salaries Expense	

Prepaid Rent		Rent Expense	

Furniture & Equipment		Utility Expense	

		Insurance Expense	

(c)

	Chambers Brokerage Services Trial Balance May 31, 2005	Debit	Credit	
1	Cash			1
2	Accounts Receivable			2
3	Office Supplies			3
4	Prepaid Insurance			4
5	Prepaid Rent			5
6	Furniture and Equipment			6
7	Accounts Payable			7
8	Dennis Chambers, Capital			8
9	Brokerage Revenue			9
10	Salaries Expense			10
11	Rent Expense			11
12	Utility Expense			12
13	Insurance Expense			13
14				14
15				15
16				16
17				17
18				18
19				19
20				20
21				21
22				22
23				23
24				24
25				25
26				26
27				27
28				28
29				29
30				30
31				31
32				32
33				33
34				34
35				35

(d)

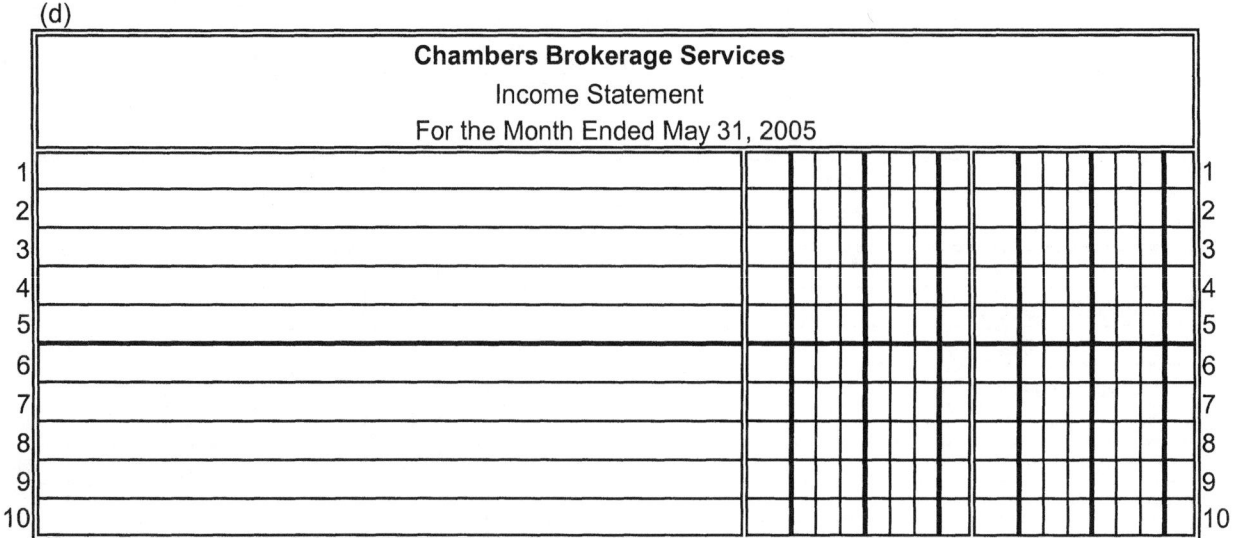

Chambers Brokerage Services

Income Statement

For the Month Ended May 31, 2005

Chambers Brokerage Services

Statement of Owner's Equity

For the Month Ended May 31, 2005

(d) (Continued)

	Chambers Brokerage Services					
	Balance Sheet					
	May 31, 2005					
1	Assets					
2						
3						
4						
5						
6						
7						
8						
9						
10	Liabilities and Owner's Equity					
11						
12						
13						
14						
15						
16						
17						
18						
19						

Ron Salem Co. Trial Balance June 30, 2005		
	Debit	Credit
1		
2		
3		
4		
5		
6		
7		
8		
9		
10		
11		
12		
13		
14		
15		
16 Journal Entry Aids:		
17		
18		
19		
20		
21		
22		
23		
24		
25		
26		
27		
28		
29		
30		
31		
32		
33		
34		
35		
36		
37		
38		
39		
40		

(a) and (c)

Cash   No. 101

Date	Explanation	Ref.	Debit	Credit	Balance
Mar. 1	Balance	√			1 6 0 0 0

Accounts Receivable   No. 112

Date	Explanation	Ref.	Debit	Credit	Balance

Land   No. 140

Date	Explanation	Ref.	Debit	Credit	Balance
Mar. 1	Balance	√			4 2 0 0 0

Buildings   No. 145

Date	Explanation	Ref.	Debit	Credit	Balance
Mar. 1	Balance	√			1 8 0 0 0

Equipment   No. 157

Date	Explanation	Ref.	Debit	Credit	Balance
Mar. 1	Balance	√			1 6 0 0 0

Accounts Payable   No. 201

Date	Explanation	Ref.	Debit	Credit	Balance
Mar. 1	Balance	√			1 2 0 0 0

A. Russo, Capital   No. 301

Date	Explanation	Ref.	Debit	Credit	Balance
Mar. 1	Balance	√			8 0 0 0 0

(a) and (c) (Continued)

Admission Revenue   No. 405

Date	Explanation	Ref.	Debit	Credit	Balance

Concession Revenue   No. 406

Date	Explanation	Ref.	Debit	Credit	Balance

Advertising Expense   No. 610

Date	Explanation	Ref.	Debit	Credit	Balance

Film Rental Expense   No. 632

Date	Explanation	Ref.	Debit	Credit	Balance

Salaries Expense   No. 726

Date	Explanation	Ref.	Debit	Credit	Balance

(b)

General Journal   J1

	Date	Account Titles and Explanation	Ref.	Debit	Credit	
1	Mar. 2					1
2						2
3						3
4						4
5						5
6	3					6
7						7
8						8
9	9					9
10						10
11						11
12						12
13	10					13
14						14
15						15
16						16
17	11					17
18						18
19						19
20	12					20
21						21
22						22
23						23
24	20					24
25						25
26						26
27						27
28	20					28
29						29
30						30
31						31
32	31					32
33						33
34						34
35						35
36	31					36
37						37
38						38
39						39
40						40

(b) (Continued)

General Journal   J1

	Date	Account Titles and Explanation	Ref.	Debit	Credit	
1	Mar. 31					1
2						2
3						3
4						4
5						5
6						6
7						7
8						8
9						9
10						10
11						11
12						12
13						13
14						14
15						15
16						16

(d)

Russo Theater
Trial Balance
March 31, 2005

		Debit	Credit	
1	Cash			1
2	Accounts Receivable			2
3	Land			3
4	Buildings			4
5	Equipment			5
6	Accounts Payable			6
7	A. Russo, Capital			7
8	Admission Revenue			8
9	Concession Revenue			9
10	Advertising Expense			10
11	Film Rental Expense			11
12	Salaries Expense			12
13				13
14				14
15				15
16				16
17				17

General Journal   J1

	Date	Account Titles and Explanation	Ref.	Debit	Credit	
1	Apr. 1					1
2						2
3						3
4	4					4
5						5
6						6
7	8					7
8						8
9						9
10	11					10
11						11
12						12
13	12					13
14						14
15						15
16	13					16
17						17
18						18
19	17					19
20						20
21						21
22	20					22
23						23
24						24
25	25					25
26						26
27						27
28	30					28
29						29
30						30
31	30					31
32						32
33						33
34						34
35						35
36						36
37						37
38						38
39						39
40						40

(a)   General Journal   J1

	Date	Account Titles and Explanation	Ref.	Debit	Credit	
1	May 1					1
2						2
3						3
4	2					4
5						5
6						6
7	3					7
8						8
9						9
10	7					10
11						11
12						12
13	11					13
14						14
15						15
16	12					16
17						17
18						18
19	17					19
20						20
21						21
22	31					22
23						23
24						24
25	31					25
26						26
27						27
28						28
29						29
30						30
31						31
32						32
33						33
34						34
35						35
36						36
37						37
38						38
39						39
40						40

(b)

Cash   No. 101

Date	Explanation	Ref.	Debit	Credit	Balance

Accounts Receivable   No. 112

Date	Explanation	Ref.	Debit	Credit	Balance

Supplies   No. 126

Date	Explanation	Ref.	Debit	Credit	Balance

Accounts Payable   No. 201

Date	Explanation	Ref.	Debit	Credit	Balance

Unearned Revenue   No. 205

Date	Explanation	Ref.	Debit	Credit	Balance

Kara Shin, Capital   No. 301

Date	Explanation	Ref.	Debit	Credit	Balance

(b) (Continued)

Service Revenue   No. 400

Date	Explanation	Ref.	Debit	Credit	Balance

Salaries Expense   No. 726

Date	Explanation	Ref.	Debit	Credit	Balance

Rent Expense   No. 729

Date	Explanation	Ref.	Debit	Credit	Balance

(c)

	Kara Shin, CPA	Debit	Credit	
	Trial Balance			
	May 31, 2005			
1	Cash			1
2	Accounts Receivable			2
3	Supplies			3
4	Accounts Payable			4
5	Unearned Revenue			5
6	Kara Shin, Capital			6
7	Service Revenue			7
8	Salaries Expense			8
9	Rent Expense			9
10				10
11				11

(a)

1		1
2		2
3		3
4		4
5		5

(b) and (d)

Cash

Bal.   8,000

Accounts Receivable

Bal.   15,000

Parts Inventory

Bal.   13,000

Prepaid Rent

Bal.   3,000

Shop Equipment

Bal.   21,000

Accounts Payable

Bal.   19,000

Mark Hockenberry, Capital

Bal.   41,000

Mark Hockenberry, Drawings

Repair Services Revenue

Advertising Expense

Miscellaneous Expense

Repair Parts Expense

Rent Expense

Wage Expense

(c)

	Date	Account Titles and Explanation	Ref.	Debit	Credit	
1	1.					1
2						2
3						3
4	2.					4
5						5
6						6
7	3.					7
8						8
9						9
10	4.					10
11						11
12						12
13	5.					13
14						14
15						15
16	6.					16
17						17
18						18
19	7.					19
20						20
21						21
22	8.					22
23						23
24						24
25	9.					25
26						26
27						27
28	10.					28
29						29
30						30
31						31
32						32
33						33
34						34
35						35
36						36
37						37
38						38
39						39
40						40

General Journal — J1

(e)

Byte Repair Service Trial Balance January 31, 2005	Debit	Credit	
1 Cash			1
2 Accounts Receivable			2
3 Parts Inventory			3
4 Prepaid Rent			4
5 Shop Equipment			5
6 Accounts Payable			6
7 Mark Hockenberry, Capital			7
8 Mark Hockenberry, Drawings			8
9 Repair Services Revenue			9
10 Advertising Expense			10
11 Miscellaneous Expense			11
12 Repair Parts Expense			12
13 Rent Expense			13
14 Wage Expense			14
15 Totals			15
16			16
17			17

(f)

1		1
2		2
3		3
4		4
5		5
6		6
7		7

(g)

1		1
2		2
3		3
4		4
5		5
6		6
7		7
8		8

Garland Company
Trial Balance
May 31, 2005

	Debit	Credit
1		
2		
3		
4		
5		
6		
7		
8		
9		
10		
11		
12		
13		
14		
15		
16 Journal Entry Aids:		
17		
18		
19		
20		
21		
22		
23		
24		
25		
26		
27		
28		
29		
30		
31		
32		
33		
34		
35		
36		
37		
38		
39		
40		

(a) and (c)

Cash   No. 101

Date	Explanation	Ref.	Debit	Credit	Balance
Apr. 1	Balance	√			6 0 0 0

Accounts Receivable   No. 112

Date	Explanation	Ref.	Debit	Credit	Balance

Prepaid Rentals   No. 136

Date	Explanation	Ref.	Debit	Credit	Balance

Land   No. 140

Date	Explanation	Ref.	Debit	Credit	Balance
Apr. 1	Balance	√			1 0 0 0 0

Buildings   No. 145

Date	Explanation	Ref.	Debit	Credit	Balance
Apr. 1	Balance	√			8 0 0 0

Equipment   No. 157

Date	Explanation	Ref.	Debit	Credit	Balance
Apr. 1	Balance	√			6 0 0 0

Accounts Payable   No. 201

Date	Explanation	Ref.	Debit	Credit	Balance
Apr. 1	Balance	√			2 0 0 0

Mortgage Payable   No. 275

Date	Explanation	Ref.	Debit	Credit	Balance
Apr. 1	Balance	√			8 0 0 0

(a) and (c) (Continued)

Alvin Wasicko, Capital   No. 301

Date	Explanation	Ref.	Debit	Credit	Balance
Apr. 1	Balance	√			2 0 0 0 0

Admission Revenue   No. 405

Date	Explanation	Ref.	Debit	Credit	Balance

Concession Revenue   No. 406

Date	Explanation	Ref.	Debit	Credit	Balance

Advertising Expense   No. 610

Date	Explanation	Ref.	Debit	Credit	Balance

Film Rental Expense   No. 632

Date	Explanation	Ref.	Debit	Credit	Balance

Salaries Expense   No. 726

Date	Explanation	Ref.	Debit	Credit	Balance

(b)

	Date	Account Titles and Explanation	Ref.	Debit	Credit	
		General Journal			J1	
1	Apr. 2					1
2						2
3						3
4	3					4
5						5
6						6
7	9					7
8						8
9						9
10	10					10
11						11
12						12
13						13
14	11					14
15						15
16						16
17	12					17
18						18
19						19
20	20					20
21						21
22						22
23	25					23
24						24
25						25
26	29					26
27						27
28						28
29	30					29
30						30
31						31
32						32
33	30					33
34						34
35						35
36						36
37						37
38						38
39						39
40						40

(d)

	Lake Theater Trial Balance April 30, 2005	Debit	Credit	
1	Cash			1
2	Accounts Receivable			2
3	Prepaid Rentals			3
4	Land			4
5	Buildings			5
6	Equipment			6
7	Accounts Payable			7
8	Mortgage Payable			8
9	Alvin Wasicko, Capital			9
10	Admission Revenue			10
11	Concession Revenue			11
12	Advertising Expense			12
13	Film Rental Expense			13
14	Salaries Expense			14
15				15
16				16
17				17

(a)

	Account	(1) Increase Side	(2) Decrease Side	Normal Balance	
1	Accounts Payable				1
2					2
3	Accounts Receivable				3
4					4
5	Property, Plant & Equipment				5
6					6
7	Income Taxes Payable				7
8					8
9	Interest Expense				9
10					10
11	Inventory				11
12					12

		Accounts	Effect	
1	(b) When			1
2	(1) Acccounts Receivable is decreased			2
3				3
4	(2) Accounts Payable is decreased			4
5				5
6	(3) Inventory are increased			6
7				7
8				8
9				9
10	(c) When			10
11	(1) Interest Expense is increased			11
12				12
13				13
14				14
15	(2) Property, Plant & Equipment is increased			15
16				16
17				17
18				18
19				19
20				20

Name

Section

Date

	Normal Balance	
(a) PepsiCo		
1. Inventory		
2. Property, Plant, and Equipment		
3. Accounts Payable		
4. Interest Expense		
Coca-Cola		
1. Accounts Receivable		
2. Cash and Equivalents		
3. Cost of Goods Sold		
4. Sales (Revenue)		

(b)

(a)

(b)

(c)

(d)

1	(a)	Industry
2		
3		
4	(b)	Total sales
5		
6		
7	(c)	Net income
8		
9		
10	(d)	Names of four competitors
11		
12		
13		
14		
15		
16	(e)	Competitor chosen
17		
18		
19	(f)	Competitor's sales
20		
21		
22		Competitor's net income
23		
24		
25	(g)	Larger company by size of sales
26		
27		
28		Company with higher net income
29		
30		
31		
32		
33		
34		
35		
36		
37		
38		
39		
40		

(a)

	Date	Account Titles	Debit	Credit	
1	May 1				1
2					2
3					3
4	5				4
5					5
6					6
7	7				7
8					8
9					9
10	14				10
11					11
12					12
13	15				13
14					14
15					15
16	20				16
17					17
18					18
19	30				19
20					20
21					21
22	31				22
23					23
24					24
25					25

(b)

1		1
2		2
3		3
4		4
5		5

(c)

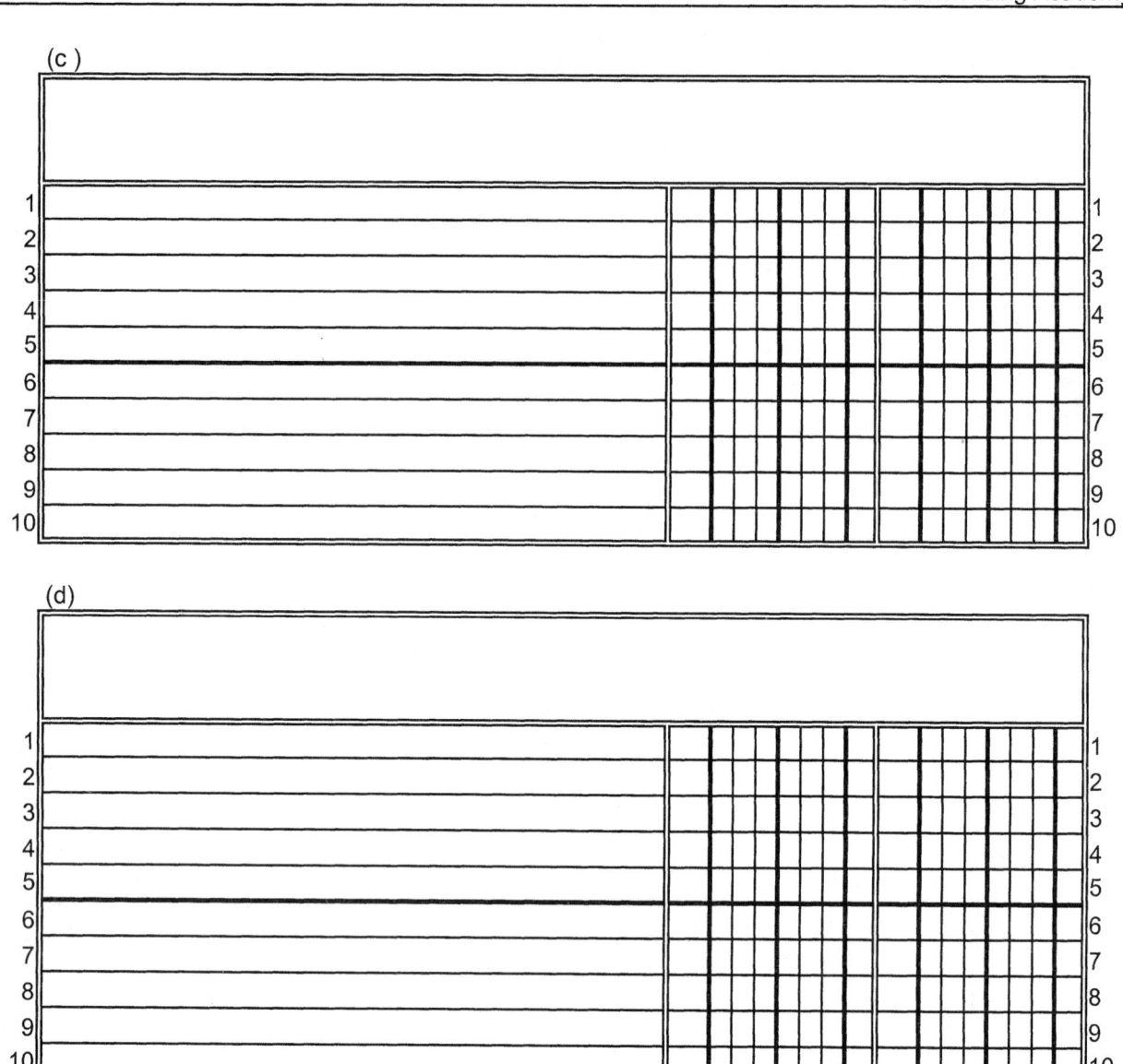

(d)

1	1
2	2
3	3
4	4
5	5
6	6
7	7
8	8
9	9
10	10
11	11
12	12
13	13
14	14
15	15
16	16
17	17
18	18
19	19
20	20
21	21
22	22
23	23
24	24
25	25
26	26
27	27
28	28
29	29
30	30
31	31
32	32
33	33
34	34
35	35
36	36
37	37
38	38

1	(a)	1
2		2
3		3
4		4
5		5
6		6
7	(b)	7
8		8
9		9
10		10
11		11
12		12
13		13
14		14
15		15
16		16
17		17
18		18
19		19
20		20
21	(c)	21
22		22
23		23
24		24
25		25
26		26
27		27
28		28
29		29
30		30
31		31
32		32
33		33
34		34
35		35
36		36
37		37
38		38

#1

(a)

(b)

(c)

(d)

#2

Item	(a) Type of Adjustment	(b) Accounts before Adjustment	
1.			
2.			
3.			
4.			

#3

	Date	Account Titles	Debit	Credit	
1	Dec. 31				1
2					2
3					3
4					4

5			5
6	Advertising Supplies	Advertising Supplies Expense	6
7			7
8			8
9			9
10			10

#4

	Date	Account Titles	Debit	Credit	
12	Date	Account Titles	Debit	Credit	12
13	Dec. 31				13
14					14
15					15

16			16
17	Depr. Expense - Equipment	Accum. Depreciation - Equipment	17
18			18
19			19
20			20
21			21
22			22
23			23
24			24
25			25
26			26

#5

	Date	Account Titles	Debit	Credit	
28	Date	Account Titles	Debit	Credit	28
29	July 1				29
30					30
31					31
32	Dec. 31				32
33					33
34					34

35			35
36	Prepaid Insurance	Insurance Expense	36
37			37
38			38
39			39
40			40

#6

	Date	Account Titles	Debit	Credit	
1	July 1				1
2					2
3					3
4					4
5	Dec. 31				5
6					6
7					7
8					8
9					9
10					10

	Unearned Insurance Revenue		Insurance Revenue	
11				11
12				12
13				13
14				14
15				15

#7

	Date	Account Titles	Debit	Credit	
16					16
17	Date	Account Titles	Debit	Credit	17
18	Dec. 31				18
19					19
20					20
21	31				21
22					22
23					23
24	31				24
25					25
26					26

#8

	Account	(a) Type of Adjustment	(b) Related Account	
27				27
28				28
29				29
30				30
31				31
32				32
33				33
34				34
35				35
36				36
37				37
38				38
39				39
40				40

#9

	Lucille Company			
	Income Statement			
	For the Year Ended December 31, 2005			

#10

	Lucille Company			
	Owner's Equity Statement			
	For the Year Ended December 31, 2005			

#11

	Date	Account Titles	Debit	Credit
(a)				
	Apr. 30			
(b)				
	Apr. 30			

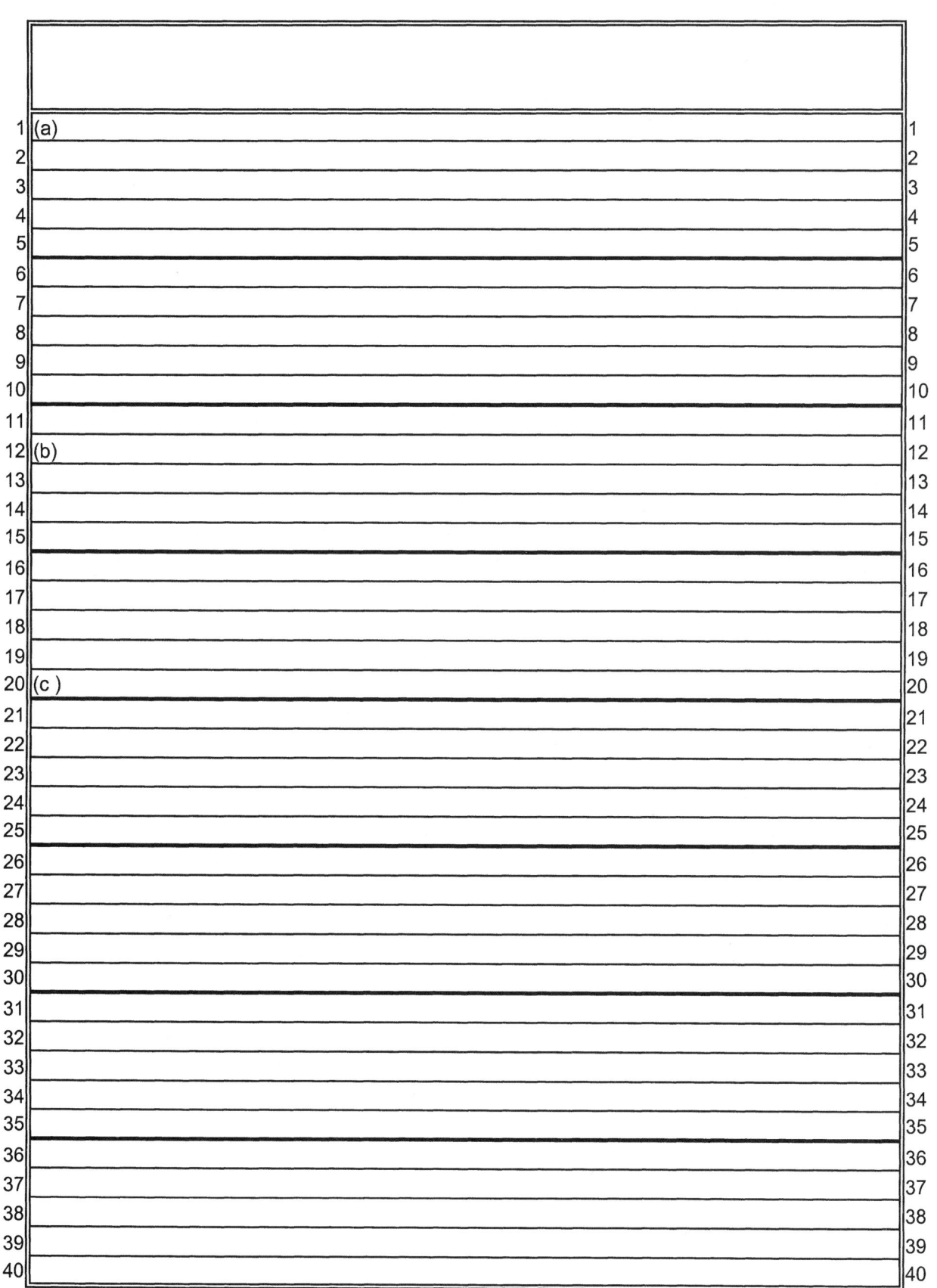

(a)

(b)

(c)

#2

	Item	(a) Type of Adjustment	(b) Accounts before Adjustment	
1	1.			1
2				2
3				3
4	2.			4
5				5
6				6
7	3.			7
8				8
9				9
10	4.			10
11				11
12				12
13	5.			13
14				14
15				15
16	6.			16
17				17
18				18
19				19

#3

	Date	Account Titles	Debit	Credit	
1	1.				1
2					2
3					3
4	2.				4
5					5
6					6
7	3.				7
8					8
9					9
10	4.				10
11					11
12					12
13	5.				13
14					14
15					15
16					16

#4

	Date	Account Titles	Debit	Credit	
1	1.				1
2					2
3					3
4	2.				4
5					5
6					6
7	3.				7
8					8
9					9
10	4.				10
11					11
12					12
13	5.				13
14					14
15					15
16					16
17					17

#5

	Date	Account Titles	Debit	Credit	
1	1.				1
2					2
3					3
4	2.				4
5					5
6					6
7	3.				7
8					8
9					9
10	4.				10
11					11
12					12
13	5.				13
14					14
15					15
16	6.				16
17					17
18					18
19	7.				19
20					20

#6

	Olympic Co.
	Income Statement
	For the Month Ended July 31, 2005

1				
1				
2				
3				
4				
5				
6				
7				
8				
9				
10				

#7

	Answer	Computation	
1	(a)		
2			
3			
4			
5			
6	(b)		
7			
8			
9			
10			
11			
12			
13			
14	(c)		
15			
16			
17			
18			
19			
20	(d)		
21			
22			
23			
24			
25			

	Date	Account Titles	Debit	Credit	
1	(a)				1
2	July 10				2
3					3
4					4
5	14				5
6					6
7					7
8	15				8
9					9
10					10
11	20				11
12					12
13					13
14					14
15					15
16	(b)				16
17	July 31				17
18					18
19					19
20	31				20
21					21
22					22
23	31				23
24					24
25					25
26	31				26
27					27
28					28
29					29
30					30
31					31
32					32
33					33
34					34
35					35
36					36
37					37
38					38
39					39
40					40

#9

	Date	Account Titles	Debit	Credit	
1	Aug. 31				1
2					2
3					3
4	31				4
5					5
6					6
7	31				7
8					8
9					9
10	31				10
11					11
12					12
13	31				13
14					14
15					15
16	31				16
17					17
18					18
19					19
20					20

#10

	Villa Company			
	Income Statement			
	For the Year Ended August 31, 2004			
1				1
2				2
3				3
4				4
5				5
6				6
7				7
8				8
9				9
10				10
11				11
12				12
13				13
14				14
15				15

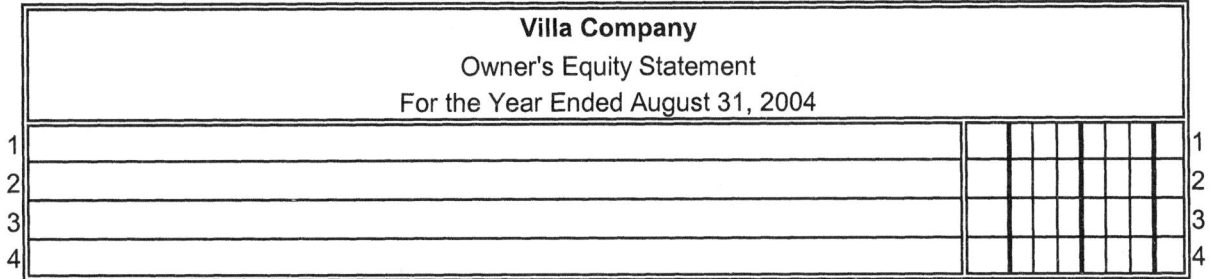

Villa Company
Owner's Equity Statement
For the Year Ended August 31, 2004

1		1
2		2
3		3
4		4

Villa Company
Balance Sheet
August 31, 2004

	Assets	
1	Assets	1
2		2
3		3
4		4
5		5
6		6
7		7
8		8
9		9
10	Liabilities and Owner's Equity	10
11		11
12		12
13		13
14		14
15		15
16		16
17		17
18		18
19		19
20		20

Account Titles	Debit	Credit
1 (a)		
2 1.		
3		
4		
5 2.		
6		
7		
8 3. (a)		
9		
10		
11 (b)		
12		
13		
14		
15 4.		
16		
17		
18 5.		
19		
20		
21		
22		
23		
24		
25 (b)		
26		
27		
28		
29		
30		
31		
32		
33		
34		
35		
36		
37		
38		
39		
40		

(a)

	Date	Account Titles	Debit	Credit	
1	Jan. 2				1
2					2
3					3
4	10				4
5					5
6					6
7	15				7
8					8

CASH   SERVICE REVENUE

INSURANCE EXPENSE   SUPPLIES EXPENSE

(b)

	Date	Account Titles	Debit	Credit	
1	Jan. 31				1
2					2
3					3
4	31				4
5					5
6					6
7	31				7
8					8

PREPAID INSURANCE   INSURANCE EXPENSE

SUPPLIES   SUPPLIES EXPENSE

UNEARNED REVENUE   SERVICE REVENUE

(c)

(a)

	Date	Account Titles and Explanations	Ref.	Debit	Credit	
1	2005					1
2	May 31					2
3						3
4						4
5	31					5
6						6
7						7
8						8
9	31					9
10						10
11						11
12						12
13	31					13
14						14
15						15
16						16
17	31					17
18						18
19						19
20						20
21	31					21
22						22
23						23
24						24
25	31					25
26						26
27						27
28						28
29						29
30						30
31						31
32						32
33						33
34						34
35						35
36						36
37						37
38						38
39						39
40						40

General Journal   J4

(b)

Cash   No. 101

Date	Explanation	Ref.	Debit	Credit	Balance
2005					
May 31	Balance	√			7 7 0 0

Accounts Receivable   No. 110

Date	Explanation	Ref.	Debit	Credit	Balance
2005					
May 31	Balance	√			4 0 0 0

Prepaid Insurance   No. 120

Date	Explanation	Ref.	Debit	Credit	Balance
2005					
May 31	Balance	√			2 4 0 0

Supplies   No. 130

Date	Explanation	Ref.	Debit	Credit	Balance
2005					
May 31	Balance	√			1 5 0 0

Office Furniture   No. 135

Date	Explanation	Ref.	Debit	Credit	Balance
2005					
May 31	Balance	√			1 2 0 0 0

Accumulated Depreciation - Office Furniture   No, 136

Date	Explanation	Ref.	Debit	Credit	Balance

Accounts Payable   No. 200

Date	Explanation	Ref.	Debit	Credit	Balance
2005					
May 31	Balance	√			3 5 0 0

(b) (Continued)

Travel Payable   No. 210

Date	Explanation	Ref.	Debit	Credit	Balance

Salaries Payable   No. 220

Date	Explanation	Ref.	Debit	Credit	Balance

Unearned Service Revenue   No. 230

Date	Explanation	Ref.	Debit	Credit	Balance
2005					
May 31	Balance	√			3 0 0 0

L. Rig, Capital   No. 300

Date	Explanation	Ref.	Debit	Credit	Balance
2005					
May 31	Balance	√			1 9 1 0 0

Service Revenue   No. 400

Date	Explanation	Ref.	Debit	Credit	Balance
2005					
May 31	Balance	√			6 0 0 0

Salaries Expense   No. 510

Date	Explanation	Ref.	Debit	Credit	Balance
2005					
May 31	Balance	√			3 0 0 0

Rent Expense   No. 520

Date	Explanation	Ref.	Debit	Credit	Balance
2005					
May 31	Balance	√			1 0 0 0

(b) (Continued)

Depreciation Expense   No. 530

Date	Explanation	Ref.	Debit	Credit	Balance

Insurance Expense   No. 540

Date	Explanation	Ref.	Debit	Credit	Balance

Travel Expense   No. 550

Date	Explanation	Ref.	Debit	Credit	Balance

Supplies Expense   No. 560

Date	Explanation	Ref.	Debit	Credit	Balance

(c)

Vektek Consulting Adjusted Trial Balance May 31, 2005	Debit	Credit
1		
2		
3		
4		
5		
6		
7		
8		
9		
10		
11		
12		
13		
14		
15		
16		
17		
18		
19		
20		
21		
22		
23		
24		
25		
26		
27		
28		
29		
30		
31		
32		
33		
34		
35		
36		
37		
38		
39		
40		

Name _____
Section _____
Date _____

Problem 3-2A

Thayer Motel

(a)

	Date	Account Titles and Explanations	Ref	Debit	Credit	
		General Journal			J1	
1	May 31					1
2						2
3						3
4	31					4
5						5
6						6
7	31					7
8						8
9						9
10	31					10
11						11
12						12
13	31					13
14						14
15						15
16	31					16
17						17
18						18
19	31					19
20						20
21						21
22						22
23						23
24						24
25						25
26						26

(b)

Cash   No. 101

Date	Explanation	Ref.	Debit	Credit	Balance
May 31	Balance	√			2500

Supplies   No. 126

Date	Explanation	Ref.	Debit	Credit	Balance
May 31	Balance	√			1900

(b)

Prepaid Insurance   No. 130

Date	Explanation	Ref.	Debit	Credit	Balance
May 31	Balance	√			2 4 0 0

Land   No. 140

Date	Explanation	Ref.	Debit	Credit	Balance
May 31	Balance	√			1 5 0 0 0

Lodge   No. 141

Date	Explanation	Ref.	Debit	Credit	Balance
May 31	Balance	√			7 0 0 0 0

Accumulated Depreciation - Lodge   No. 142

Date	Explanation	Ref.	Debit	Credit	Balance

Furniture   No. 149

Date	Explanation	Ref.	Debit	Credit	Balance
May 31	Balance	√			1 6 8 0 0

Accumulated Depreciation - Furniture   No. 150

Date	Explanation	Ref.	Debit	Credit	Balance

Accounts Payable   No. 201

Date	Explanation	Ref.	Debit	Credit	Balance
May 31	Balance	√			5 3 0 0

Unearned Rent   No. 208

Date	Explanation	Ref.	Debit	Credit	Balance
May 31	Balance	√			3 6 0 0

Salaries Payable   No. 212

Date	Explanation	Ref.	Debit	Credit	Balance

Interest Payable   No. 230

Date	Explanation	Ref.	Debit	Credit	Balance

(b) (Continued)

Mortgage Payable   No. 275

Date	Explanation	Ref.	Debit	Credit	Balance
May 31	Balance	√			3 5 0 0 0

Sue Phillips, Capital   No. 301

Date	Explanation	Ref.	Debit	Credit	Balance
May 31	Balance	√			6 0 0 0 0

Rent Revenue   No. 429

Date	Explanation	Ref.	Debit	Credit	Balance
May 31	Balance	√			9 2 0 0

Advertising Expense   No. 610

Date	Explanation	Ref.	Debit	Credit	Balance
May 31	Balance	√			5 0 0

Depreciation Expense - Lodge   No. 619

Date	Explanation	Ref.	Debit	Credit	Balance

Depreciation Expense - Furniture   No. 621

Date	Explanation	Ref.	Debit	Credit	Balance

Supplies Expense   No. 631

Date	Explanation	Ref.	Debit	Credit	Balance

Interest Expense   No. 718

Date	Explanation	Ref.	Debit	Credit	Balance

Insurance Expense   No. 722

Date	Explanation	Ref.	Debit	Credit	Balance

Salaries Expense   No. 726

Date	Explanation	Ref.	Debit	Credit	Balance
May 31	Balance	√			3 0 0 0

(b) (Continued)

Utilities Expense   No. 732

Date	Explanation	Ref.	Debit	Credit	Balance
May 31	Balance	√			1 0 0 0

(c)

Thayer Motel
Adjusted Trial Balance
May 31, 2005

	Debit	Credit
1		
2		
3		
4		
5		
6		
7		
8		
9		
10		
11		
12		
13		
14		
15		
16		
17		
18		
19		
20		
21		
22		
23		
24		
25		
26		
27		

(d)

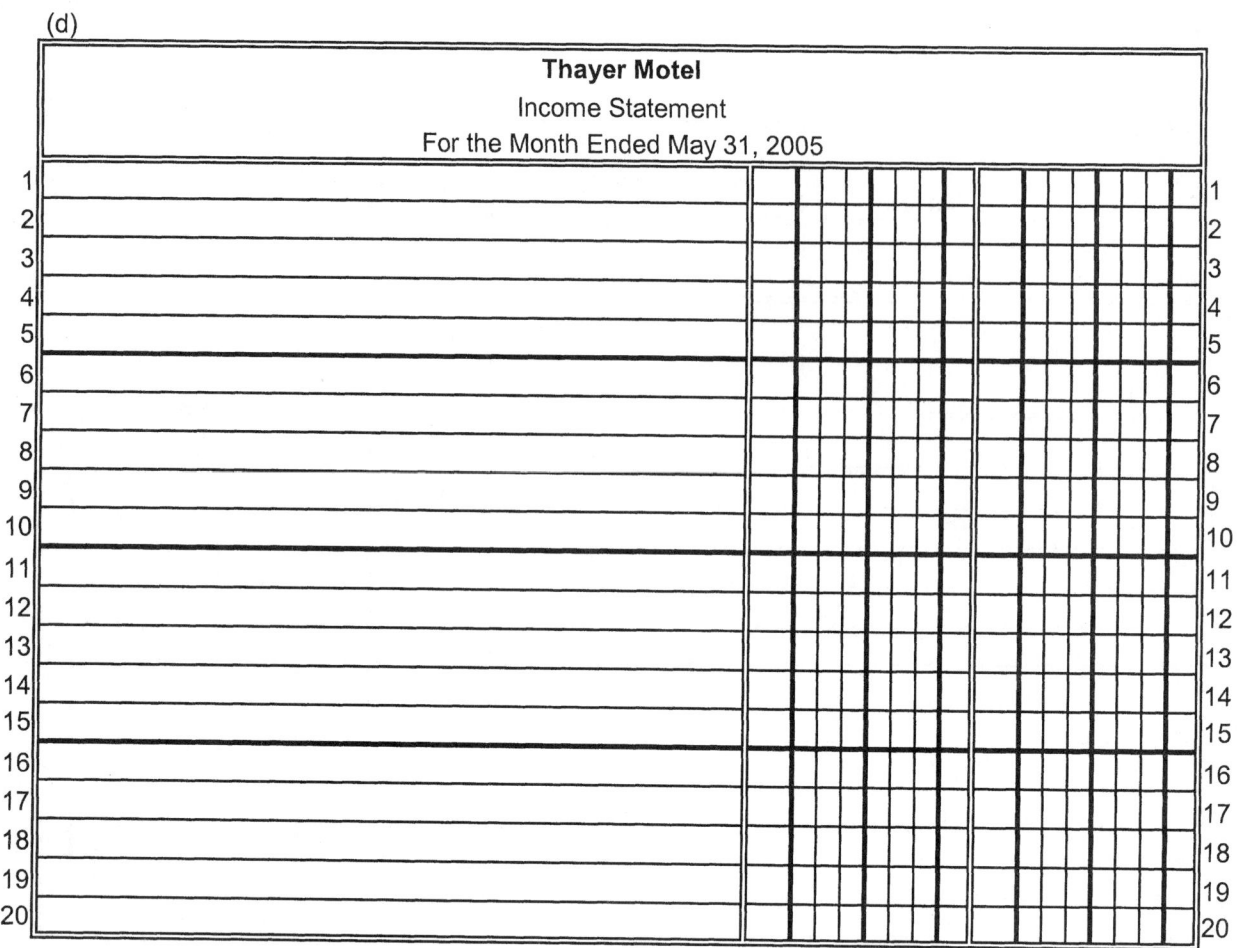

Thayer Motel

Income Statement

For the Month Ended May 31, 2005

Thayer Motel

Owner's Equity Statement

For the Month Ended May 31, 2005

(d) (Continued)

Thayer Motel
Balance Sheet
May 31, 2005

Assets		

Liabilities and Owner's Equity		

(a)

	Date	Accounts Titles and Explanation	Debit	Credit	
1	Sept. 30				1
2					2
3					3
4	30				4
5					5
6					6
7	30				7
8					8
9					9
10	30				10
11					11
12					12
13	30				13
14					14
15					15
16	30				16
17					17
18					18
19	30				19
20					20
21					21

(b)

	Mendoza Co. Income Statement For the Quarter Ended September 30, 2005			
1				1
2				2
3				3
4				4
5				5
6				6
7				7
8				8
9				9
10				10
11				11
12				12
13				13
14				14

(b) (Continued)

Mendoza Co.

Owner's Equity Statement

For the Quarter Ended September 30, 2005

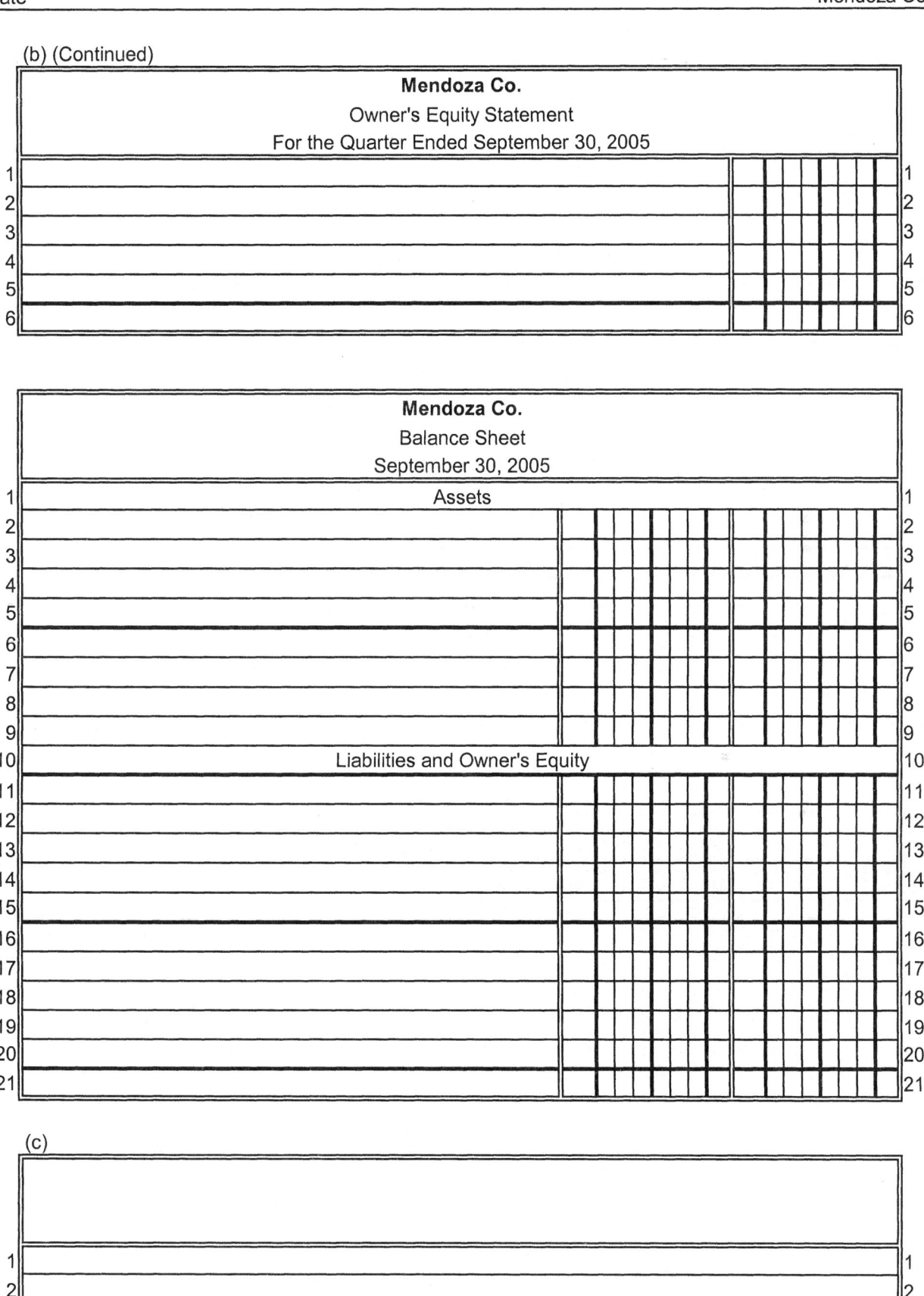

Mendoza Co.

Balance Sheet

September 30, 2005

Assets

Liabilities and Owner's Equity

(c)

General Journal

	Date	Accounts Titles and Explanation	Debit	Credit	
1	1.				1
2	Dec. 31				2
3					3
4					4
5					5
6	2.				6
7	Dec. 31				7
8					8
9					9
10					10
11	3.				11
12	Dec. 31				12
13					13
14					14
15					15
16	4.				16
17	Dec. 31				17
18					18
19					19
20					20
21					21
22					22
23					23
24					24
25					25
26					26
27					27
28					28
29					29
30					30
31					31
32					32
33					33
34					34
35					35
36					36
37					37
38					38
39					39
40					40

(a), (c) and (e)

Cash
No. 101

Date	Explanation	Ref.	Debit	Credit	Balance
Nov. 1	Balance	√			2790

Accounts Receivable
No. 112

Date	Explanation	Ref.	Debit	Credit	Balance
Nov. 1	Balance	√			2510

Supplies
No. 126

Date	Explanation	Ref.	Debit	Credit	Balance
Nov. 1	Balance	√			2000

Store Equipment
No. 153

Date	Explanation	Ref.	Debit	Credit	Balance
Nov. 1	Balance	√			10000

Accumulated Depreciation - Store Equipment
No. 154

Date	Explanation	Ref.	Debit	Credit	Balance
Nov. 1	Balance	√			500

Accounts Payable
No. 201

Date	Explanation	Ref.	Debit	Credit	Balance
Nov. 1	Balance	√			2100

(a), (c) and (e) (Continued)

Unearned Service Revenue   No. 209

Date	Explanation	Ref.	Debit	Credit	Balance
Nov. 1	Balance	√			1 4 0 0

Salaries Payable   No. 212

Date	Explanation	Ref.	Debit	Credit	Balance
Nov. 1	Balance	√			5 0 0

P. Samone, Capital   No. 301

Date	Explanation	Ref.	Debit	Credit	Balance
Nov. 1	Balance	√			1 2 8 0 0

Service Revenue   No. 407

Date	Explanation	Ref.	Debit	Credit	Balance

Depreciation Expense   No. 615

Date	Explanation	Ref.	Debit	Credit	Balance

Supplies Expense   No. 631

Date	Explanation	Ref.	Debit	Credit	Balance

Salaries Expense   No. 726

Date	Explanation	Ref.	Debit	Credit	Balance

Rent Expense   No. 729

Date	Explanation	Ref.	Debit	Credit	Balance

(b)

		General Journal			J1
	Date		Ref	Debit	Credit
1	Nov. 8				
2					
3					
4					
5	10				
6					
7					
8	12				
9					
10					
11	15				
12					
13					
14	17				
15					
16					
17	20				
18					
19					
20	22				
21					
22					
23	25				
24					
25					
26	27				
27					
28					
29	29				
30					
31					
32					
33					
34					
35					

(d) & (f)

| | | Before Adjustment | | After Adjustment | |
		Dr.	Cr.	Dr.	Cr.
1	Cash				
2	Accounts Receivable				
3	Supplies				
4	Equipment				
5	Accumulated				
6	Depreciation				
7	Accounts Payable				
8	Unearned Service				
9	Revenue				
10	Salaries Payable				
11	P. Samone, Capital				
12	Service Revenue				
13	Depreciation Expense				
14	Supplies Expense				
15	Salaries Expense				
16	Rent Expense				
17	Totals				
18					
19					
20					

Samone Equipment Repair — Trial Balances — November 30, 2005

(e)   General Journal   J1

	Date	Account Titles	Ref	Debit	Credit
1	1.				
2	Nov. 30				
3					
4	2.				
5	Nov. 30				
6					
7	3.				
8	Nov. 30				
9					
10	4.				
11	Nov. 30				
12					
13					

(g)

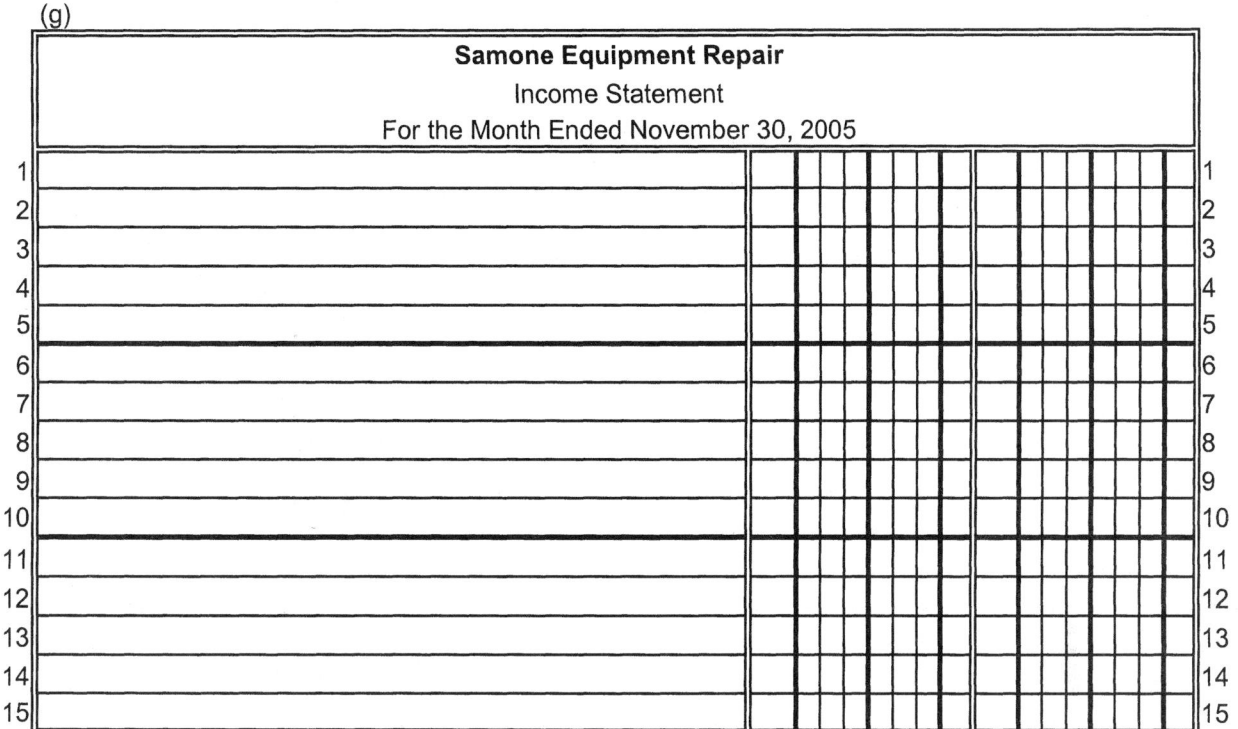

Samone Equipment Repair
Income Statement
For the Month Ended November 30, 2005

Samone Equipment Repair
Owner's Equity Statement
For the Month Ended November 30, 2005

(g) (Continued)

Samone Equipment Repair		
Balance Sheet		
November 30, 2005		
Assets		
Liabilities and Owner's Equity		

(a)

	Date	Account Titles and Explanations	Debit	Credit	
1	1.				1
2	June 30				2
3					3
4					4
5					5
6	2.				6
7	June 30				7
8					8
9					9
10					10
11	3.				11
12	June 30				12
13					13
14					14
15					15
16	4.				16
17	June 30				17
18					18
19					19
20					20
21	5.				21
22	June 30				22
23					23
24					24
25					25
26	6.				26
27	June 30				27
28					28
29					29
30					30
31					31
32					32
33					33
34					34
35					35
36					36
37					37
38					38
39					39
40					40

(b)

Salzer Graphics Company Adjusted Trial Balance June 30, 2005	Debit	Credit
1		
2		
3		
4		
5		
6		
7		
8		
9		
10		
11		
12		
13		
14		
15		
16		
17		
18		
19		
20		
21		
22		
23		
24		
25		

(c)

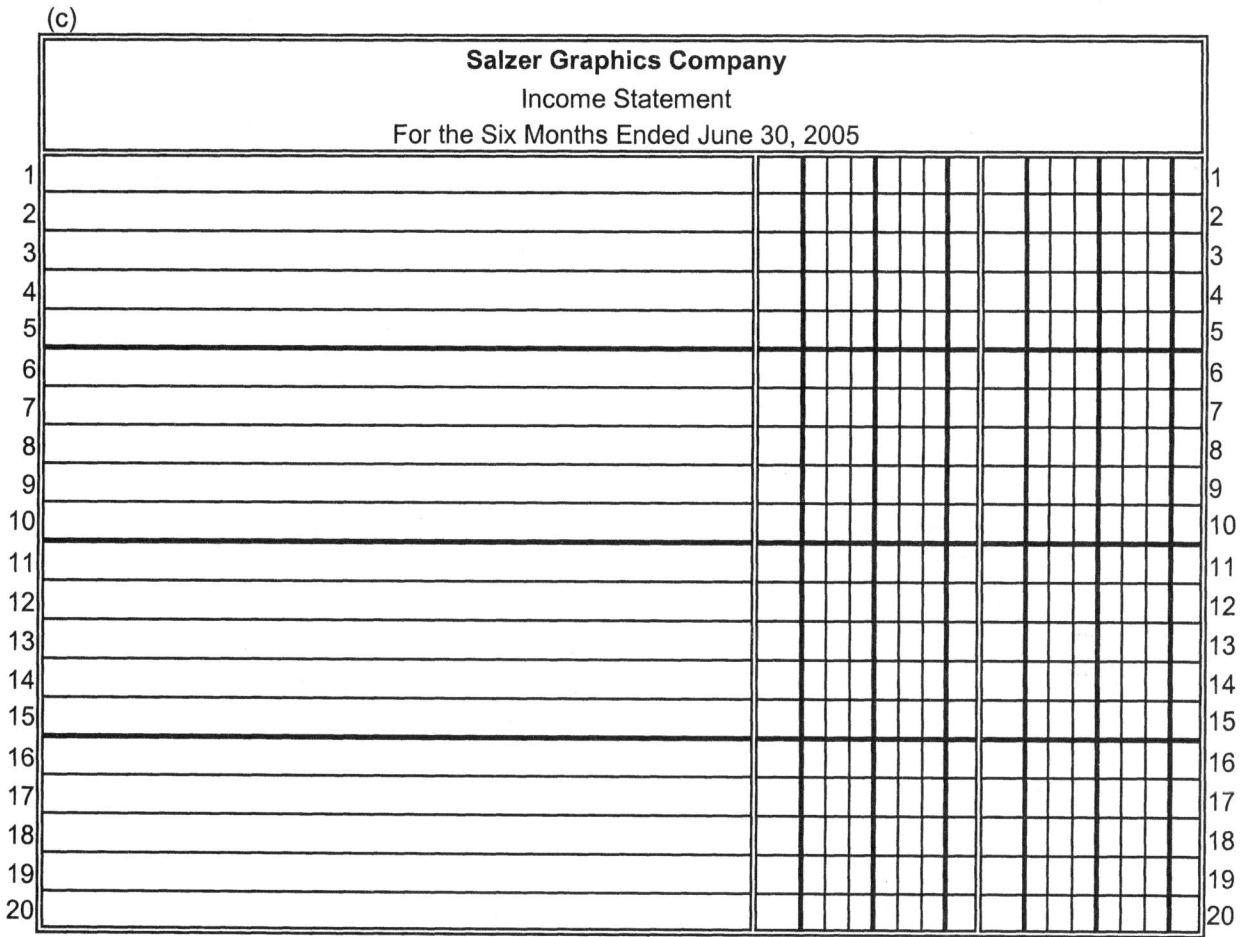

Salzer Graphics Company

Income Statement

For the Six Months Ended June 30, 2005

Salzer Graphics Company

Owner's Equity Statement

For the Six Months Ended June 30, 2005

(c) (Continued)

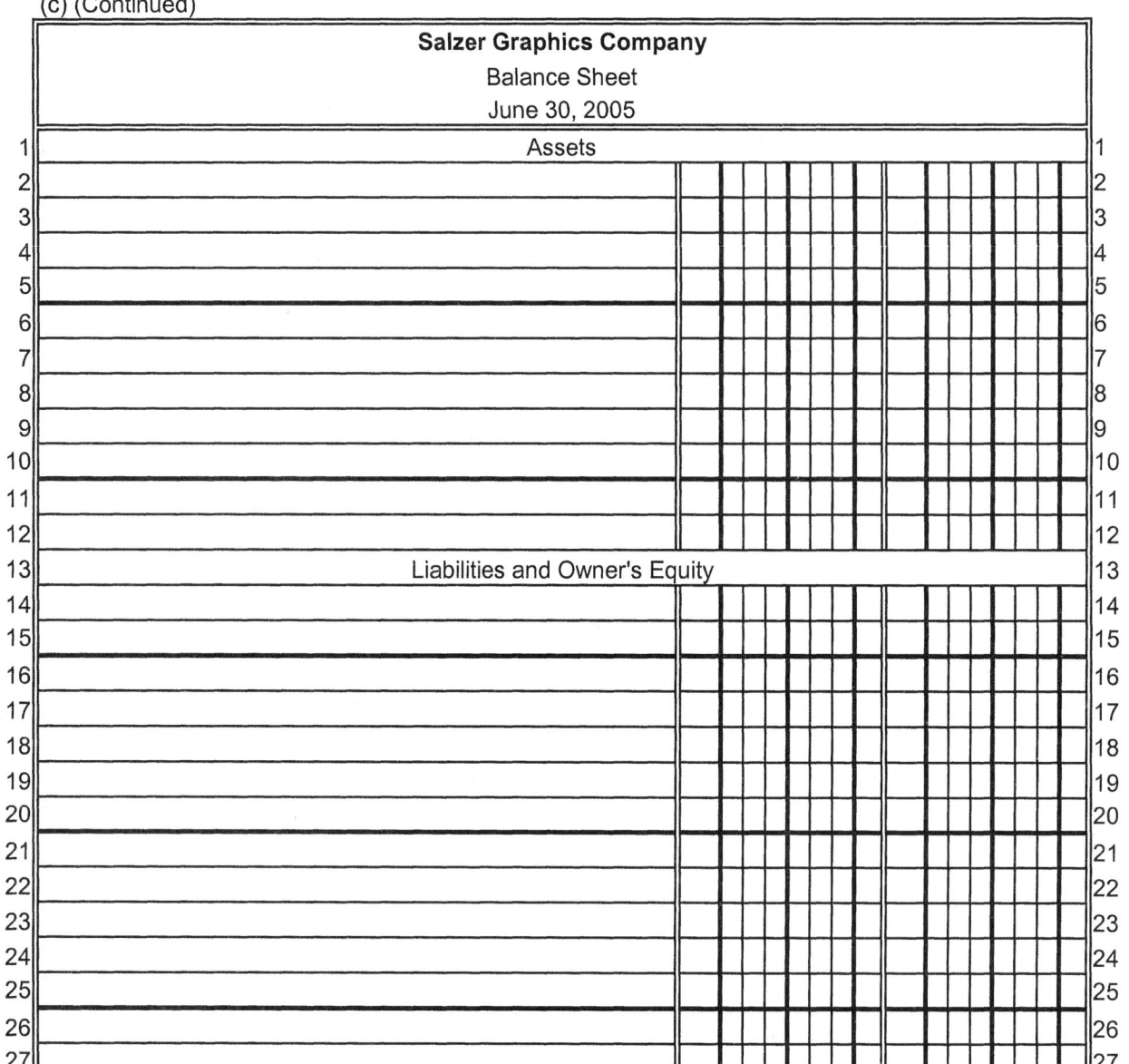

Salzer Graphics Company
Balance Sheet
June 30, 2005

Assets

Liabilities and Owner's Equity

(a)

	Date	Account Titles and Explanations	Ref.	Debit	Credit	
1	2005					1
2	June 30					2
3						3
4						4
5	30					5
6						6
7						7
8	30					8
9						9
10						10
11	30					11
12						12
13						13
14	30					14
15						15
16						16
17	30					17
18						18
19						19
20	30					20
21						21
22						22
23						23
24						24
25						25
26						26
27						27
28						28
29						29
30						30
31						31
32						32
33						33
34						34
35						35
36						36
37						37
38						38
39						39
40						40

General Journal   J3

(b)

Cash   No. 100

Date	Explanation	Ref.	Debit	Credit	Balance
2005					
June 30	Balance	√			7 1 5 0

Accounts Receivable   No. 110

Date	Explanation	Ref.	Debit	Credit	Balance
2005					
June 30	Balance	√			6 0 0 0

Prepaid Insurance   No. 120

Date	Explanation	Ref.	Debit	Credit	Balance
2005					
June 30	Balance	√			3 0 0 0

Supplies   No. 130

Date	Explanation	Ref.	Debit	Credit	Balance
2005					
June 30	Balance	√			2 0 0 0

Office Equipment   No. 135

Date	Explanation	Ref.	Debit	Credit	Balance
2005					
June 30	Balance	√			1 5 0 0 0

Accumulated Depreciation - Office Furniture   No, 136

Date	Explanation	Ref.	Debit	Credit	Balance

Accounts Payable   No. 200

Date	Explanation	Ref.	Debit	Credit	Balance
2005					
June 30	Balance	√			4 5 0 0

(b) (Continued)

Utilities Payable   No. 210

Date	Explanation	Ref.	Debit	Credit	Balance

Salaries Payable   No. 220

Date	Explanation	Ref.	Debit	Credit	Balance

Unearned Service Revenue   No. 230

Date	Explanation	Ref.	Debit	Credit	Balance
2005					
June 30	Balance	√			4 0 0 0

J. Cuono, Capital   No. 300

Date	Explanation	Ref.	Debit	Credit	Balance
2005					
June 30	Balance	√			2 1 7 5 0

Service Revenue   No. 400

Date	Explanation	Ref.	Debit	Credit	Balance
2005					
June 30	Balance	√			7 9 0 0

Salaries Expense   No. 510

Date	Explanation	Ref.	Debit	Credit	Balance
2005					
June 30	Balance	√			4 0 0 0

Rent Expense   No. 520

Date	Explanation	Ref.	Debit	Credit	Balance
2005					
June 30	Balance	√			1 0 0 0

(b) (Continued)

Depreciation Expense   No. 530

Date	Explanation	Ref.	Debit	Credit	Balance

Insurance Expense   No. 540

Date	Explanation	Ref.	Debit	Credit	Balance

Utilities Expense   No. 550

Date	Explanation	Ref.	Debit	Credit	Balance

Supplies Expense   No. 560

Date	Explanation	Ref.	Debit	Credit	Balance

(c)

Cuono Company Adjusted Trial Balance June 30, 2005	Debit	Credit
1		
2		
3		
4		
5		
6		
7		
8		
9		
10		
11		
12		
13		
14		
15		
16		
17		
18		
19		
20		
21		
22		
23		
24		
25		
26		
27		
28		
29		
30		
31		
32		
33		
34		
35		
36		
37		
38		
39		
40		

(a)

General Journal   J1

	Date	Account Titles and Explanations	Ref	Debit	Credit	
1	Aug. 31					1
2						2
3						3
4	31					4
5						5
6						6
7	31					7
8						8
9						9
10	31					10
11						11
12						12
13	31					13
14						14
15						15
16	31					16
17						17
18						18
19	31					19
20						20
21						21
22	31					22
23						23
24						24
25						25
26						26

(b)

Cash   No. 101

Date	Explanation	Ref.	Debit	Credit	Balance
Aug. 31	Balance	√			1 9 6 0 0

Accounts Receivable   No. 112

Date	Explanation	Ref.	Debit	Credit	Balance

134

(b) (Continued)

Supplies   No. 126

Date	Explanation	Ref.	Debit	Credit	Balance
Aug. 31	Balance	√			3 3 0 0

Prepaid Insurance   No. 130

Date	Explanation	Ref.	Debit	Credit	Balance
Aug.31	Balance	√			6 0 0 0

Land   No. 140

Date	Explanation	Ref.	Debit	Credit	Balance
Aug.31	Balance	√			2 5 0 0 0

Cottages   No. 143

Date	Explanation	Ref.	Debit	Credit	Balance
Aug. 31	Balance	√			1 2 5 0 0 0

Accumulated Depreciation - Cottages   No. 144

Date	Explanation	Ref.	Debit	Credit	Balance

Furniture   No. 149

Date	Explanation	Ref.	Debit	Credit	Balance
Aug. 31	Balance	√			2 6 0 0 0

Accumulated Depreciation - Furniture   No. 150

Date	Explanation	Ref.	Debit	Credit	Balance

Accounts Payable   No. 201

Date	Explanation	Ref.	Debit	Credit	Balance
Aug. 31	Balance	√			6 5 0 0

Unearned Rent   No. 208

Date	Explanation	Ref.	Debit	Credit	Balance
Aug. 31	Balance	√			7 4 0 0

Salaries Payable   No. 212

Date	Explanation	Ref.	Debit	Credit	Balance

(b) (Continued)

Interest Payable   No. 230

Date	Explanation	Ref.	Debit	Credit	Balance

Mortgage Payable   No. 275

Date	Explanation	Ref.	Debit	Credit	Balance
Aug. 31	Balance	√			8 0 0 0 0

P. Orbis, Capital   No. 301

Date	Explanation	Ref.	Debit	Credit	Balance
Aug. 31	Balance	√			1 0 0 0 0 0

P. Orbis, Drawing   No. 306

Date	Explanation	Ref.	Debit	Credit	Balance
Aug. 31	Balance	√			5 0 0 0

Rent Revenue   No. 429

Date	Explanation	Ref.	Debit	Credit	Balance
Aug. 31	Balance	√			8 0 0 0 0

Depreciation Expense - Cottages   No. 620

Date	Explanation	Ref.	Debit	Credit	Balance

Depreciation Expense - Furniture   No. 621

Date	Explanation	Ref.	Debit	Credit	Balance

Repair Expense   No. 622

Date	Explanation	Ref.	Debit	Credit	Balance
Aug. 31	Balance	√			3 6 0 0

Supplies Expense   No. 631

Date	Explanation	Ref.	Debit	Credit	Balance

Interest Expense   No. 718

Date	Explanation	Ref.	Debit	Credit	Balance

(b) (Continued)

Insurance Expense   No. 722

Date	Explanation	Ref.	Debit	Credit	Balance

Salaries Expense   No. 726

Date	Explanation	Ref.	Debit	Credit	Balance
Aug. 31	Balance	√			5 1 0 0 0

Utilities Expense   No. 732

Date	Explanation	Ref.	Debit	Credit	Balance
Aug. 31	Balance	√			9 4 0 0

(c)

Spring River Resort
Adjusted Trial Balance
August 31, 2005

	Debit	Credit
1		
2		
3		
4		
5		
6		
7		
8		
9		
10		
11		
12		
13		
14		
15		
16		
17		
18		
19		
20		
21		
22		
23		
24		
25		
26		
27		

(d)

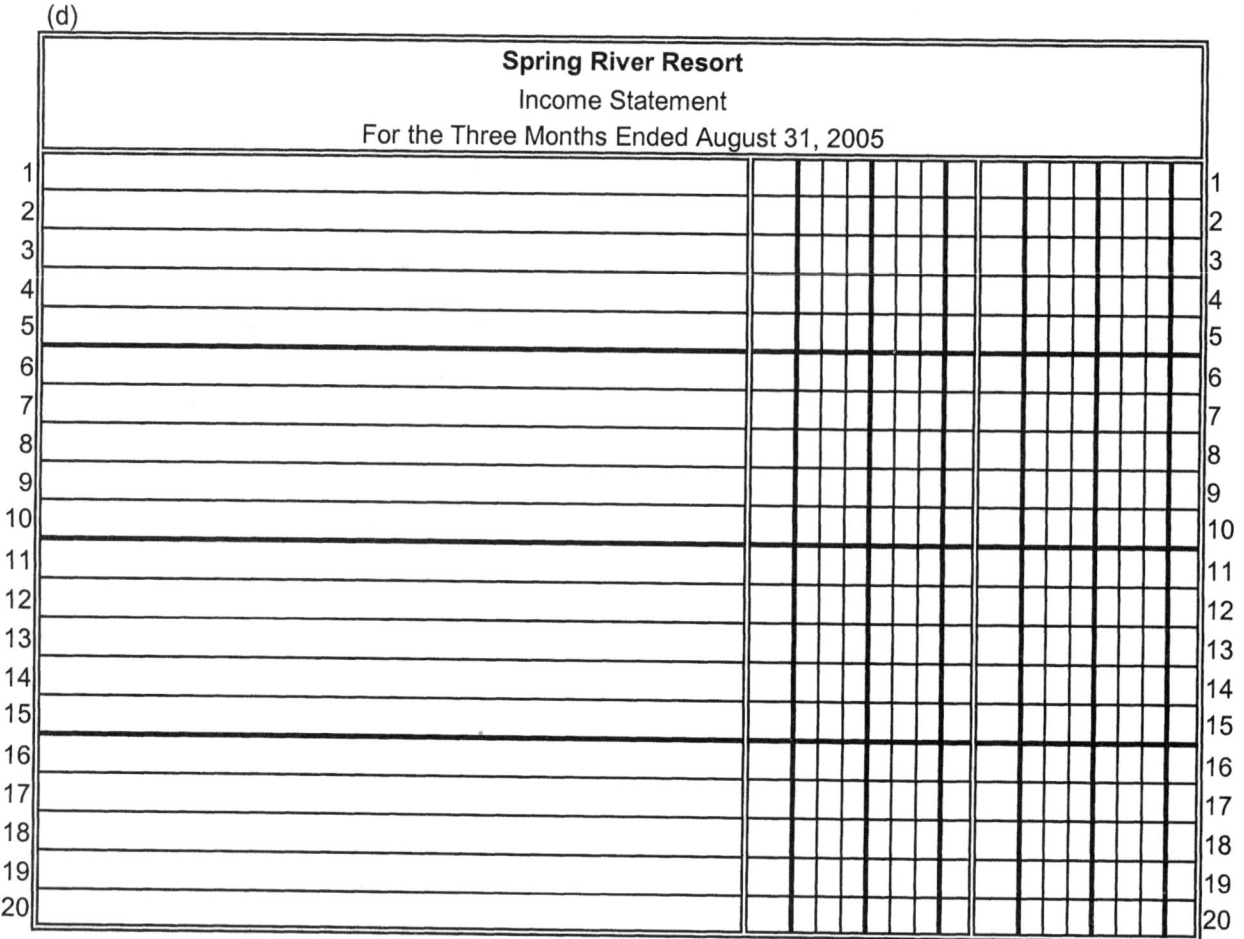

Spring River Resort

Income Statement

For the Three Months Ended August 31, 2005

Spring River Resort

Owner's Equity Statement

For the Three Months Ended August 31, 2005

(d) (Continued)

Spring River Resort
Balance Sheet
August 31, 2005

Assets				
Liabilities and Owner's Equity				

(a)

	Date	Accounts Titles and Explanation	Debit	Credit	
1	Dec. 31				1
2					2
3					3
4	31				4
5					5
6					6
7	31				7
8					8
9					9
10	31				10
11					11
12					12
13	31				13
14					14
15					15
16	31				16
17					17
18					18
19	31				19
20					20
21					21

(b)

Costello Advertising Agency
Income Statement
For the Year Ended December 31, 2005

1			1
2			2
3			3
4			4
5			5
6			6
7			7
8			8
9			9
10			10
11			11
12			12
13			13
14			14

(b) (Continued)

Costello Advertising Agency		
Owner's Equity Statement		
For the Year Ended December 31, 2005		
1		1
2		2
3		3
4		4
5		5
6		6

Costello Advertising Agency		
Balance Sheet		
December 31, 2005		
1	Assets	1
2		2
3		3
4		4
5		5
6		6
7		7
8		8
9		9
10	Liabilities and Owner's Equity	10
11		11
12		12
13		13
14		14
15		15
16		16
17		17
18		18
19		19
20		20
21		21

(c)

1	(1)
2	
3	
4	
5	
6	
7	
8	
9	
10	
11	(2)
12	
13	
14	
15	
16	
17	
18	
19	
20	

General Journal

	Date	Accounts Titles and Explanation	Debit	Credit	
1	1.				1
2	Dec. 31				2
3					3
4					4
5					5
6	2.				6
7	Dec. 31				7
8					8
9					9
10					10
11	3.				11
12	Dec. 31				12
13					13
14					14
15					15
16	4.				16
17	Dec. 31				17
18					18
19					19
20					20
21					21
22					22
23					23
24					24
25					25
26					26
27					27
28					28
29					29
30					30
31					31
32					32
33					33
34					34
35					35
36					36
37					37
38					38
39					39
40					40

(a), (c) and (e)

Cash   No. 101

Date	Explanation	Ref.	Debit	Credit	Balance
Sept. 1	Balance	√			4 8 8 0

Accounts Receivable   No. 112

Date	Explanation	Ref.	Debit	Credit	Balance
Sept. 1	Balance	√			3 5 2 0

Supplies   No. 126

Date	Explanation	Ref.	Debit	Credit	Balance
Sept. 1	Balance	√			2 0 0 0

Store Equipment   No. 153

Date	Explanation	Ref.	Debit	Credit	Balance
Sept. 1	Balance	√			1 5 0 0 0

Accumulated Depreciation - Equipment   No. 154

Date	Explanation	Ref.	Debit	Credit	Balance
Sept. 1	Balance	√			1 5 0 0

Accounts Payable   No. 201

Date	Explanation	Ref.	Debit	Credit	Balance
Sept. 1	Balance	√			3 4 0 0

(a), (c) and (e) (Continued)

Unearned Service Revenue   No. 209

Date	Explanation	Ref.	Debit	Credit	Balance
Sept. 1	Balance	√			1 4 0 0

Salaries Payable   No. 212

Date	Explanation	Ref.	Debit	Credit	Balance
Sept. 1	Balance	√			5 0 0

J. Beck, Capital   No. 301

Date	Explanation	Ref.	Debit	Credit	Balance
Sept. 1	Balance	√			1 8 6 0 0

Service Revenue   No. 407

Date	Explanation	Ref.	Debit	Credit	Balance

Depreciation Expense   No. 615

Date	Explanation	Ref.	Debit	Credit	Balance

Supplies Expense   No. 631

Date	Explanation	Ref.	Debit	Credit	Balance

Salaries Expense   No. 726

Date	Explanation	Ref.	Debit	Credit	Balance

Rent Expense   No. 729

Date	Explanation	Ref.	Debit	Credit	Balance

(b)

General Journal

J1

	Date		Ref.	Debit	Credit	
1	Sept. 8					1
2						2
3						3
4						4
5	10					5
6						6
7						7
8	12					8
9						9
10						10
11	15					11
12						12
13						13
14	17					14
15						15
16						16
17	20					17
18						18
19						19
20	22					20
21						21
22						22
23	25					23
24						24
25						25
26	27					26
27						27
28						28
29	29					29
30						30
31						31
32						32
33						33
34						34
35						35

(d) & (f)

	Beck Equipment Repair Trial Balances September 30, 2005				
		Before Adjustment		After Adjustment	
		Dr.	Cr.	Dr.	Cr.
1	Cash				
2	Accounts Receivable				
3	Supplies				
4	Equipment				
5	Accumulated				
6	Depreciation				
7	Accounts Payable				
8	Unearned Service				
9	Revenue				
10	Salaries Payable				
11	J. Beck, Capital				
12	Service Revenue				
13	Depreciation Expense				
14	Supplies Expense				
15	Salaries Expense				
16	Rent Expense				
17	Totals				
18					
19					
20					

(e) General Journal J1

	Date	Account Titles	Ref	Debit	Credit
1	1.				
2	Sept. 30				
3					
4	2.				
5	Sept. 30				
6					
7	3.				
8	Sept. 30				
9					
10	4.				
11	Sept. 30				
12					
13					

(g)

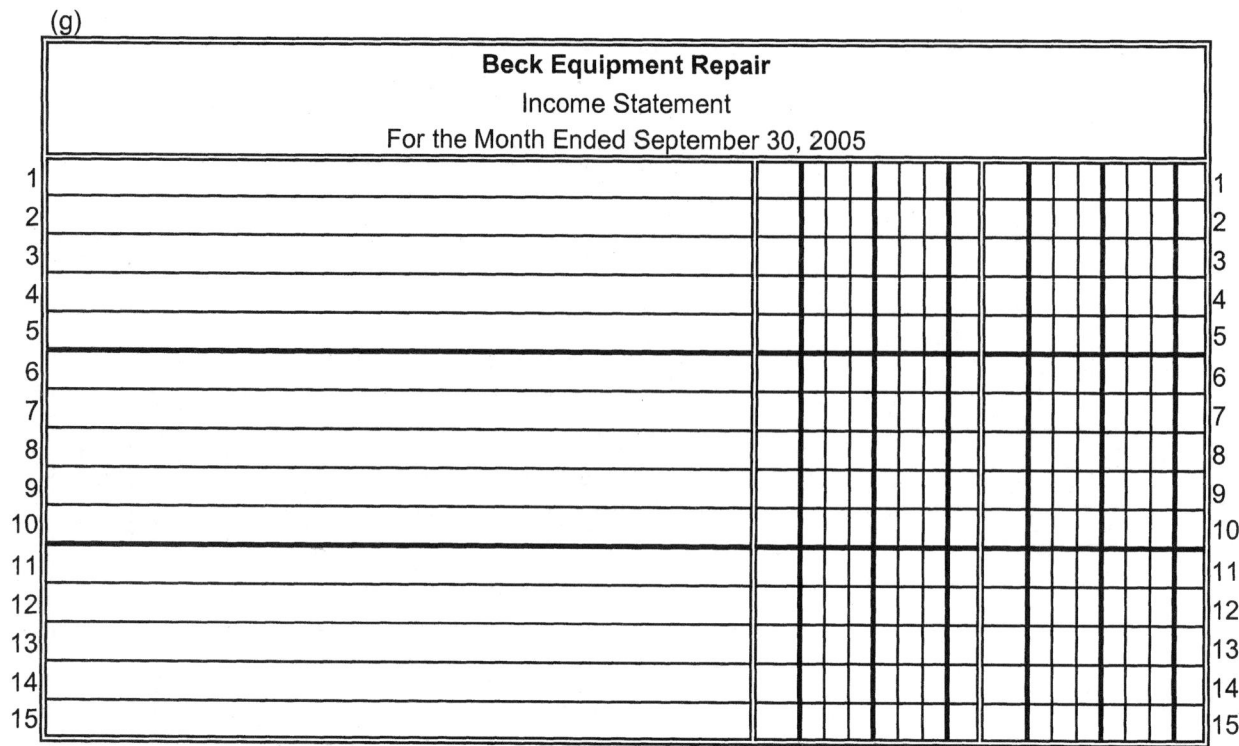

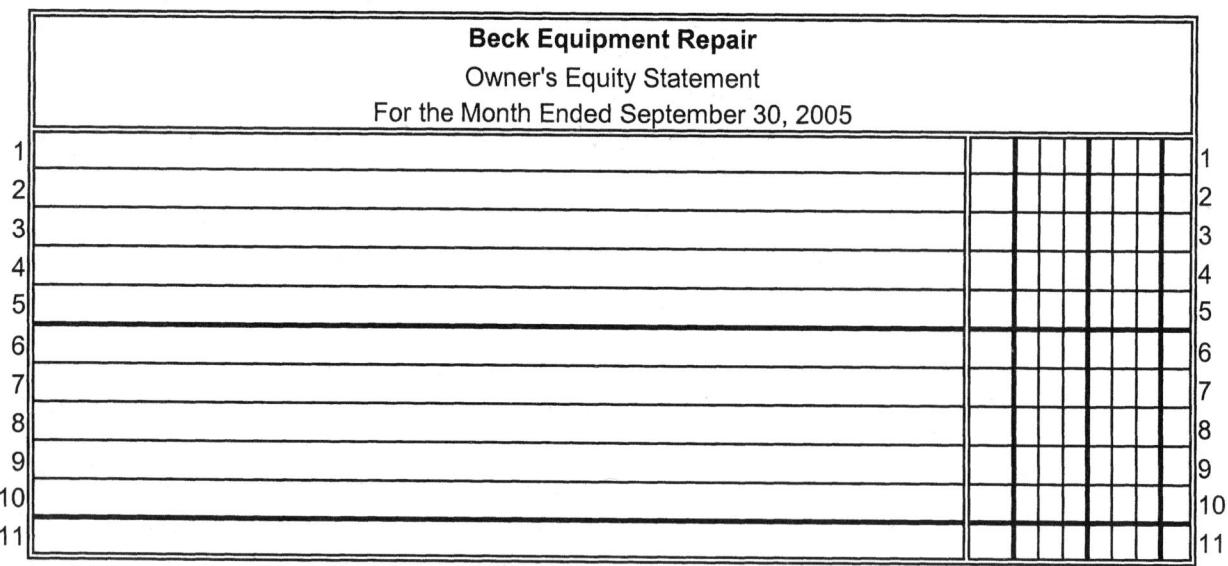

(g) (Continued)

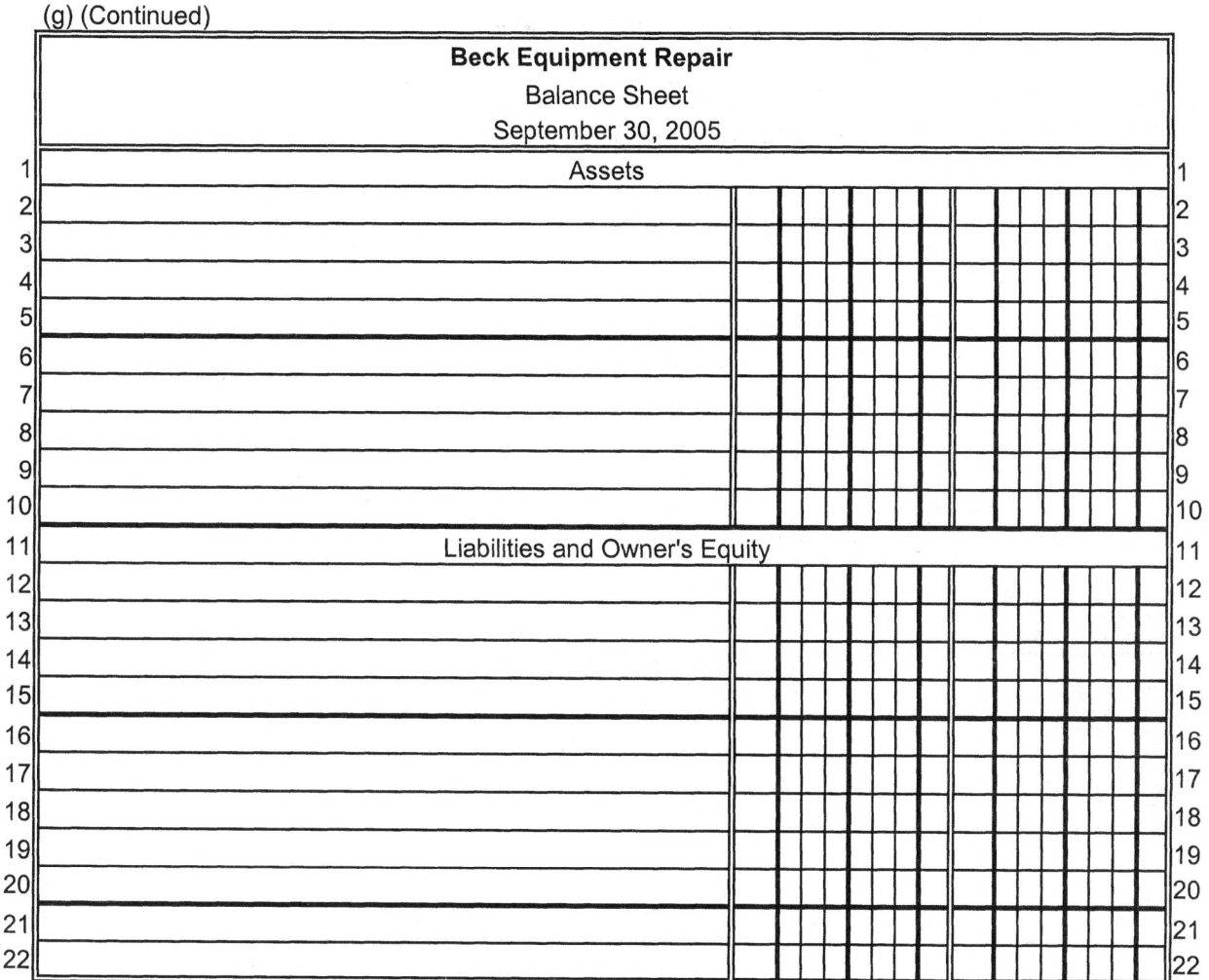

Beck Equipment Repair

Balance Sheet

September 30, 2005

	Assets					
1						1
2						2
3						3
4						4
5						5
6						6
7						7
8						8
9						9
10						10
11	Liabilities and Owner's Equity					11
12						12
13						13
14						14
15						15
16						16
17						17
18						18
19						19
20						20
21						21
22						22

Section

Date   PepsiCo

1	(a)
2	
3	
4	
5	
6	
7	
8	
9	
10	
11	
12	
13	
14	
15	(b)
16	
17	
18	
19	
20	
21	(c)
22	
23	
24	
25	
26	
27	
28	
29	
30	
31	
32	
33	
34	
35	
36	
37	
38	
39	
40	

	PepsiCo	Coca-Cola
1 Increase (decrease) from 2001 to 2002 in:		
2		
3		
4 (a) Property, plant, and equipment, net		
5		
6		
7		
8 (b) Selling, general, and administrative expenses		
9		
10		
11		
12 (c) Long-term debt (obligations)		
13		
14		
15		
16 (d) Net income		
17		
18		
19		
20 (e) Cash and cash equivalents		
21		
22		
23		
24		
25		
26		
27		
28		
29		
30		
31		
32		
33		
34		
35		
36		
37		
38		
39		
40		

(a)

(b)

(c)

(a)

(b)

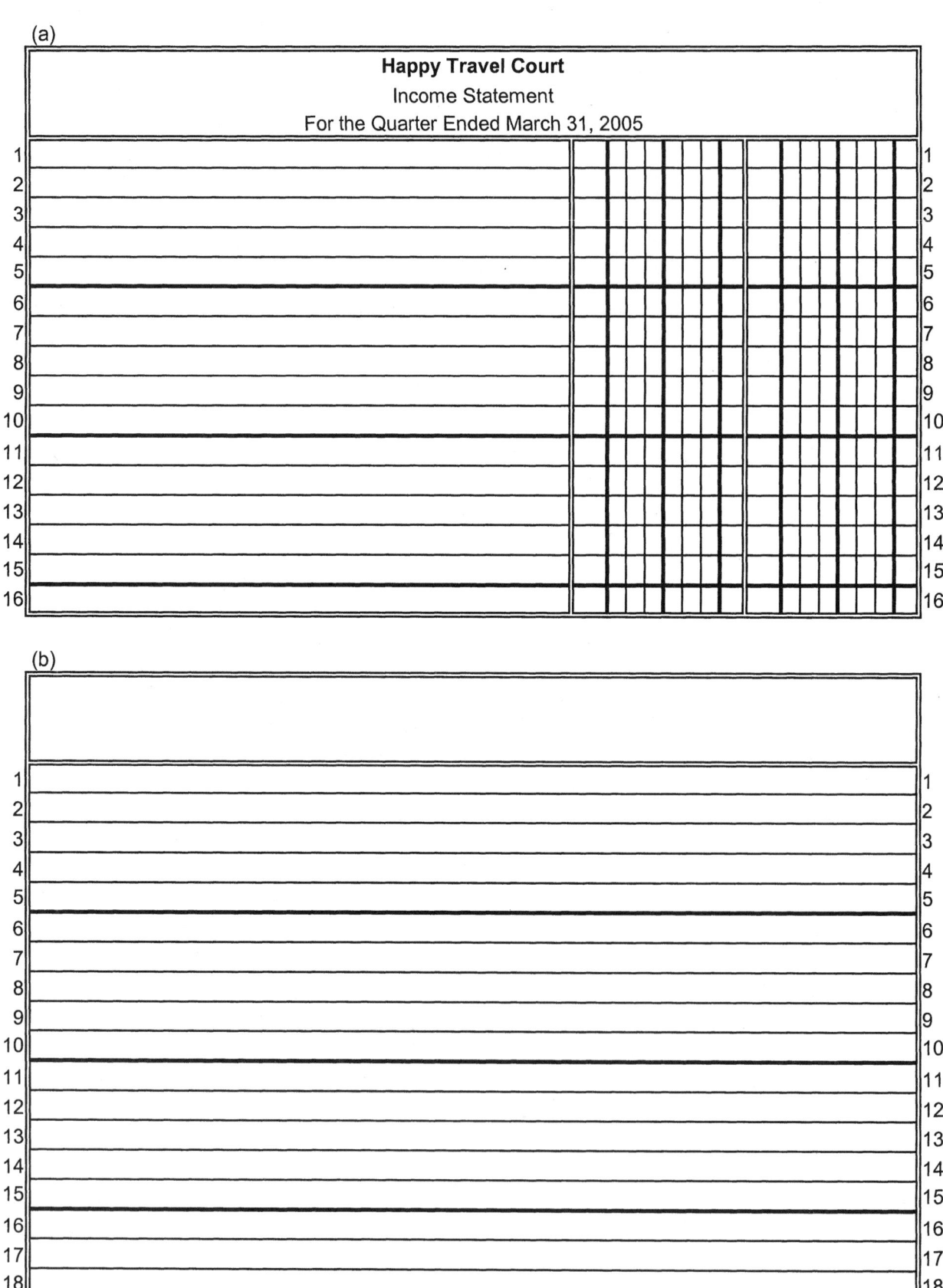

(a)

Happy Travel Court

Income Statement

For the Quarter Ended March 31, 2005

(b)

Name

Section

Date

1	1
2	2
3	3
4	4
5	5
6	6
7	7
8	8
9	9
10	10
11	11
12	12
13	13
14	14
15	15
16	16
17	17
18	18
19	19
20	20
21	21
22	22
23	23
24	24
25	25
26	26
27	27
28	28
29	29
30	30
31	31
32	32
33	33
34	34
35	35
36	36
37	37
38	38
39	39
40	40

1	1
2	2
3	3
4	4
5	5
6	6
7	7
8	8
9	9
10	10
11	11
12	12
13	13
14	14
15	15
16	16
17	17
18	18
19	19
20	20
21	21
22	22
23	23
24	24
25	25
26	26
27	27
28	28
29	29
30	30
31	31
32	32
33	33
34	34
35	35
36	36
37	37
38	38
39	39
40	40

(a)

1 (a)

2

3

4

5

6

7

8

9

10 (b)

11

12

13

14

15

16

17

18

19

20

21

22

23

24

25 (c)

26

27

28

29

30

31

32

33

34

35

36

37

38

39

40

1	**#1**				
2					
3					
4					
5					
6					
7					
8					

	#3	Income Statement		Balance Sheet	
10	Account	Debit	Credit	Debit	Credit
11	Accumulated Depreciation				
12	Depreciation Expense				
13	N. Cesar, Capital				
14	N. Cesar, Drawing				
15	Service Revenue				
16	Supplies				
17	Accounts Payable				
18					
19					
20					
21					
22					

	#4			
	Date	Account Titles	Debit	Credit
25	Dec. 31			
26				
27				
28	31			
29				
30				
31				
32	31			
33				
34				
35	31			
36				
37				
38				
39				

BRIEF EXERCISE 4-2
See Appendix

#5

Service Revenue

Income Summary

Salaries Expense

D. Rowen, Capital

Supplies Expense

D. Rowen, Drawing

#6

	Date	Account Titles	Debit	Credit	
1	July 31				1
2					2
3					3
4	31				4
5					5
6					6

Green Fee Revenue

Date	Explanation	Ref.	Debit	Credit	Balance

Salaries Expense

Date	Explanation	Ref.	Debit	Credit	Balance

Supplies Expense

Date	Explanation	Ref.	Debit	Credit	Balance

#7

#8

1.

2.

3.

4.

5.

6.

7.

8.

9.

#9	Account Titles	Debit	Credit
1.			
2.			

#10

Kren Company
Partial Balance Sheet

Current assets			

Date	Account Titles	Debit	Credit
Nov. 1			

Cajon Company
(Partial) Work Sheet
For the Month Ended April 30, 2005

	Account Titles	Adjusted Trial Balance Dr.	Adjusted Trial Balance Cr.	Income Statement Dr.	Income Statement Cr.	Balance Sheet Dr.	Balance Sheet Cr.	
1	Cash	1 4 7 5 2						1
2	Accounts Receivable	7 8 4 0						2
3	Prepaid Rent	2 2 8 0						3
4	Equipment	2 3 0 5 0						4
5	Accumulated Depreciation		4 9 2 1					5
6	Notes Payable		5 7 0 0					6
7	Accounts Payable		5 6 7 2					7
8	P. Cajon, Capital		3 3 9 6 0					8
9	P. Cajon, Drawing	3 6 5 0						9
10	Service Revenue		1 2 5 9 0					10
11	Salaries Expense	9 8 4 0						11
12	Rent Expense	7 6 0						12
13	Depreciation Expense	6 7 1						13
14	Interest Expense	5 7						14
15	Interest Payable		5 7					15
16	Totals	6 2 9 0 0	6 2 9 0 0					16
17	Net Income							17
18	Totals							18
19								19
20								20

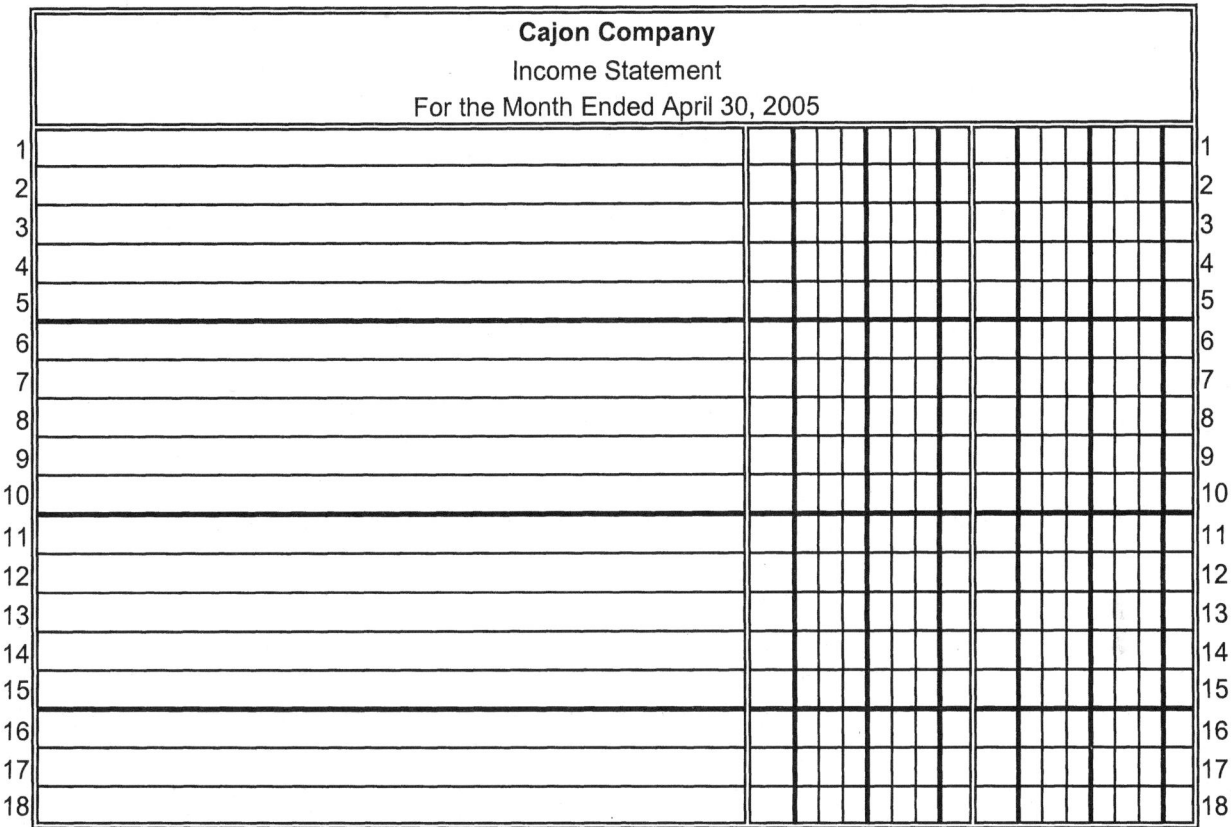

Cajon Company
Income Statement
For the Month Ended April 30, 2005

Cajon Company
Owner's Equity Statement
For the Month Ended April 30, 2005

(Continued)

Cajon Company

Balance Sheet

April 30, 2005

	Assets					
1						1
2						2
3						3
4						4
5						5
6						6
7						7
8						8
9						9
10						10
11						11
12						12
13	Liabilities and Owner's Equity					13
14						14
15						15
16						16
17						17
18						18
19						19
20						20
21						21
22						22
23						23
24						24
25						25
26						26

Section

(a)

	Date	Account Titles	Debit	Credit	
1	Apr. 30				1
2					2
3					3
4	30				4
5					5
6					6
7					7
8					8
9					9
10	30				10
11					11
12					12
13	30				13
14					14
15					15

(b)

INCOME SUMMARY	RETAINED EARNINGS

(c)

Cajon Company
Post-Closing Trial Balance
April 30, 2005

		Debit	Credit	
1				1
2				2
3				3
4				4
5				5
6				6
7				7
8				8
9				9
10				10
11				11

(a)

	Account Titles	Debit	Credit	
1				1
2				2
3				3
4				4
5				5
6				6
7				7
8				8
9				9
10				10
11				11
12				12

(b)

		Income Statement		Balance Sheet		
		Debit	Credit	Debit	Credit	
1	Accounts Receivable					1
2	Prepaid Insurance					2
3	Accumulated Depreciation					3
4	Salaries Payable					4
5	Service Revenue					5
6	Salaries Expense					6
7	Insurance Expense					7
8	Depreciation Expense					8
9						9

(a)

(b)

	Account Titles	Debit	Credit	
1				1
2				2
3				3
4				4
5				5
6				6
7				7
8				8
9				9
10				10
11				11
12				12
13				13
14				14
15				15

(a)

J15

	Date	Account Titles and Explanations	Ref	Debit	Credit	
1	July 31					1
2						2
3						3
4						4
5	31					5
6						6
7						7
8						8
9						9
10	31					10
11						11
12						12
13	31					13
14						14

(b)

C. J. Lanza, Capital

No. 301

Date	Explanation	Ref.	Debit	Credit	Balance

Income Summary

No. 350

Date	Explanation	Ref.	Debit	Credit	Balance

(c)

Lanza Company

Post-Closing Trial Balance

July 31, 2005

		Debit	Credit	
1				1
2				2
3				3
4				4
5				5
6				6
7				7
8				8

(a)

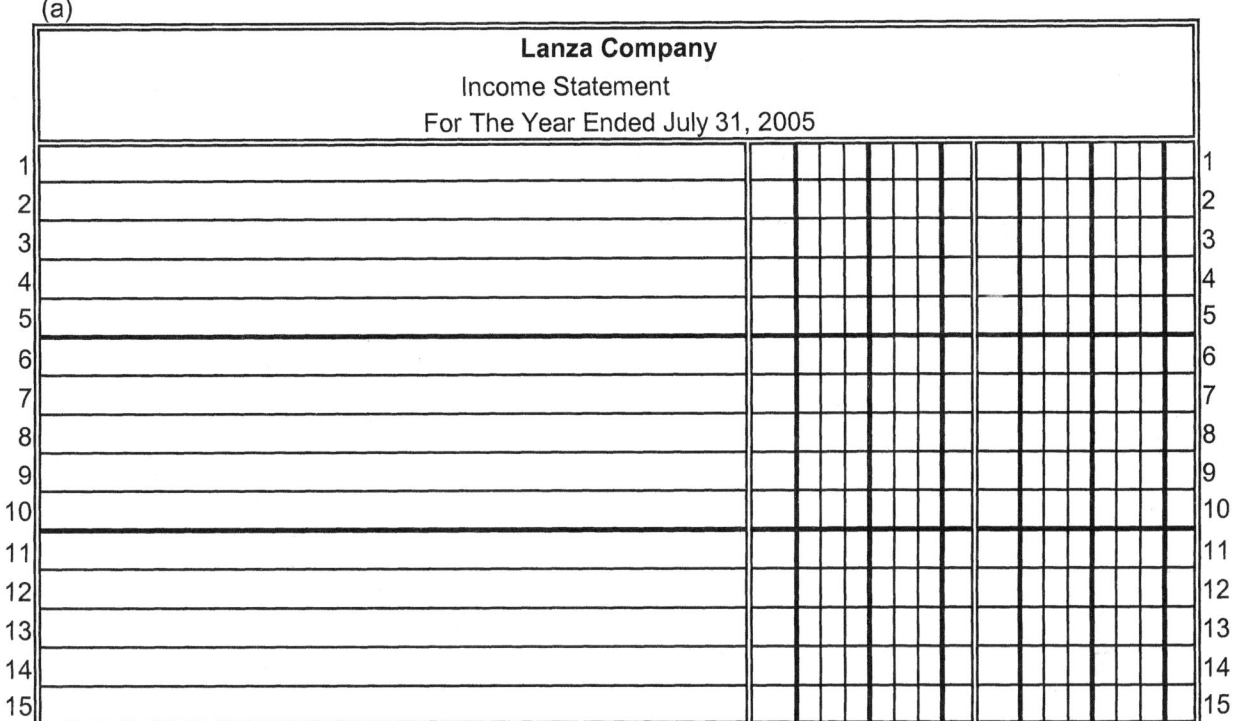

Lanza Company
Income Statement
For The Year Ended July 31, 2005

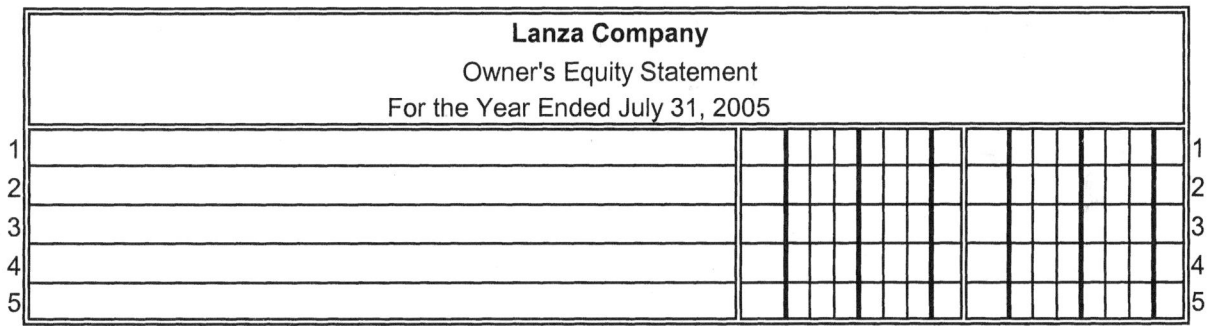

Lanza Company
Owner's Equity Statement
For the Year Ended July 31, 2005

(b)

Lanza Company		
Balance Sheet		
July 31, 2005		
Assets		
Liabilities and Owner's Equity		

#8

	Date	Account Titles and Explanation	Debit	Credit	
1	(a)				1
2	June 30				2
3					3
4					4
5	30				5
6					6
7					7
8					8
9					9
10	30				10
11					11
12					12
13	30				13
14					14

(b)

INCOME SUMMARY

#9

	Date	Account Titles and Explanation	Debit	Credit	
1	1.				1
2					2
3					3
4	2.				4
5					5
6					6
7					7
8	3.				8
9					9
10					10

(a)

Rego Bowling Alley
Balance Sheet
December 31, 2005

Assets

Liabilities and Owner's Equity

(b)

Date   Garg Employment Agency

(a) & (b)

	Date	Account Titles	Debit	Credit	
1	Dec. 31				1
2					2
3					3
4					4
5	31				5
6					6
7					7
8					8
9	Jan. 1				9
10					10
11					11
12	1				12
13					13
14					14
15					15

(c) & (e)

	ACCOUNTS RECEIVABLE		COMMISSION REVENUE	
17				17
18	Dec 31 Bal 19,800		Dec 31 Bal 87,800	18
19				19
20				20
21				21
22				22
23				23

	INTEREST PAYABLE		INTEREST EXPENSE	
24				24
25			Dec 31 Bal 6,300	25
26				26
27				27
28				28
29				29

(d)

	Date	Account Titles	Debit	Credit	
31	Date	Account Titles	Debit	Credit	31
32	Jan. 10				32
33					33
34					34
35	15				35
36					36
37					37
38					38
39					39
40					40

PROBLEM 4-1A
See Appendix

(b)

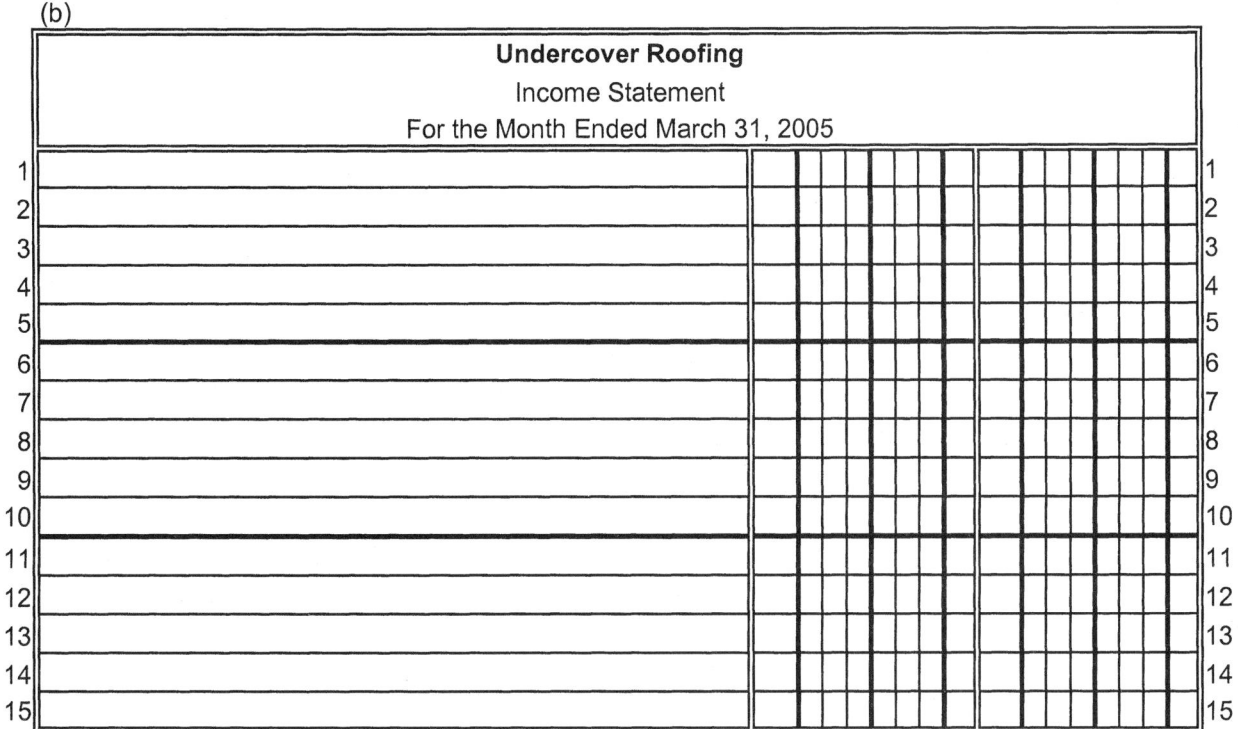

	Undercover Roofing			
	Income Statement			
	For the Month Ended March 31, 2005			
1				
2				
3				
4				
5				
6				
7				
8				
9				
10				
11				
12				
13				
14				
15				

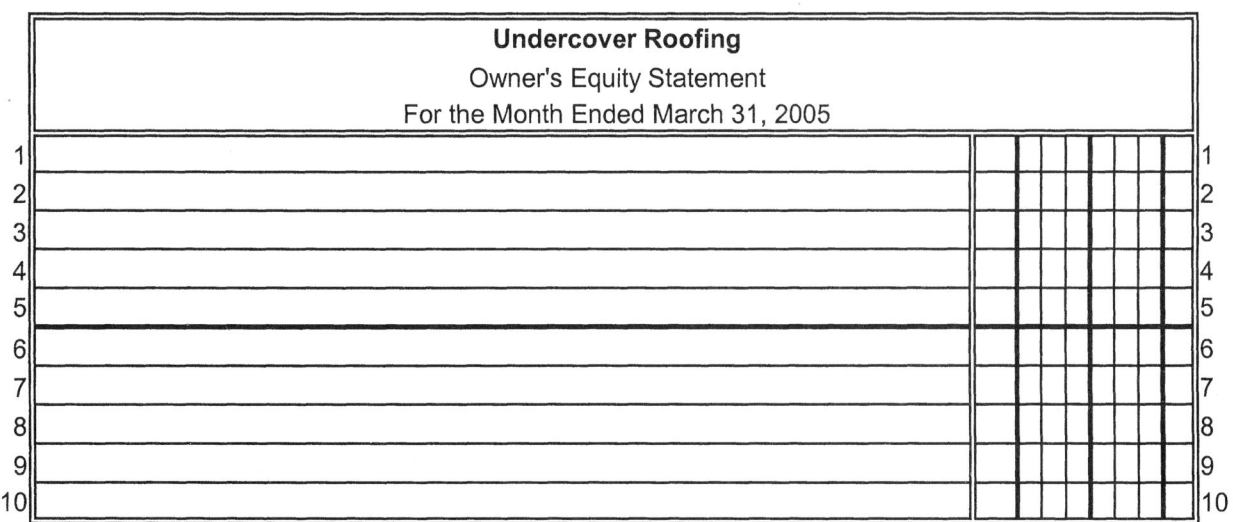

	Undercover Roofing	
	Owner's Equity Statement	
	For the Month Ended March 31, 2005	
1		
2		
3		
4		
5		
6		
7		
8		
9		
10		

(b) (Continued)

Undercover Roofing		
Balance Sheet		
March 31, 2005		

Assets

Liabilities and Owner's Equity

(c)

General Journal

	Date	Account Titles and Explanation	Ref.	Debit	Credit	
1		Adjusting Entries				1
2	Mar. 31					2
3						3
4						4
5	31					5
6						6
7						7
8	31					8
9						9
10						10
11	31					11
12						12
13						13
14						14
15						15

(d)

General Journal

	Date	Account Titles and Explanation	Ref.	Debit	Credit	
1		Closing Entries				1
2	Mar. 31					2
3						3
4						4
5	31					5
6						6
7						7
8						8
9						9
10						10
11	31					11
12						12
13						13
14	31					14
15						15
16						16

(a)

Eagle Company
Partial Work Sheet
For the Year Ended December 31, 2005

No.	Account Titles	Adjusted Trial Balance Dr.	Adjusted Trial Balance Cr.	Income Statement Dr.	Income Statement Cr.	Balance Sheet Dr.	Balance Sheet Cr.
101	Cash	13600					
112	Accounts Receivable	15400					
126	Supplies	2000					
130	Prepaid Insurance	2800					
151	Office Equipment	34000					
152	Accum. Depr. - Office Equip.		8000				
200	Notes Payable		20000				
201	Accounts Payable		6000				
212	Salaries Payable		3500				
230	Interest Payable		800				
301	A. Eagle, Capital		25000				
306	A. Eagle, Drawing	10000					
400	Service Revenue		88000				
610	Advertising Expense	12000					
631	Supplies Expense	5700					
711	Depreciation Expense	8000					
722	Insurance Expense	5000					
726	Salaries Expense	42000					
905	Interest Expense	800					
	Totals	151300	151300				
	Net Income						
	Totals						

(b)

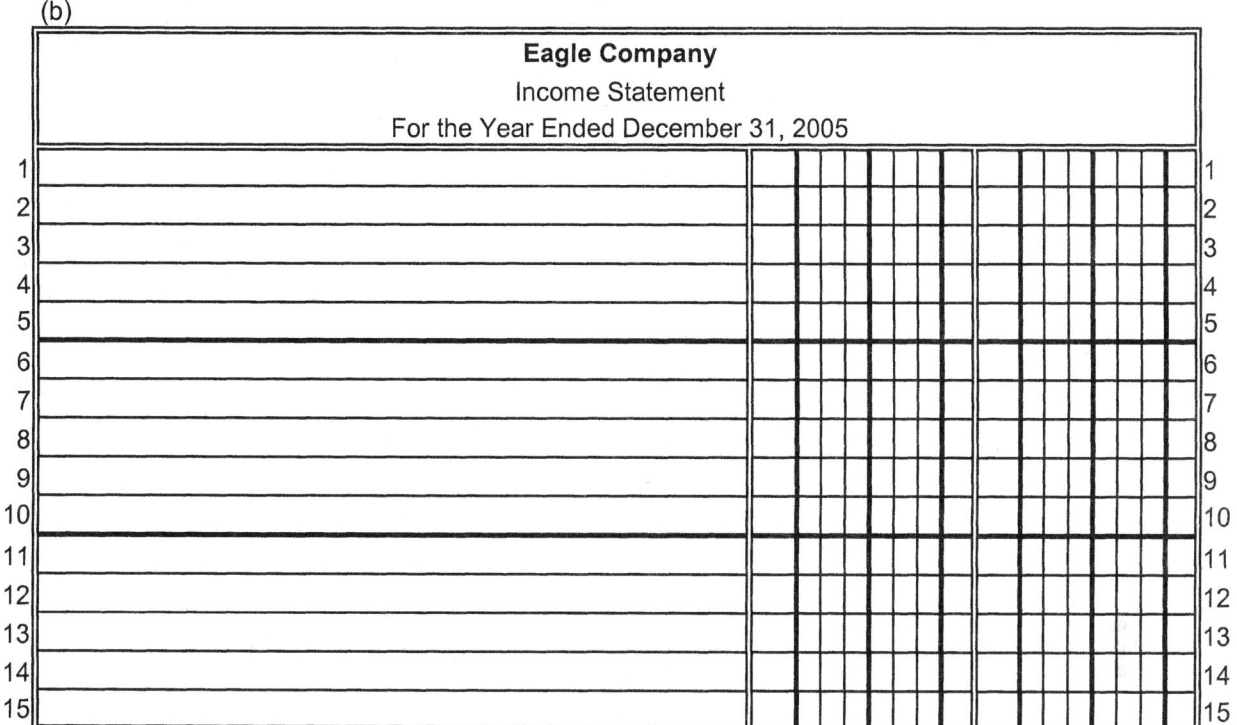

Eagle Company

Income Statement

For the Year Ended December 31, 2005

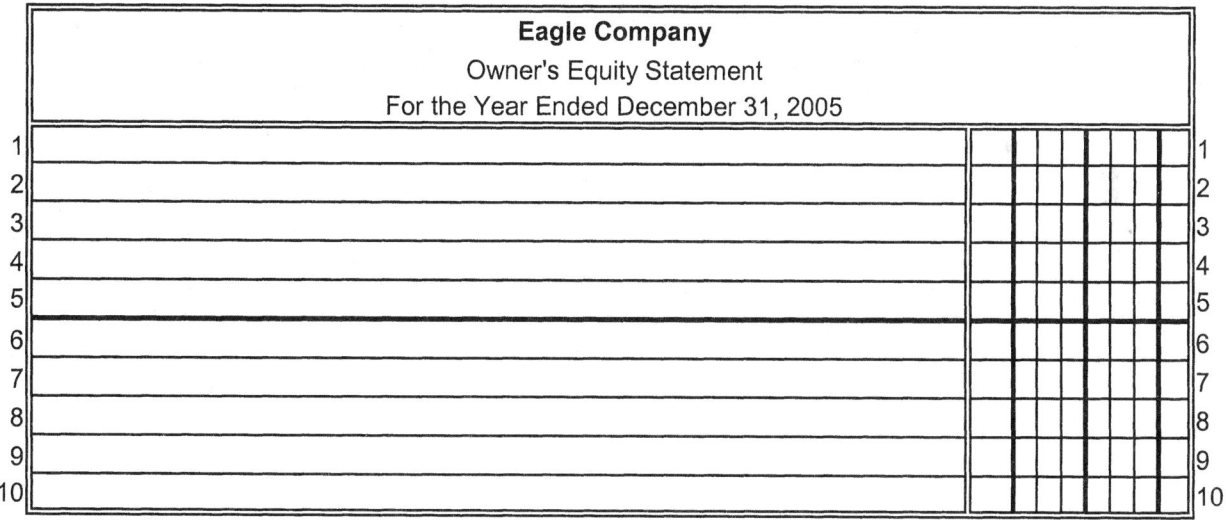

Eagle Company

Owner's Equity Statement

For the Year Ended December 31, 2005

(b) (Continued)

	Eagle Company
	Balance Sheet
	December 31, 2005

	Assets																	
1																		1
2																		2
3																		3
4																		4
5																		5
6																		6
7																		7
8																		8
9																		9
10																		10
11																		11
12																		12
13																		13
14																		14
15																		15
16	Liabilities and Owner's Equity																	16
17																		17
18																		18
19																		19
20																		20
21																		21
22																		22
23																		23
24																		24
25																		25
26																		26
27																		27
28																		28
29																		29
30																		30
31																		31
32																		32
33																		33

(c)

General Journal ___ J14

	Date	Account Titles and Explanation	Ref	Debit	Credit	
1	Dec. 31					1
2						2
3						3
4	31					4
5						5
6						6
7						7
8						8
9						9
10						10
11						11
12	31					12
13						13
14						14
15	31					15
16						16
17						17
18						18

(d)

A. Eagle, Capital ___ No.301

Date	Explanation	Ref.	Debit	Credit	Balance
Jan 1	Balance	√			2 5 0 0 0

A. Eagle, Drawing ___ No. 306

Date	Explanation	Ref.	Debit	Credit	Balance
Dec 31	Balance	√			1 0 0 0 0

Income Summary ___ No. 350

Date	Explanation	Ref.	Debit	Credit	Balance

(d) (Continued)

Service Revenue   No. 400

Date	Explanation	Ref.	Debit	Credit	Balance
Dec 31	Balance	√			8 8 0 0 0

Advertising Expense   No. 610

Date	Explanation	Ref.	Debit	Credit	Balance
Dec 31	Balance	√			1 2 0 0 0

Supplies Expense   No. 631

Date	Explanation	Ref.	Debit	Credit	Balance
Dec 31	Balance	√			5 7 0 0

Depreciation Expense   No. 711

Date	Explanation	Ref.	Debit	Credit	Balance
Dec 31	Balance	√			8 0 0 0

Insurance Expense   No. 722

Date	Explanation	Ref.	Debit	Credit	Balance
Dec 31	Balance	√			5 0 0 0

Salaries Expense   No. 726

Date	Explanation	Ref.	Debit	Credit	Balance
Dec 31	Balance	√			4 2 0 0 0

Interest Expense   No. 905

Date	Explanation	Ref.	Debit	Credit	Balance
Dec 31	Balance	√			8 0 0

(e)

Eagle Company Post-Closing Trial Balance December 31, 2005	Debit	Credit
1		
2		
3		
4		
5		
6		
7		
8		
9		
10		
11		
12		
13		
14		
15		
16		
17		
18		
19		
20		

(a)

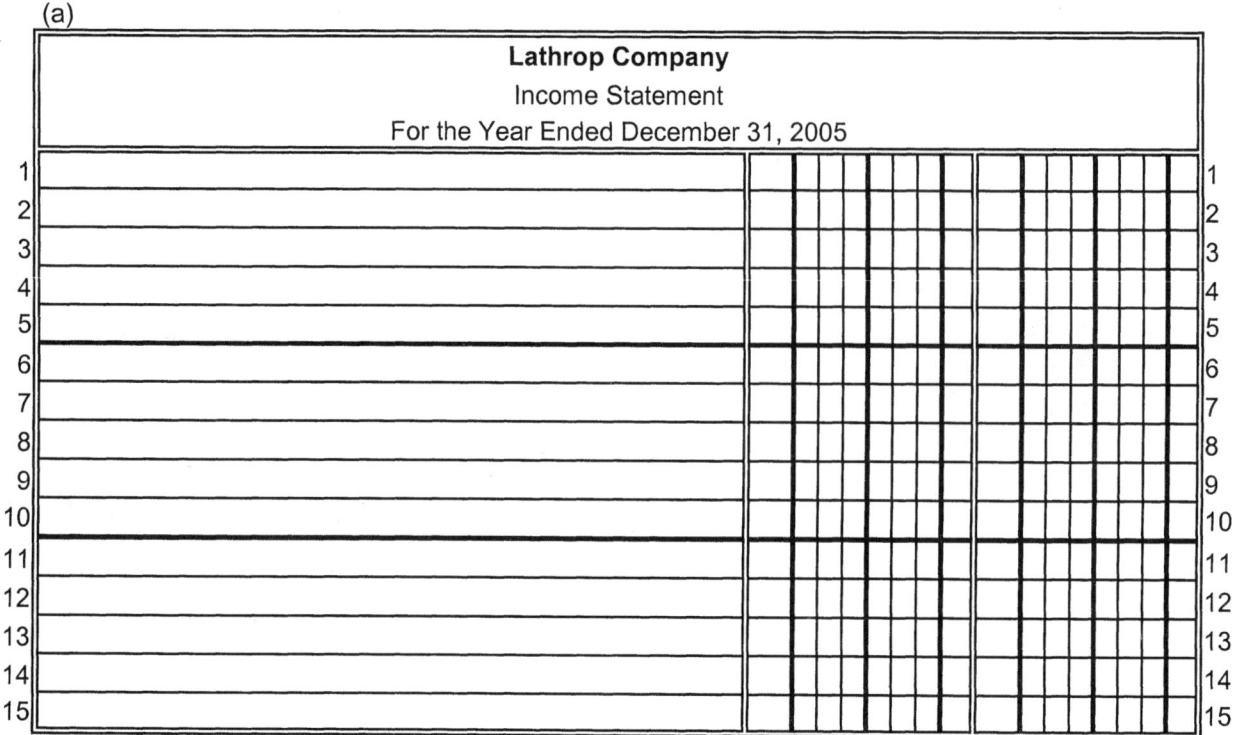

Lathrop Company
Income Statement
For the Year Ended December 31, 2005

Lathrop Company
Owner's Equity Statement
For the Year Ended December 31, 2005

(a) (Continued)

	Lathrop Company				
	Balance Sheet				
	December 31, 2005				
1	Assets				1
2					2
3					3
4					4
5					5
6					6
7					7
8					8
9					9
10					10
11					11
12	Liabilities and Owner's Equity				12
13					13
14					14
15					15
16					16
17					17
18					18
19					19
20					20
21					21
22					22
23					23

(b)

General Journal

	Date	Accounts Titles	Ref.	Debit	Credit	
1		Closing Entries				1
2	Dec. 31					2
3						3
4						4
5	31					5
6						6
7						7
8						8
9						9
10						10
11						11
12	31					12
13						13
14						14
15	31					15
16						16
17						17
18						18
19						19
20						20
21						21
22						22
23						23
24						24
25						25

(c)

Sue Lathrop, Capital	No. 301
	1/1 Bal 36,000

Sue Lathrop, Drawing	No.306
12/31 Bal 14,000	

Income Summary	No. 350

Service Revenue	No. 400

Repair Expense	No. 622

Depreciation Expense	No. 711

Insurance Expense	No. 722

Salaries Expense	No. 726

Utilities Expense	No. 732

(d)

Lathrop Company
Post-Closing Trial Balance
December 31, 2005

	Debit	Credit
1		
2		
3		
4		
5		
6		
7		
8		
9		
10		

PROBLEM 4-4A
See Appendix

(b)

Nish Kumar Management Services					
Balance Sheet					
December 31, 2005					

	Assets				
1					
2					
3					
4					
5					
6					
7					
8					
9					
10					
11					
12					
13					
14					
15					
16					
17					
18					
19	Liabilities and Owner's Equity				
20					
21					
22					
23					
24					
25					
26					
27					
28					
29					
30					
31					
32					
33					
34					
35					
36					
37					
38					
39					
40					

	Date	Accounts Titles and Explanation	Debit	Credit	
1	(c)	Adjusting Entries			1
2	Dec. 31				2
3					3
4					4
5	31				5
6					6
7					7
8	31				8
9					9
10					10
11	31				11
12					12
13					13
14	31				14
15					15
16					16
17					17
18					18
19	(d)	Closing Entries			19
20	Dec. 31				20
21					21
22					22
23					23
24	31				24
25					25
26					26
27					27
28					28
29					29
30					30
31					31
32					32
33	31				33
34					34
35					35
36	31				36
37					37
38					38
39					39
40					40

(e)

Nish Kumar Management Services	Debit	Credit
Post-Closing Trial Balance		
December 31, 2005		
1		
2		
3		
4		
5		
6		
7		
8		
9		
10		
11		
12		
13		
14		
15		
16		
17		
18		
19		
20		
21		
22		
23		
24		
25		
26		
27		
28		
29		
30		

(a)   General Journal   J1

	Date	Accounts Titles and Explanation	Ref.	Debit	Credit	
1	July 1					1
2						2
3						3
4	1					4
5						5
6						6
7						7
8	3					8
9						9
10						10
11	5					11
12						12
13						13
14	12					14
15						15
16						16
17	18					17
18						18
19						19
20	20					20
21						21
22						22
23	21					23
24						24
25						25
26	25					26
27						27
28						28
29	31					29
30						30
31						31
32	31					32
33						33
34						34
35						35
36						36
37						37
38						38
39						39
40						40

PROBLEM 4-5A
See Appendix

(a), (e) and (f)

Cash   No. 101

Date	Explanation	Ref.	Debit	Credit	Balance

Accounts Receivable   No. 112

Date	Explanation	Ref.	Debit	Credit	Balance

Cleaning Supplies   No. 128

Date	Explanation	Ref.	Debit	Credit	Balance

Prepaid Insurance   No. 130

Date	Explanation	Ref.	Debit	Credit	Balance

Equipment   No. 157

Date	Explanation	Ref.	Debit	Credit	Balance

(a), (e) and (f) (Continued)

Accumulated Depreciation - Equipment   No. 158

Date	Explanation	Ref.	Debit	Credit	Balance

Accounts Payable   No. 201

Date	Explanation	Ref.	Debit	Credit	Balance

Salaries Payable   No. 212

Date	Explanation	Ref.	Debit	Credit	Balance

Eve Tsai, Capital   No. 301

Date	Explanation	Ref.	Debit	Credit	Balance

Eve Tsai, Drawing   No. 306

Date	Explanation	Ref.	Debit	Credit	Balance

Income Summary   No. 350

Date	Explanation	Ref.	Debit	Credit	Balance

Service Revenue   No. 400

Date	Explanation	Ref.	Debit	Credit	Balance

(a), (e) and (f) (Continued)

Gas & Oil Expense   No. 633

Date	Explanation	Ref.	Debit	Credit	Balance

Cleaning Supplies Expense   No. 634

Date	Explanation	Ref.	Debit	Credit	Balance

Depreciation Expense   No. 711

Date	Explanation	Ref.	Debit	Credit	Balance

Insurance Expense   No. 722

Date	Explanation	Ref.	Debit	Credit	Balance

Salaries Expense   No. 726

Date	Explanation	Ref.	Debit	Credit	Balance

(e)

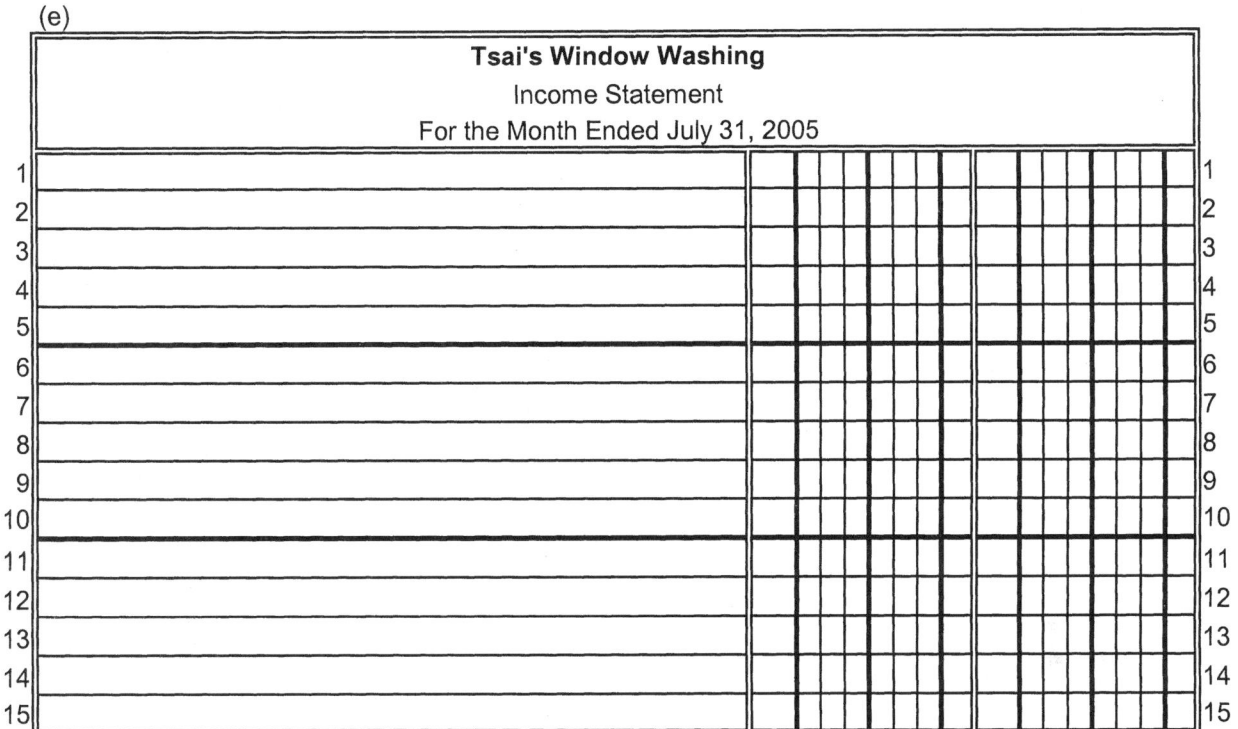

Tsai's Window Washing
Income Statement
For the Month Ended July 31, 2005

Tsai's Window Washing
Owner's Equity Statement
For the Month Ended July 31, 2005

(e) (Continued)

Tsai's Window Washing
Balance Sheet
July 31, 2005

Assets

Liabilities and Owner's Equity

General Journal
J2

	Date	Accounts Titles and Explanation	Ref.	Debit	Credit	
1	(d)	Adjusting Entries				1
2	July 31					2
3						3
4						4
5	31					5
6						6
7						7
8	31					8
9						9
10						10
11	31					11
12						12
13						13
14	31					14
15						15
16						16

General Journal
J3

	Date	Account Titles and Explanation	Ref.	Debit	Credit	
1	(f)	Closing Entries				1
2	July 31					2
3						3
4						4
5	31					5
6						6
7						7
8						8
9						9
10						10
11						11
12	31					12
13						13
14						14
15	31					15
16						16
17						17
18						18
19						19

(g)

Tsai's Window Washing Post-Closing Trial Balance July 31, 2005	Debit	Credit

(a)

24/7 Cable

	(1) Incorrect Entry			(2) Correct Entry			(3) Correcting Entry		
	Account Titles	Dr.	Cr.	Account Titles	Dr.	Cr.	Account Titles	Dr.	Cr.
1.									
2									
3									
4 2.									
5									
6									
7 3.									
8									
9									
10									
11									
12 4.									
13									
14									
15 5.									
16									
17									
18									
19									
20									

(b)

24/7 Cable Trial Balance April 30, 2005	Debit	Credit
1 Cash		
2 Accounts Receivable		
3 Supplies		
4 Equipment		
5 Accumulated Depreciation		
6 Accounts Payable		
7 Salaries Payable		
8 Unearned Revenue		
9 A. Manion, Capital		
11 Service Revenue		
12 Salaries Expense		
13 Advertising Expense		
14 Miscellaneous Expense		
15 Repair Expense		
16 Depreciation Expense		

PROBLEM 4-1B
See Appendix

(b)

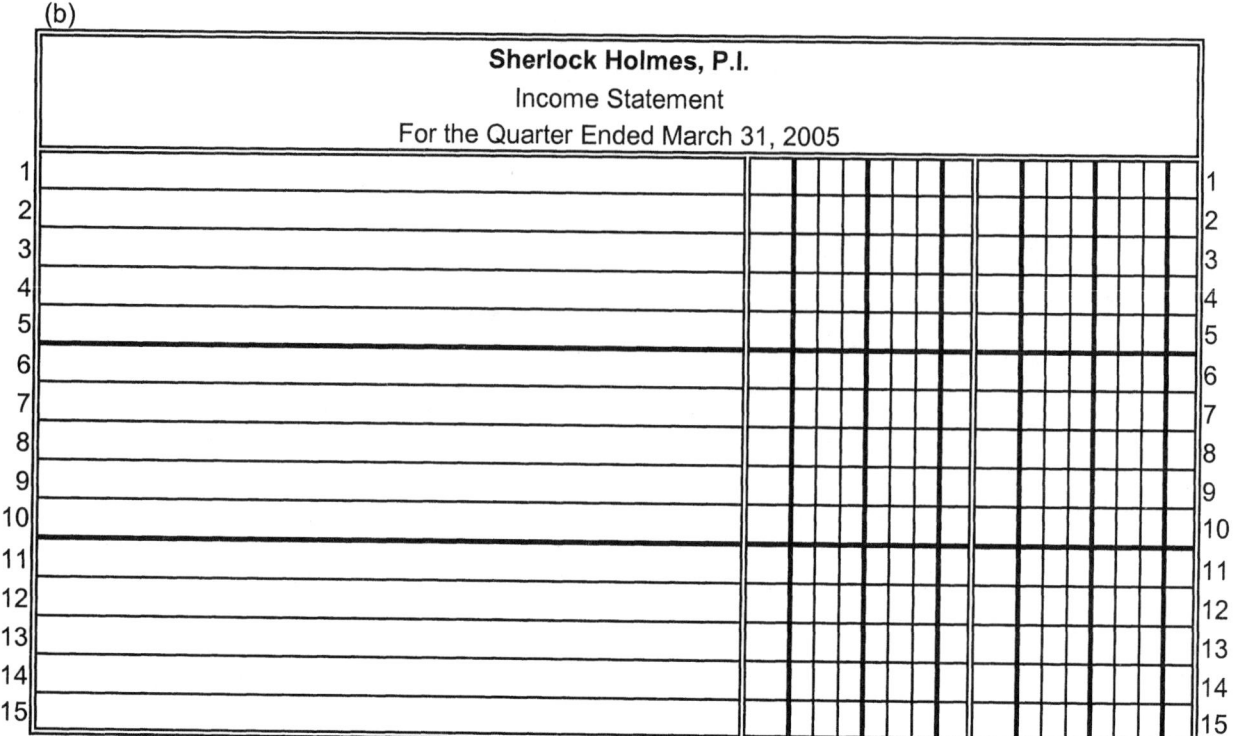

Sherlock Holmes, P.I.
Income Statement
For the Quarter Ended March 31, 2005

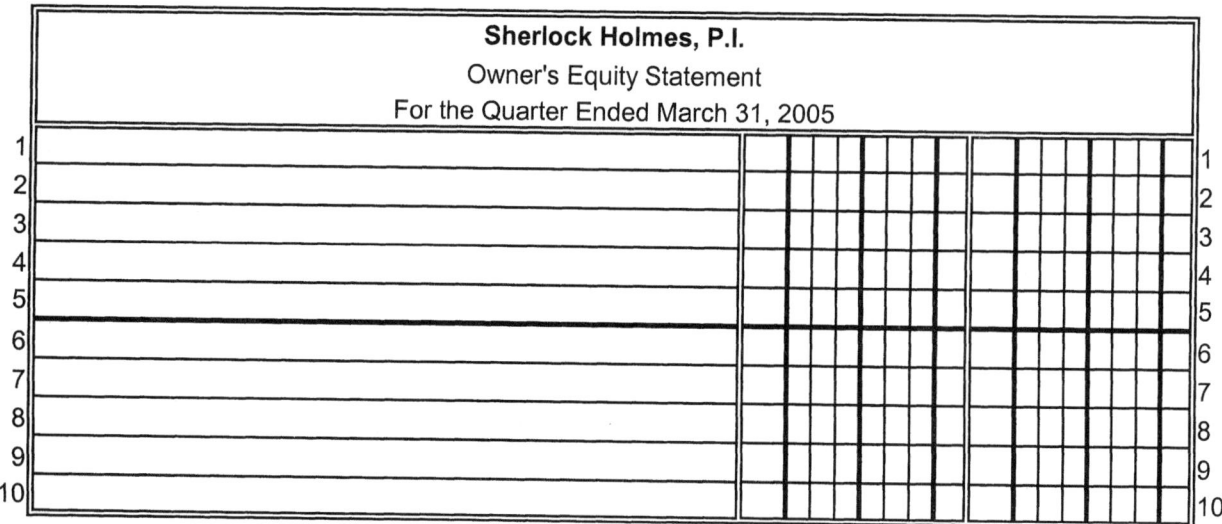

Sherlock Holmes, P.I.
Owner's Equity Statement
For the Quarter Ended March 31, 2005

(b) (Continued)

	Sherlock Holmes, P.I.											
	Balance Sheet											
	March 31, 2005											
1	Assets											1
2												2
3												3
4												4
5												5
6												6
7												7
8												8
9												9
10												10
11												11
12												12
13												13
14												14
15												15
16	Liabilities and Owner's Equity											16
17												17
18												18
19												19
20												20
21												21
22												22
23												23
24												24
25												25
26												26
27												27
28												28
29												29
30												30

(c)

General Journal

	Date	Account Titles and Explanation	Debit	Credit	
1		Adjusting Entries			1
2	Mar. 31				2
3					3
4					4
5	31				5
6					6
7					7
8	31				8
9					9
10					10
11	31				11
12					12
13					13
14	31				14
15					15

(d)

General Journal

	Date	Account Titles and Explanation	Debit	Credit	
1		Closing Entries			1
2	Mar. 31				2
3					3
4					4
5	31				5
6					6
7					7
8					8
9					9
10					10
11					11
12					12
13					13
14					14
15	31				15
16					16
17					17
18	31				18
19					19

(a)

Mr. Watson Company
Work Sheet (Partial)
For the Year Ended December 31, 2005

	Account		Adjusted Trial Balance		Income Statement		Balance Sheet	
No.	Titles		Dr.	Cr.	Dr.	Cr.	Dr.	Cr.
101	Cash	1						
112	Accounts Receivable	2						
126	Supplies	3						
130	Prepaid Insurance	4						
151	Office Equipment	5						
152	Accum. Depr. - Office Equip.	6						
200	Notes Payable	7						
201	Accounts Payable	8						
212	Salaries Payable	9						
230	Interest Payable	10						
301	M. Watson, Capital	11						
306	M. Watson, Drawing	12						
400	Service Revenue	13						
610	Advertising Expense	14						
631	Supplies Expense	15						
711	Depreciation Expense	16						
722	Insurance Expense	17						
726	Salaries Expense	18						
905	Interest Expense	19						
	Totals	20						
		21						
	Net Income	22						
	Totals	23						
		24						
		25						

(b)

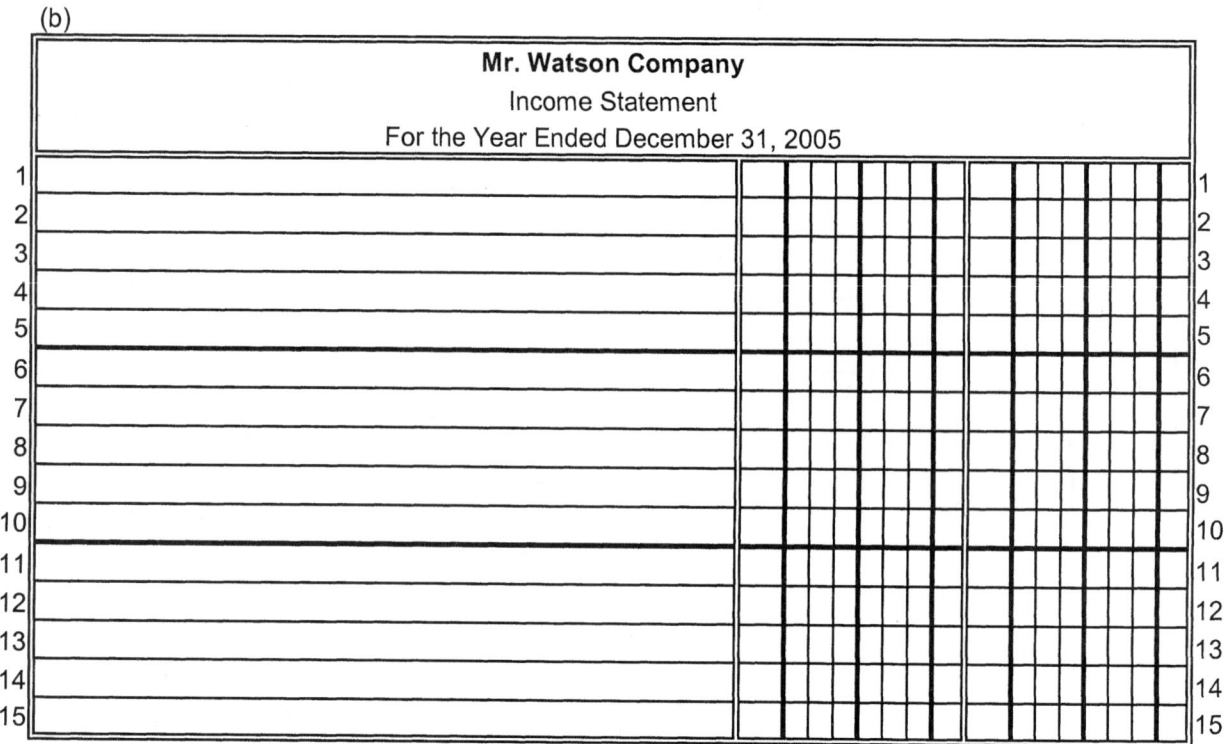

Mr. Watson Company

Income Statement

For the Year Ended December 31, 2005

Mr. Watson Company

Owner's Equity Statement

For the Year Ended December 31, 2005

(b) (Continued)

	Mr. Watson Company		
	Balance Sheet		
	December 31, 2005		

	Assets			
1				
2				
3				
4				
5				
6				
7				
8				
9				
10				
11				
12				
13				
14				
15				
16	Liabilities and Owner's Equity			
17				
18				
19				
20				
21				
22				
23				
24				
25				
26				
27				
28				
29				
30				
31				
32				
33				

(c)

General Journal

J14

	Date	Account Titles and Explanation	Ref	Debit	Credit	
1	Dec. 31					1
2						2
3						3
4	31					4
5						5
6						6
7						7
8						8
9						9
10						10
11						11
12	31					12
13						13
14						14
15	31					15
16						16
17						17
18						18

(d)

M. Watson, Capital

No.301

Date	Explanation	Ref.	Debit	Credit	Balance
Jan 1	Balance	√			3 6 0 0 0

M. Watson, Drawing

No. 306

Date	Explanation	Ref.	Debit	Credit	Balance
Dec 31	Balance	√			1 2 0 0 0

Income Summary

No. 350

Date	Explanation	Ref.	Debit	Credit	Balance

(d) (Continued)

Service Revenue   No. 400

Date	Explanation	Ref.	Debit	Credit	Balance
Dec 31	Balance	√			7 9 8 0 0

Advertising Expense   No. 610

Date	Explanation	Ref.	Debit	Credit	Balance
Dec 31	Balance	√			1 2 0 0 0

Supplies Expense   No. 631

Date	Explanation	Ref.	Debit	Credit	Balance
Dec 31	Balance	√			3 7 0 0

Depreciation Expense   No. 711

Date	Explanation	Ref.	Debit	Credit	Balance
Dec 31	Balance	√			6 0 0 0

Insurance Expense   No. 722

Date	Explanation	Ref.	Debit	Credit	Balance
Dec 31	Balance	√			4 0 0 0

Salaries Expense   No. 726

Date	Explanation	Ref.	Debit	Credit	Balance
Dec 31	Balance	√			# 2 0 0 0

Interest Expense   No. 905

Date	Explanation	Ref.	Debit	Credit	Balance
Dec 31	Balance	√			1 0 0 0

(e)

Mr. Watson Company Post-Closing Trial Balance December 31, 2005	Debit	Credit
1		
2		
3		
4		
5		
6		
7		
8		
9		
10		
11		
12		
13		
14		
15		
16		
17		
18		
19		
20		

(a)

Hubbs Company		
Income Statement		
For the Year Ended December 31, 2005		
1		
2		
3		
4		
5		
6		
7		
8		
9		
10		
11		
12		
13		
14		
15		

Hubbs Company		
Owner's Equity Statement		
For the Year Ended December 31, 2005		
1		
2		
3		
4		
5		
6		
7		
8		
9		
10		

(a) (Continued)

	Hubbs Company
	Balance Sheet
	December 31, 2005

	Assets							
1								
2								
3								
4								
5								
6								
7								
8								
9								
10								
11								
12								
13	Liabilities and Owner's Equity							
14								
15								
16								
17								
18								
19								
20								
21								
22								
23								
24								

(b)

General Journal

	Date	Accounts Titles	Ref.	Debit	Credit	
1		Closing Entries				1
2	Dec. 31					2
3						3
4						4
5	31					5
6						6
7						7
8						8
9						9
10						10
11						11
12	31					12
13						13
14						14
15	31					15
16						16
17						17
18						18
19						19
20						20
21						21
22						22
23						23
24						24
25						25

(c)

D. Hubbs, Capital	No. 301			Repair Expense	No. 622
	1/1 Bal	36,000			

D. Hubbs, Drawing	No.306			Depreciation Expense	No. 711
12/31 Bal	14,000				

Income Summary	No. 350			Insurance Expense	No. 722

				Salaries Expense	No. 726

Service Revenue	No. 400			Utilities Expense	No. 732

(d)

Hubbs Company
Post-Closing Trial Balance
December 31, 2005

	Debit	Credit
1		
2		
3		
4		
5		
6		
7		
8		
9		
10		

PROBLEM 4-4B
See Appendix

(b)

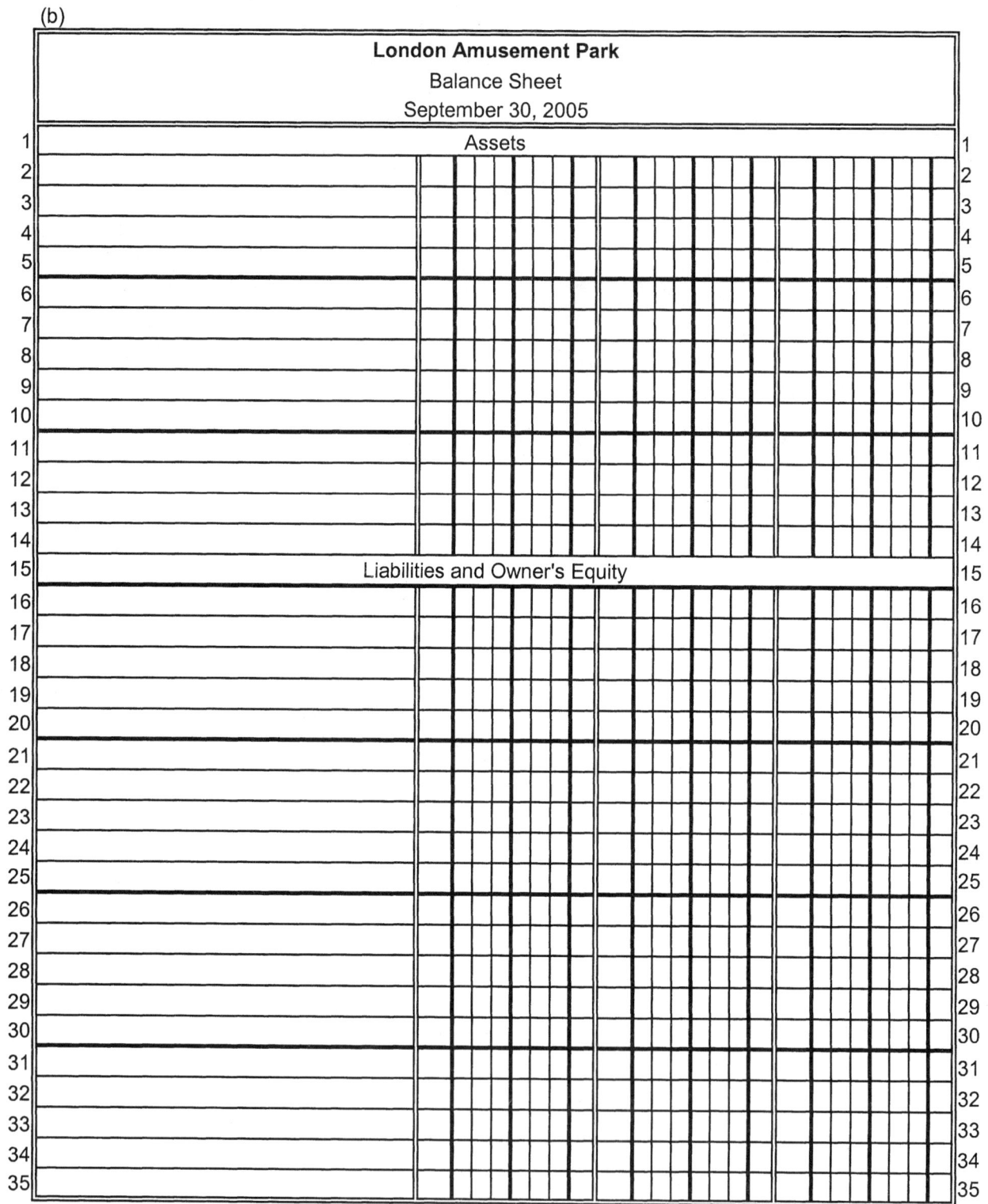

	London Amusement Park
	Balance Sheet
	September 30, 2005
	Assets
	Liabilities and Owner's Equity

	Date	Accounts Titles and Explanation	Ref.	Debit	Credit	
1	(c)	Adjusting Entries				1
2	Sept. 30					2
3						3
4						4
5	30					5
6						6
7						7
8	30					8
9						9
10						10
11	30					11
12						12
13						13
14	30					14
15						15
16						16
17	30					17
18						18
19						19
20	(d)	Closing Entries				20
21	Sept. 30					21
22						22
23						23
24	30					24
25						25
26						26
27						27
28						28
29						29
30						30
31						31
32						32
33						33
34						34
35	30					35
36						36
37						37
38	30					38
39						39
40						40

(e)

London Amusement Park Post-Closing Trial Balance September 30, 2005	Debit	Credit
1		
2		
3		
4		
5		
6		
7		
8		
9		
10		
11		
12		
13		
14		
15		
16		
17		
18		
19		
20		
21		
22		
23		
24		
25		
26		
27		
28		
29		
30		

(a)   General Journal   J1

	Date	Accounts Titles and Explanation	Ref.	Debit	Credit	
1	Mar. 1					1
2						2
3						3
4	1					4
5						5
6						6
7						7
8	3					8
9						9
10						10
11	5					11
12						12
13						13
14	14					14
15						15
16						16
17	18					17
18						18
19						19
20	20					20
21						21
22						22
23	21					23
24						24
25						25
26	28					26
27						27
28						28
29	31					29
30						30
31						31
32	31					32
33						33
34						34
35						35
36						36
37						37
38						38
39						39
40						40

PROBLEM 4-5B
See Appendix

(a), (e) and (f)

Cash   No. 101

Date	Explanation	Ref.	Debit	Credit	Balance

Accounts Receivable   No. 112

Date	Explanation	Ref.	Debit	Credit	Balance

Cleaning Supplies   No. 128

Date	Explanation	Ref.	Debit	Credit	Balance

Prepaid Insurance   No. 130

Date	Explanation	Ref.	Debit	Credit	Balance

Equipment   No. 157

Date	Explanation	Ref.	Debit	Credit	Balance

(a), (e) and (f) (Continued)

Accumulated Depreciation - Equipment   No. 158

Date	Explanation	Ref.	Debit	Credit	Balance

Accounts Payable   No. 201

Date	Explanation	Ref.	Debit	Credit	Balance

Salaries Payable   No. 212

Date	Explanation	Ref.	Debit	Credit	Balance

M. Young, Capital   No. 301

Date	Explanation	Ref.	Debit	Credit	Balance

M. Young, Drawing   No. 306

Date	Explanation	Ref.	Debit	Credit	Balance

Income Summary   No. 350

Date	Explanation	Ref.	Debit	Credit	Balance

Service Revenue   No. 400

Date	Explanation	Ref.	Debit	Credit	Balance

(a), (e) and (f) (Continued)

Gas & Oil Expense   No. 633

Date	Explanation	Ref.	Debit	Credit	Balance

Cleaning Supplies Expense   No. 634

Date	Explanation	Ref.	Debit	Credit	Balance

Depreciation Expense   No. 711

Date	Explanation	Ref.	Debit	Credit	Balance

Insurance Expense   No. 722

Date	Explanation	Ref.	Debit	Credit	Balance

Salaries Expense   No. 726

Date	Explanation	Ref.	Debit	Credit	Balance

(d)

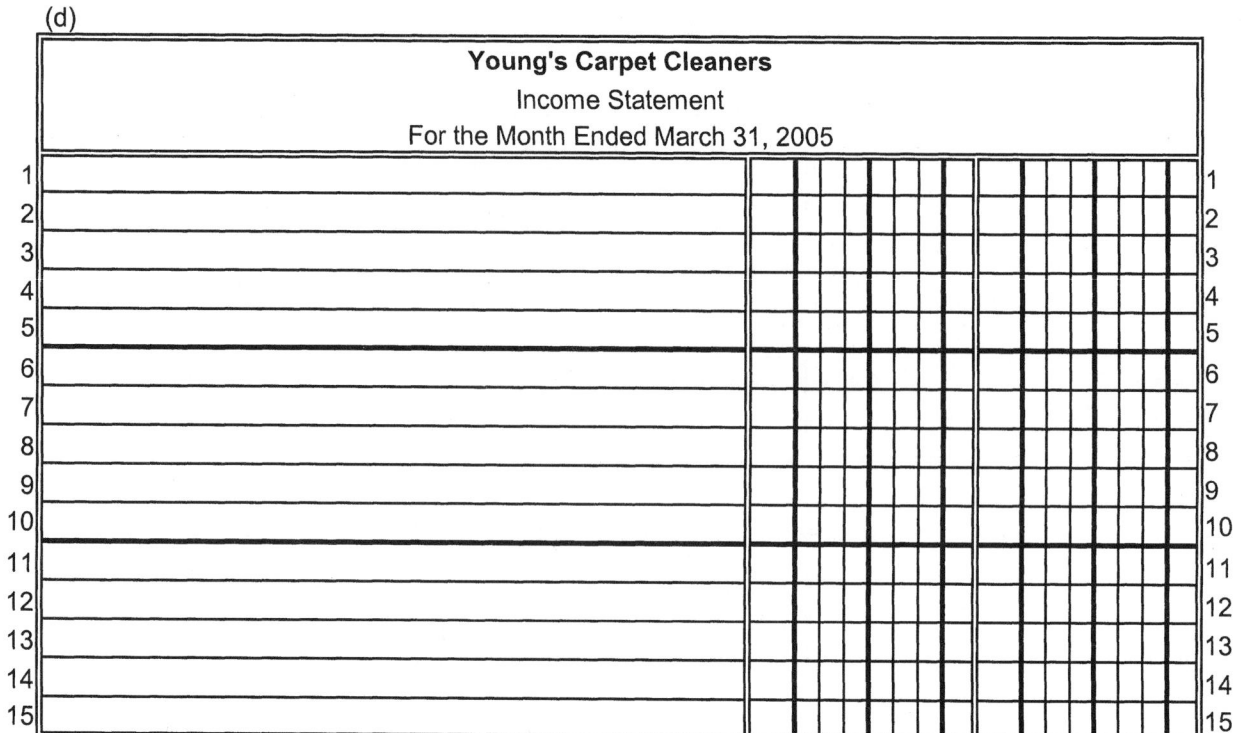

Young's Carpet Cleaners
Income Statement
For the Month Ended March 31, 2005

Young's Carpet Cleaners
Owner's Equity Statement
For the Month Ended March 31, 2005

(d) (Continued)

Young's Carpet Cleaners				
Balance Sheet				
March 31, 2005				
Assets				
Liabilities and Owner's Equity				

General Journal   J2

	Date	Accounts Titles and Explanation	Ref.	Debit	Credit	
1	(e)	Adjusting Entries				1
2	Mar. 31					2
3						3
4						4
5	31					5
6						6
7						7
8	31					8
9						9
10						10
11	31					11
12						12
13						13
14	31					14
15						15
16						16

General Journal   J3

	Date	Account Titles and Explanation	Ref.	Debit	Credit	
1	(f)	Closing Entries				1
2	Mar. 31					2
3						3
4						4
5	31					5
6						6
7						7
8						8
9						9
10						10
11						11
12	31					12
13						13
14						14
15	31					15
16						16
17						17
18						18
19						19

(g)

Young's Carpet Cleaners Post-Closing Trial Balance March 31, 2005	Debit	Credit

(a)   General Journal   J1

	Date	Accounts Titles and Explanation	Ref.	Debit	Credit	
1	July 1					1
2						2
3						3
4	1					4
5						5
6						6
7						7
8	3					8
9						9
10						10
11	5					11
12						12
13						13
14	12					14
15						15
16						16
17	18					17
18						18
19						19
20	20					20
21						21
22						22
23	21					23
24						24
25						25
26	25					26
27						27
28						28
29	31					29
30						30
31						31
32	31					32
33						33
34						34
35						35
36						36
37						37
38						38
39						39
40						40

COMPREHENSIVE PROBLEM: Chapters 2 to 4
Mary's Maids Cleaning Service
See Appendix

(a), (e) and (f)

Cash   No. 101

Date	Explanation	Ref.	Debit	Credit	Balance

Accounts Receivable   No. 112

Date	Explanation	Ref.	Debit	Credit	Balance

Cleaning Supplies   No. 128

Date	Explanation	Ref.	Debit	Credit	Balance

Prepaid Insurance   No. 130

Date	Explanation	Ref.	Debit	Credit	Balance

Equipment   No. 157

Date	Explanation	Ref.	Debit	Credit	Balance

Accumulated Depreciation - Equipment   No. 158

Date	Explanation	Ref.	Debit	Credit	Balance

(a), (e) and (f) (Continued)

Accounts Payable   No. 201

Date	Explanation	Ref.	Debit	Credit	Balance

Salaries Payable   No. 212

Date	Explanation	Ref.	Debit	Credit	Balance

Mary Coleman, Capital   No. 301

Date	Explanation	Ref.	Debit	Credit	Balance

Mary Coleman, Drawing   No. 306

Date	Explanation	Ref.	Debit	Credit	Balance

Income Summary   No. 350

Date	Explanation	Ref.	Debit	Credit	Balance

Service Revenue   No. 400

Date	Explanation	Ref.	Debit	Credit	Balance

(a), (e) and (f) (Continued)

Gas & Oil Expense   No. 633

Date	Explanation	Ref.	Debit	Credit	Balance

Cleaning Supplies Expense   No. 634

Date	Explanation	Ref.	Debit	Credit	Balance

Depreciation Expense   No. 711

Date	Explanation	Ref.	Debit	Credit	Balance

Insurance Expense   No. 722

Date	Explanation	Ref.	Debit	Credit	Balance

Salaries Expense   No. 726

Date	Explanation	Ref.	Debit	Credit	Balance

(d)

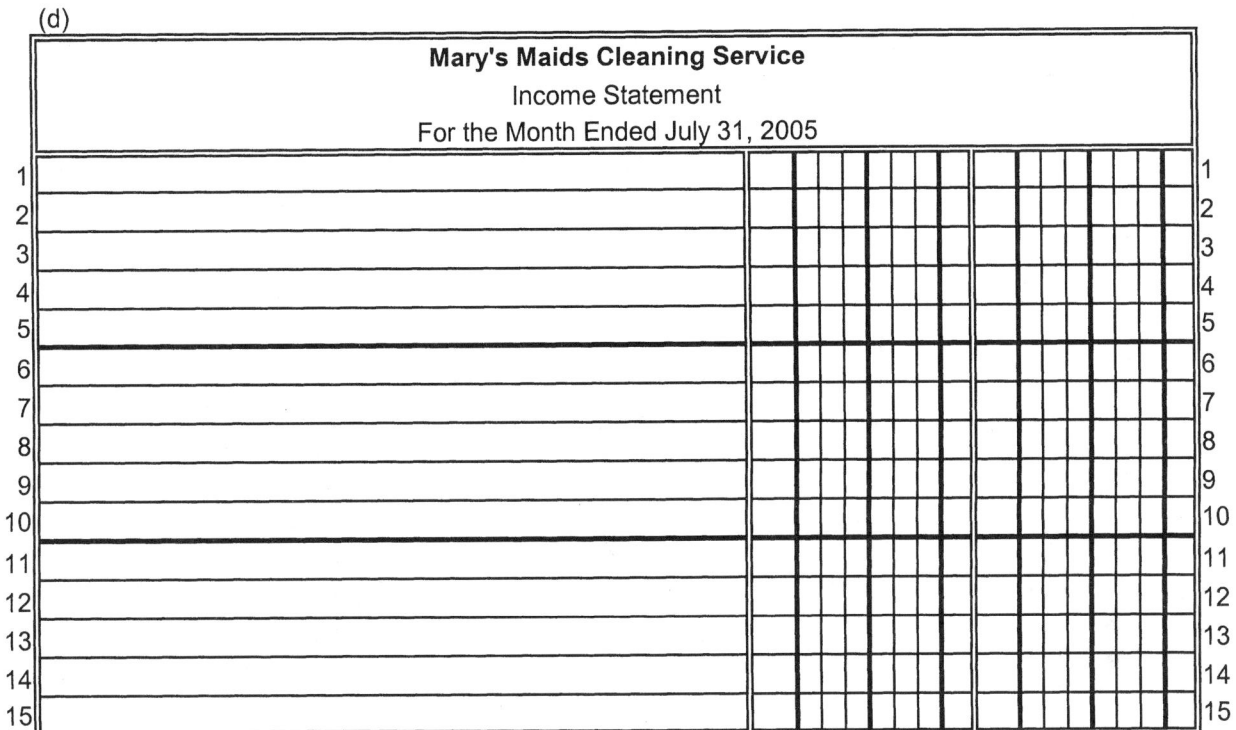

Mary's Maids Cleaning Service

Income Statement

For the Month Ended July 31, 2005

Mary's Maids Cleaning Service

Retained Earnings Statement

For the Month Ended July 31, 2005

(d) (Continued)

Mary's Maids Cleaning Service
Balance Sheet
July 31, 2005

Assets

Liabilities and Owner's Equity

(g)

Mary's Maids Cleaning Service
Post-Closing Trial Balance
July 31, 2005

	Debit	Credit

General Journal   J2

	Date	Accounts Titles and Explanation	Ref.	Debit	Credit	
1	(e)	Adjusting Entries				1
2	July 31					2
3						3
4						4
5	31					5
6						6
7						7
8	31					8
9						9
10						10
11	31					11
12						12
13						13
14	31					14
15						15
16						16

General Journal   J3

				Debit	Credit	
1	(f)	Closing Entries				1
2	July 31					2
3						3
4						4
5	31					5
6						6
7						7
8						8
9						9
10						10
11						11
12	31					12
13						13
14						14
15	31					15
16						16
17						17
18						18
19						19
20						20

(a)

(b)

(c)

(d)

(e)

	PepsiCo	Coca-Cola	
1			1
2 (a) In millions			2
3			3
4 1. Total current assets			4
5			5
6 2. Net property, plant, and equipment			6
7			7
8 3. Total current liabilities			8
9			9
10 4. Total stockholders' (shareholders') equity			10
11			11
12			12
13			13
14			14
15			15
16 (b)			16
17			17
18			18
19			19
20			20
21			21
22			22
23			23
24			24
25			25
26			26
27			27
28			28
29			29
30			30
31			31
32			32
33			33
34			34
35			35
36			36
37			37
38			38
39			39
40			40

1	1
2	2
3	3
4	4
5	5
6	6
7	7
8	8
9	9
10	10
11	11
12	12
13	13
14	14
15	15
16	16
17	17
18	18
19	19
20	20
21	21
22	22
23	23
24	24
25	25
26	26
27	27
28	28
29	29
30	30
31	31
32	32
33	33
34	34
35	35
36	36
37	37
38	38
39	39
40	40

1		1
2		2
3		3
4		4
5		5
6		6
7		7
8		8
9		9
10		10
11		11
12		12
13		13
14		14
15		15
16		16
17		17
18		18
19		19
20		20
21		21
22		22
23		23
24		24
25		25
26		26
27		27
28		28
29		29
30		30
31		31
32		32
33		33
34		34
35		35
36		36
37		37
38		38
39		39
40		40

(a)

Everclean Janitorial Service
Balance Sheet
December 31, 2005

Assets

Liabilities and Owner's Equity

(b)

Everclean Janitorial Service		
Capital Account Detail		
December 31, 2005		
Capital account balance as reported		

1
2
3
4
5
6
7
8
9
10
11
12
13
14
15
16
17
18
19
20
21
22
23
24
25
26
27
28
29
30
31
32
33
34
35
36
37
38
39
40

(a)

(b)

(c)

#1

	Sales	Cost of Goods Sold	Gross Profit	Operating Expenses	Net Income
(a)	$ 75000		28600		10800
(b)	$ 108000	70000			29500
(c)	$	71900	99600	39500	

#2

Account Titles	Debit	Credit
Giovanni Company		
Gordon Company		

#3

Account Titles	Debit	Credit
(a)		
(b)		
(c)		

#4

	Account Titles	Debit	Credit	
1	(a)			1
2				2
3				3
4	(b)			4
5				5
6				6
7	(c)			7
8				8
9				9
10				10

#5

11				11
12	**Piccola Company**			12
13	Income Statement (Partial)			13
14	For the Month Ended October 31, 2005			14
15				15
16				16
17				17
18				18
19				19
20				20

#6

	Account Titles	Debit	Credit	
21				21
22				22
23				23
24				24
25				25

#7

	Account Titles	Debit	Credit	
26				26
27				27
28				28
29				29
30				30
31				31
32				32
33				33
34				34
35				35
36				36
37				37
38				38
39				39
40				40

#8

	Item	Section	
1			1
2			2
3			3
4			4
5			5
6			6
7			7
8			8
9			9
10			10

11	(1) Multiple-Step Income Statement		11
12			12
13	Item	Section	13
14	a.		14
15	b.		15
16	c.		16
17			17
18	(2) Single-Step Income Statement		18
19			19
20	Item	Section	20
21	a.		21
22	b.		22
23	c.		23
24			24
25			25
26	**#9**		26
27	(a)		27
28			28
29	(b)		29
30			30
31	(c)		31
32			32
33			33
34			34
35			35
36			36
37			37
38			38
39			39
40			40

#10

		1
1		1
2		2
3		3
4		4
5		5
6		6
7		7
8		8
9		9
10		10

#11

11		11
12		12
13		13
14		14
15		15
16		16
17		17
18		18
19		19
20		20

#12

	Account Titles	Debit	Credit	
21				21
22	(a)			22
23				23
24				24
25	(b)			25
26				26
27				27
28	(c)			28
29				29
30				30
31				31

#13

32		32
33	(a) Cash:	33
34		34
35	(b) Merchandise Inventory:	35
36		36
37	(c) Sales:	37
38		38
39	(d) Cost of Goods Sold	39
40		40

#1

General Journal

	Date	Account Titles and Explanation	Debit	Credit	
1	(a)				1
2	Apr. 5				2
3					3
4					4
5	6				5
6					6
7					7
8	7				8
9					9
10					10
11	8				11
12					12
13					13
14	15				14
15					15
16					16
17					17
18	(b)				18
19	May 4				19
20					20
21					21

#2

	Date	Account Titles and Explanation	Debit	Credit	
1	Sept. 6				1
2					2
3					3
4	9				4
5					5
6					6
7	10				7
8					8
9					9
10	12				10
11					11
12					12
13					13
14					14

#2 (Continued)

General Journal

	Date	Account Titles and Explanation	Debit	Credit	
1	Sept. 14				1
2					2
3					3
4					4
5					5
6	20				6
7					7
8					8
9					9
10					10
11					11
12					12

#3

	Date	Account Titles and Explanation	Debit	Credit	
1	(a)				1
2	June 10				2
3					3
4					4
5	11				5
6					6
7					7
8	12				8
9					9
10					10
11	19				11
12					12
13					13
14					14
15	(b)				15
16	June 10				16
17					17
18					18
19					19
20					20
21					21
22					22
23					23

#3 (continued)

General Journal

	Date	Account Titles and Explanation	Debit	Credit	
1	June 12				1
2					2
3					3
4					4
5					5
6	19				6
7					7
8					8
9					9
10					10

#4

	Date	Account Titles and Explanation	Debit	Credit	
1	(a)				1
2	Dec. 3				2
3					3
4					4
5					5
6					6
7					7
8	8				8
9					9
10					10
11	13				11
12					12
13					13
14					14
15					15
16					16
17	(b)				17
18					18
19					19
20					20
21					21
22					22
23					23
24					24
25					25

#5

(a)

Schinzer Company		
Income Statement (Partial)		
For the Year Ended October 31, 2005		

(b)

	Date	Account Titles	Debit	Credit
1	Oct. 31			
2				
3				
4	31			
5				
6				
7				

#6

	Account Titles	Debit	Credit
1	(a)		
2			
3			
4	(b)		
5			
6			
7			
8			
9			
10			
11			
12			
13			
14			
15			
16			
17			

(a)

Bach Company Income Statement For the Year Ended December 31, 2005				
1				
2				
3				
4				
5				
6				
7				
8				
9				
10				
11				
12				
13				
14				
15				
16				
17				
18				
19				
20				

(b)

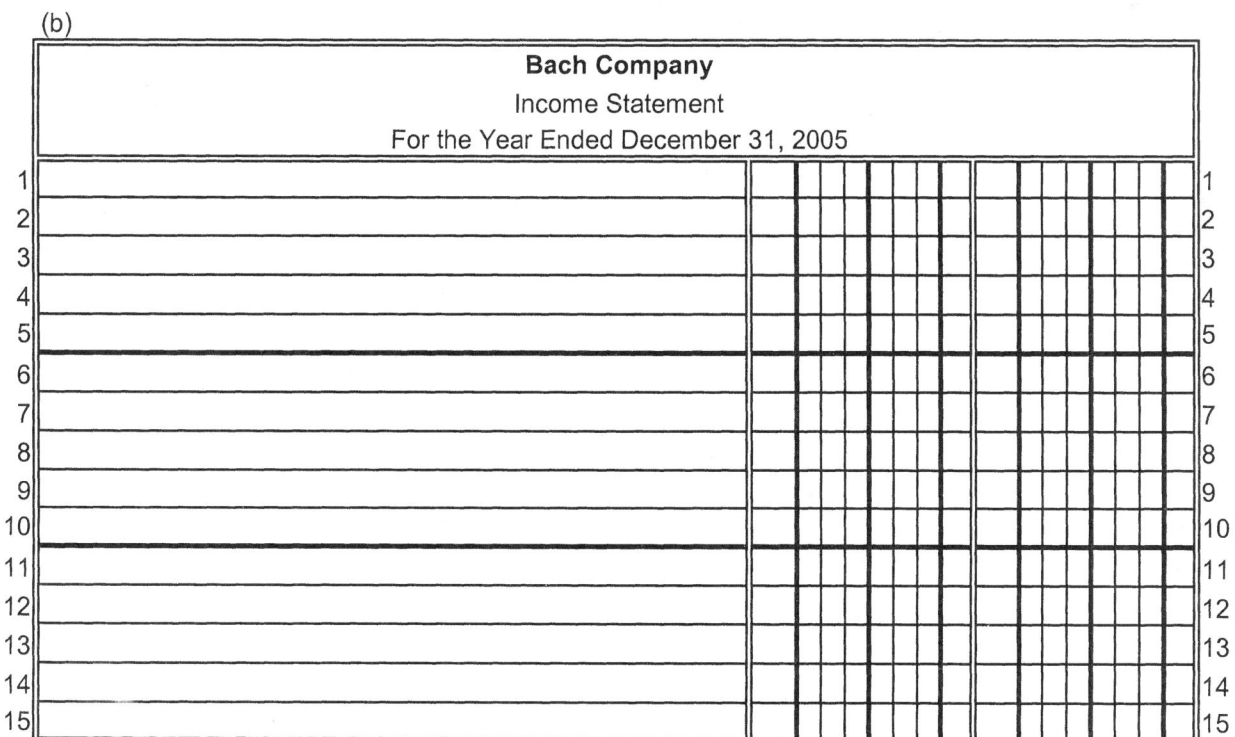

Bach Company Income Statement For the Year Ended December 31, 2005		
1		
2		
3		
4		
5		
6		
7		
8		
9		
10		
11		
12		
13		
14		
15		

#8

	Account Titles	Debit	Credit	
1	1.			1
2				2
3				3
4	2.			4
5				5
6				6
7				7
8				8
9	3.			9
10				10
11				11
12	4.			12
13				13
14				14
15				15

#9

		Lee Company	Chan Company	
1				1
2	Sales	$ 90000	$	2
3				3
4	Sales Returns		5000	4
5				5
6	Net Sales	81900	95000	6
7				7
8	Cost of Goods Sold	56000		8
9				9
10	Gross Profit		41500	10
11				11
12	Operating Expenses	15000		12
13				13
14	Net Income	$	$ 15000	14
15				15
16				16
17				17
18				18
19				19
20				20

#10

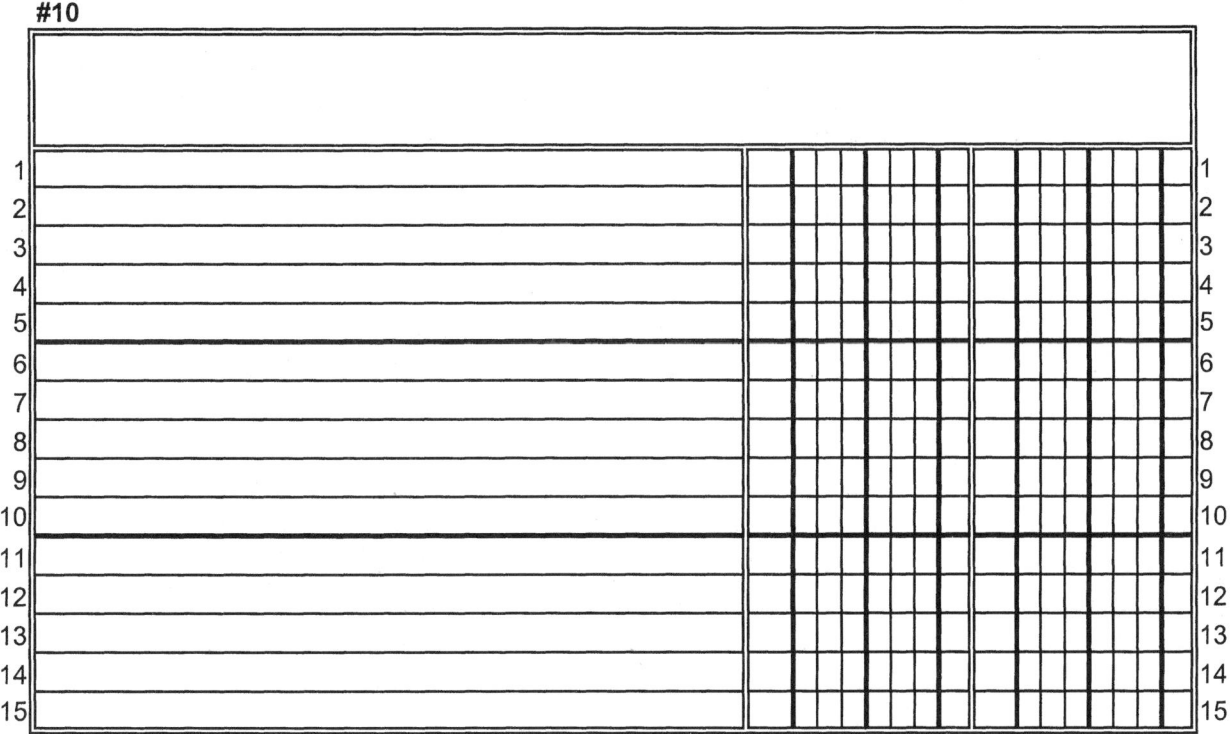

#11

	X	F	L	S	
1 Beginning inventory	$ 250	$ 120	$ 1000	$	1
2					2
3 Purchases	1500	1080		43590	3
4					4
5 Purchase returns					5
6 & allowances	40		290		6
7					7
8 Net purchases		1030	7210	42090	8
9					9
10 Freight-in	110			2240	10
11					11
12 Cost of goods					12
13 purchased		1230	7940		13
14 Cost of goods					14
15 available for sale	1820	1350		49530	15
16 Ending inventory	310		1450	6230	16
17					17
18 Cost of goods sold		1230	7490	43300	18

	Date	Account Titles	Debit	Credit	
1	(a)				1
2	Apr. 5				2
3					3
4					4
5	5				5
6					6
7					7
8	7				8
9					9
10					10
11	8				11
12					12
13					13
14	15				14
15					15
16					16
17					17
18					18
19	(b)				19
20	May 4				20
21					21
22					22
23					23
24					24
25					25

	Date	Account Titles	Debit	Credit	
1	(a)				1
2	Apr. 5				2
3					3
4					4
5	5				5
6					6
7					7
8	7				8
9					9
10					10
11	8				11
12					12
13					13
14	15				14
15					15
16					16
17					17
18					18
19	(b)				19
20	May 4				20
21					21
22					22
23					23
24					24
25					25

Streisand Company
Work Sheet (Partial)
For the Period Ended May 31, 2005

	Account Titles	Adjusted Trial Balance		Income Statement		Balance Sheet	
		Dr.	Cr.	Dr.	Cr.	Dr.	Cr.
1	Cash	9 0 0 0					
2	Merchandise Inventory	7 6 0 0 0					
3	Sales		4 5 0 0 0 0				
4	Sales Returns and Allowances	1 0 0 0 0					
5	Sales Discounts	9 0 0 0					
6	Cost of Goods Sold	2 5 0 0 0 0					
7							
8							
9							
10							
11							
12							
13							
14							
15							

General Journal

	Date	Account Titles and Explanation	Debit	Credit	
1	June 1				1
2					2
3					3
4	3				4
5					5
6					6
7					7
8					8
9					9
10	6				10
11					11
12					12
13	9				13
14					14
15					15
16					16
17	15				17
18					18
19					19
20	17				20
21					21
22					22
23					23
24					24
25					25
26	20				26
27					27
28					28
29	24				29
30					30
31					31
32					32
33	26				33
34					34
35					35
36					36
37					37
38					38
39					39
40					40

General Journal

	Date	Account Titles and Explanation	Debit	Credit	
1	June 28				1
2					2
3					3
4					4
5					5
6					6
7	30				7
8					8
9					9
10					10
11					11
12					12
13					13
14					14
15					15
16					16
17					17
18					18
19					19
20					20
21					21
22					22
23					23
24					24
25					25
26					26
27					27
28					28
29					29
30					30
31					31
32					32
33					33
34					34
35					35
36					36
37					37
38					38
39					39
40					40

(a)   General Journal   J1

	Date	Account Titles and Explanation	Ref.	Debit	Credit	
1	May 1					1
2						2
3						3
4	2					4
5						5
6						6
7						7
8						8
9						9
10	5					10
11						11
12						12
13	9					13
14						14
15						15
16						16
17	10					17
18						18
19						19
20						20
21	11					21
22						22
23						23
24	12					24
25						25
26						26
27	15					27
28						28
29						29
30	17					30
31						31
32						32
33	19					33
34						34
35						35
36	24					36
37						37
38						38
39						39
40						40

(a) (Continued)

General Journal   J1

	Date	Account Titles and Explanation	Ref	Debit	Credit	
1	May 25					1
2						2
3						3
4	27					4
5						5
6						6
7						7
8	29					8
9						9
10						10
11						11
12						12
13						13
14	31					14
15						15
16						16
17						17
18						18
19						19
20						20

(b)

Cash   No. 101

Date	Explanation	Ref.	Debit	Credit	Balance
May 1	Balance	√			5 0 0 0

Accounts Receivable   No. 112

Date	Explanation	Ref.	Debit	Credit	Balance

(b) (Continued)

Merchandise Inventory   No. 120

Date	Explanation	Ref.	Debit	Credit	Balance

Supplies   No. 126

Date	Explanation	Ref.	Debit	Credit	Balance

Accounts Payable   No. 201

Date	Explanation	Ref.	Debit	Credit	Balance

B. Copple, Capital   No. 301

Date	Explanation	Ref.	Debit	Credit	Balance
May 1	Balance	√			5 0 0 0

Sales   No. 401

Date	Explanation	Ref.	Debit	Credit	Balance

(b) (Continued)

Sales Returns and Allowances   No. 412

Date	Explanation	Ref.	Debit	Credit	Balance

Sales Discounts   No. 414

Date	Explanation	Ref.	Debit	Credit	Balance

Cost of Goods Sold   No. 505

Date	Explanation	Ref.	Debit	Credit	Balance

(c)

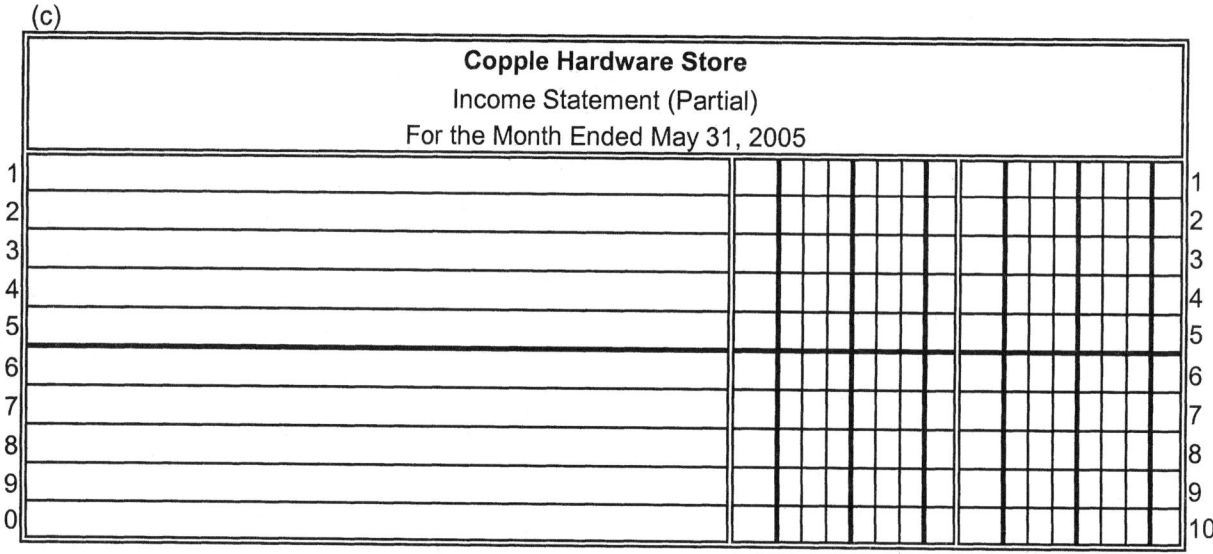

Copple Hardware Store

Income Statement (Partial)

For the Month Ended May 31, 2005

(a)

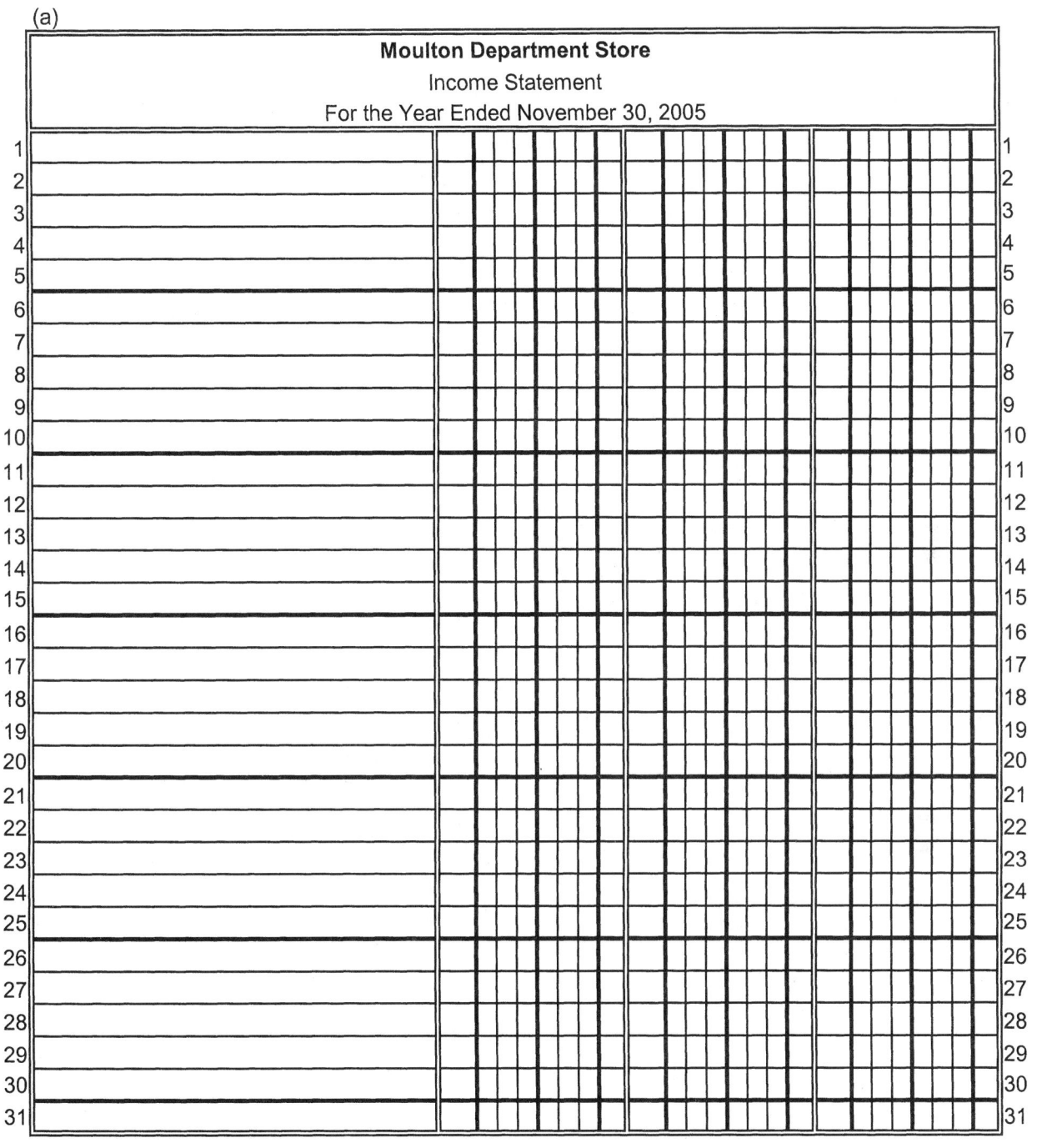

(a) (Continued)

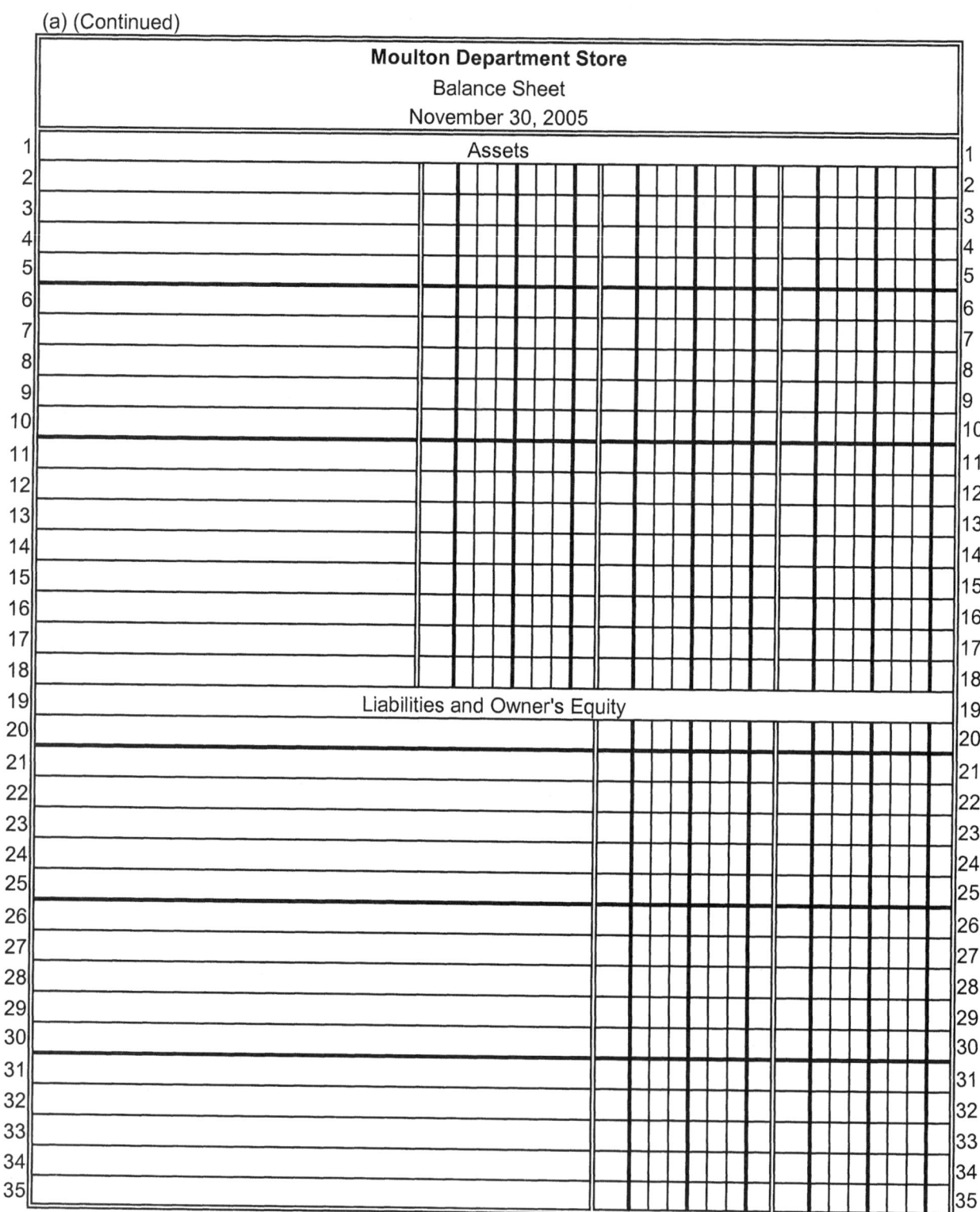

Moulton Department Store
Balance Sheet
November 30, 2005

Assets

Liabilities and Owner's Equity

(b)   General Journal

	Date	Account Titles and Explanation	Debit	Credit	
1		Adjusting Entries			1
2	Nov. 30				2
3					3
4					4
5	30				5
6					6
7					7
8	30				8
9					9
10					10
11	30				11
12					12
13					13
14	30				14
15					15
16					16
17					17
18					18
19					19
20					20
21					21
22					22
23					23
24					24
25					25

(c)   General Journal

	Date	Account Titles and Explanation	Debit	Credit	
1		Closing Entries			1
2	Nov. 30				2
3					3
4					4
5					5
6	30				6
7					7
8					8
9					9
10					10
11					11
12					12
13					13
14					14
15					15
16					16
17					17
18					18
19					19
20	30				20
21					21
22					22
23	30				23
24					24
25					25
26					26
27					27
28					28
29					29
30					30
31					31
32					32
33					33
34					34
35					35

(a)   General Journal   J1

	Date	Account Titles and Explanation	Ref.	Debit	Credit	
1	Apr. 5					1
2						2
3						3
4	7					4
5						5
6						6
7	9					7
8						8
9						9
10	10					10
11						11
12						12
13						13
14						14
15						15
16	12					16
17						17
18						18
19	14					19
20						20
21						21
22						22
23	17					23
24						24
25						25
26	20					26
27						27
28						28
29						29
30						30
31						31
32	21					32
33						33
34						34
35						35
36	27					36
37						37
38						38
39	30					39
40						40
41						41

(b)

Cash   No. 101

Date	Explanation	Ref.	Debit	Credit	Balance
Apr 1	Balance	√			2500

Accounts Receivable   No. 112

Date	Explanation	Ref.	Debit	Credit	Balance

Merchandise Inventory   No. 120

Date	Explanation	Ref.	Debit	Credit	Balance
Apr 1	Balance	√			3500

Accounts Payable   No. 201

Date	Explanation	Ref.	Debit	Credit	Balance

(b) (Continued)

B. Kokott, Capital   No. 301

Date	Explanation	Ref.	Debit	Credit	Balance
Apr 1	Balance	√			6 0 0 0

Sales   No. 401

Date	Explanation	Ref.	Debit	Credit	Balance

Sales Returns and Allowances   No. 412

Date	Explanation	Ref.	Debit	Credit	Balance

Cost of Goods Sold   No. 505

Date	Explanation	Ref.	Debit	Credit	Balance

(c)

Bill's Pro Shop Trial Balance April 30, 2005	Debit	Credit
1		
2		
3		
4		
5		
6		
7		
8		
9		
10		

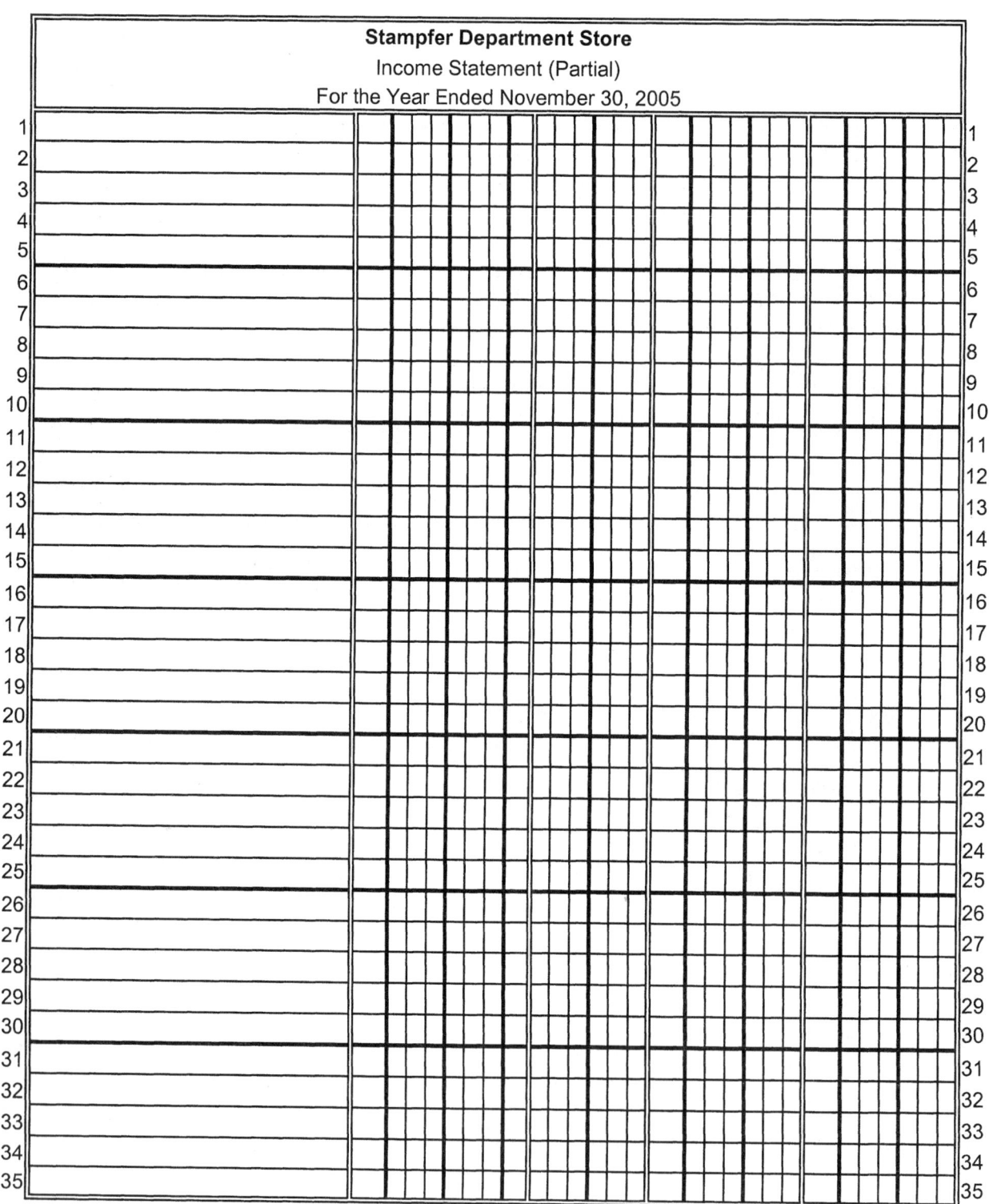

Stampfer Department Store
Income Statement (Partial)
For the Year Ended November 30, 2005

(a)

	2003	2004	2005	2006
1 **Inc. Stmt. Data**				
2 Sales	$	$ 96850	$	$ 82220
3 Cost of goods				
4 sold			27140	26550
5 Gross profit		69260	61540	
6 Operating exp.		63500		52060
7 Net income			4570	
8				
9 **Bal. Sheet Data**				
10 Merch. Inv.	$ 13000	$	$ 14700	$
11 Accounts payable	5000	6500	4600	
12				
13 **Add'l Information**				
14 Purchases of merch.				
15 inv. on account	$	$ 25890	$	$ 24050
16 Cash payments				24650
17 to suppliers				
18				
19				
20				

(b)

		2004	2005	2006
1				
2				
3				
4				
5				
6				
7				
8				
9				
10 Gross profit rate				
11				
12				
13 Profit margin ratio				
14				
15				

(a)   General Journal

	Date	Account Titles and Explanation	Debit	Credit	
1	Apr. 5				1
2					2
3					3
4	7				4
5					5
6					6
7	9				7
8					8
9					9
10	10				10
11					11
12					12
13	12				13
14					14
15					15
16	14				16
17					17
18					18
19					19
20	17				20
21					21
22					22
23	20				23
24					24
25					25
26	21				26
27					27
28					28
29					29
30	27				30
31					31
32					32
33	30				33
34					34
35					35
36					36
37					37
38					38
39					39
40					40

(b)

Cash	Tiger Woods, Capital
Accounts Receivable	**Sales**
Merchandise Inventory	**Sales Returns and Allowances**
Accounts Payable	**Purchases**
	Freight-in
Purchase Returns and Allowances	
Purchase Discounts	

(c)

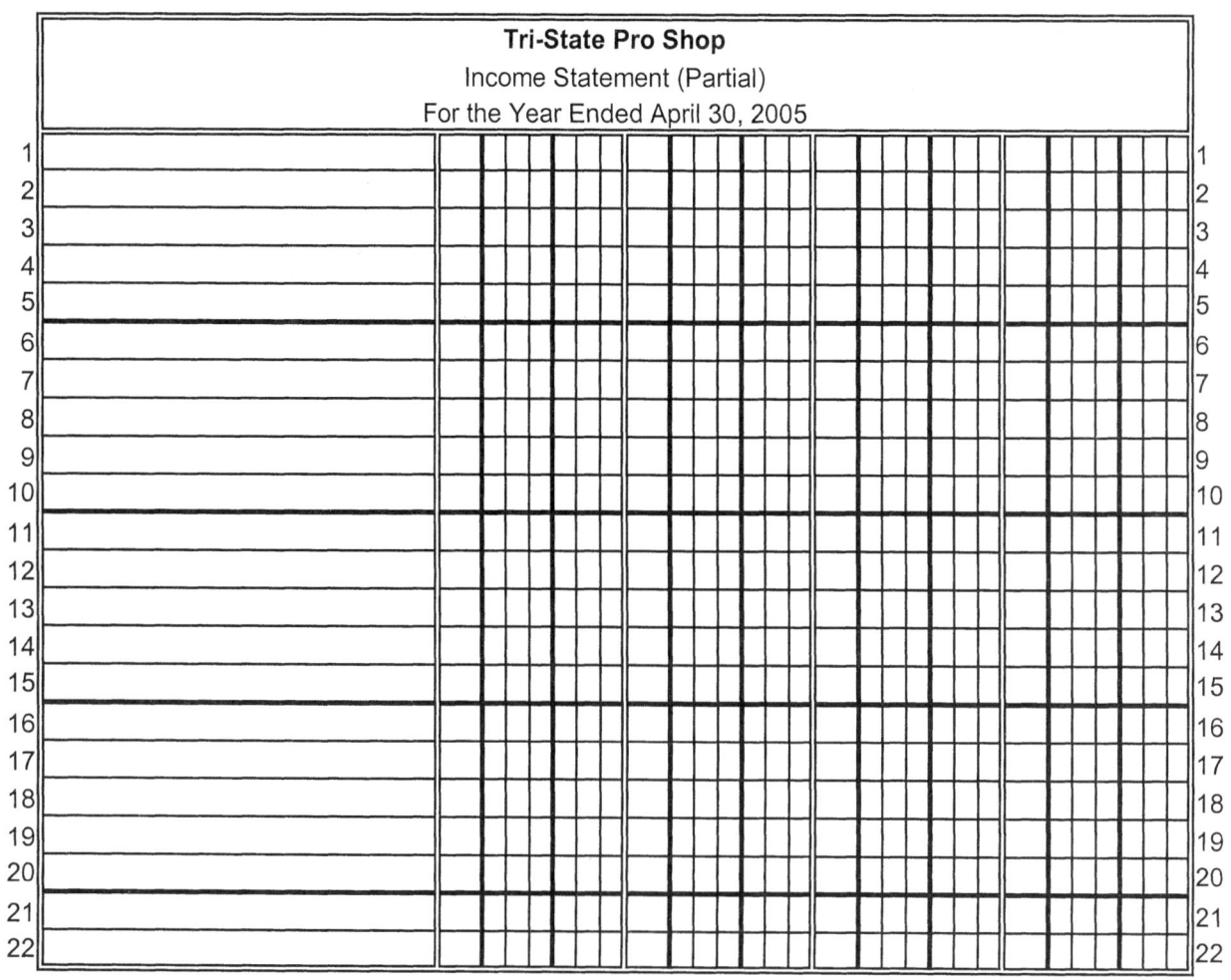

Tri-State Pro Shop
Trial Balance
April 30, 2005

	Debit	Credit
1		
2		
3		
4		
5		
6		
7		
8		
9		
10		
11		
12		
13		

Tri-State Pro Shop
Income Statement (Partial)
For the Year Ended April 30, 2005

PROBLEM 5 – 8A
See Appendix

(b)

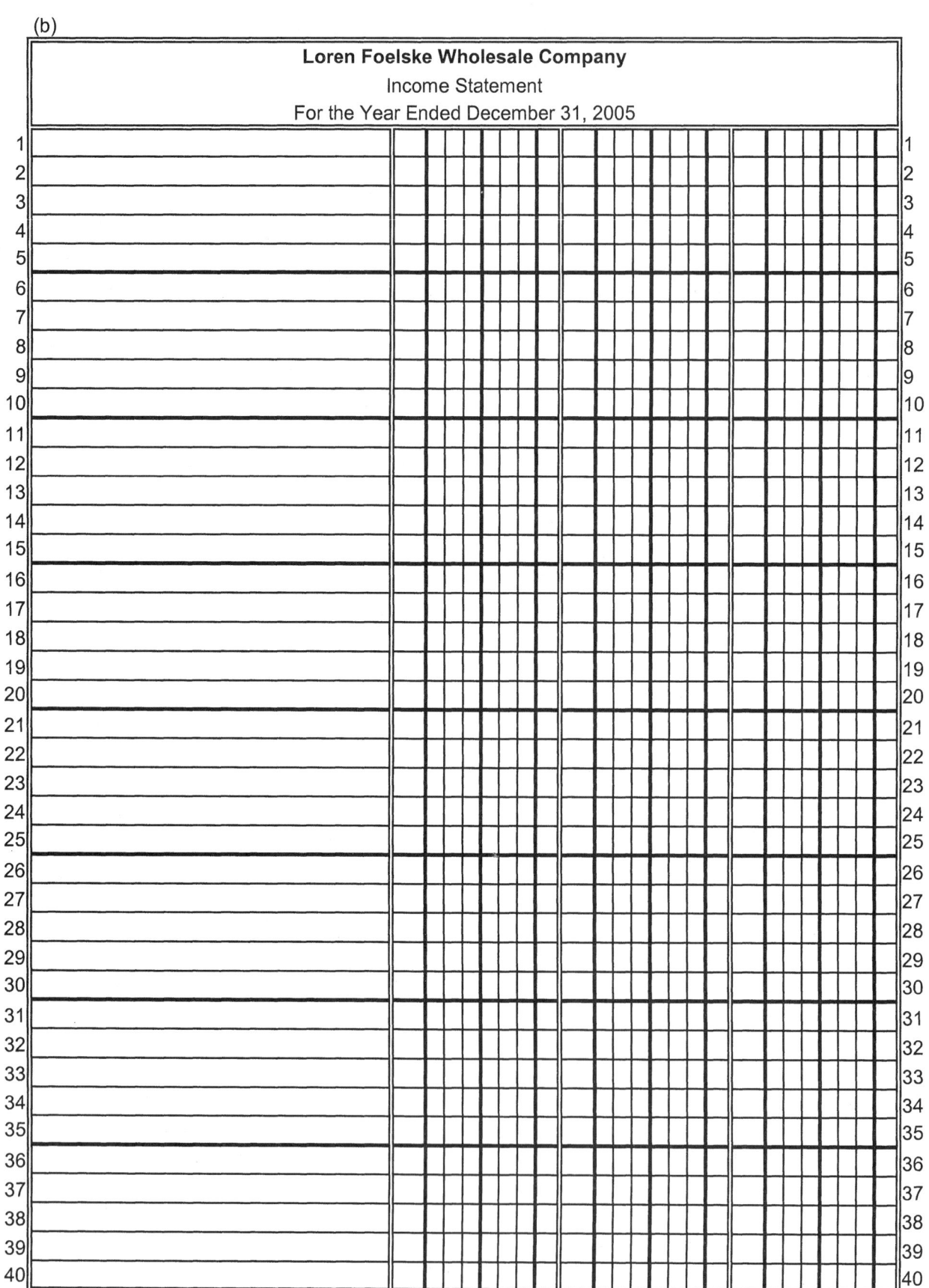

Loren Foelske Wholesale Company

Income Statement

For the Year Ended December 31, 2005

(b) (Continued)

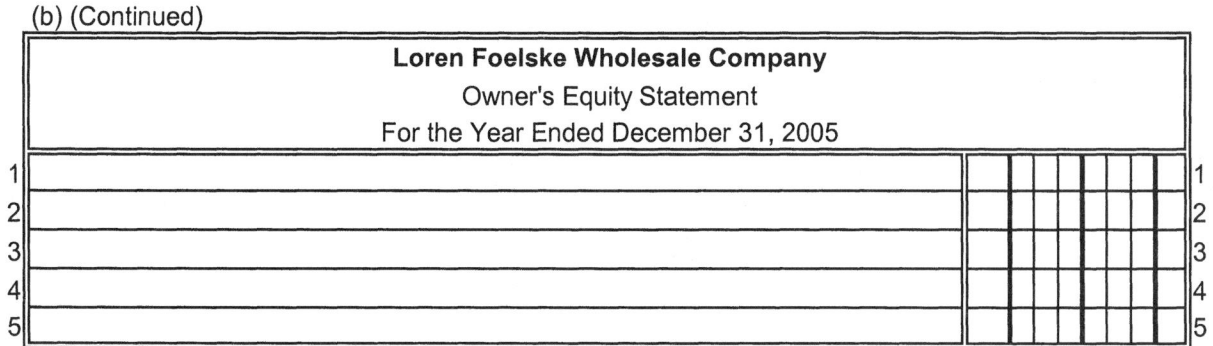

Loren Foelske Wholesale Company
Owner's Equity Statement
For the Year Ended December 31, 2005

1			1
2			2
3			3
4			4
5			5

Loren Foelske Wholesale Company
Balance Sheet
December 31, 2005

	Assets			
1	Assets			1
2				2
3				3
4				4
5				5
6				6
7				7
8				8
9				9
10				10
11				11
12				12
13				13
14				14
15				15
16				16
17	Liabilities and Owner's Equity			17
18				18
19				19
20				20
21				21
22				22
23				23
24				24
25				25
26				26
27				27
28				28
29				29
30				30

(c)   General Journal

	Date	Account Titles and Explanation	Debit	Credit	
1		Adjusting Entries			1
2	Dec. 31				2
3					3
4					4
5	31				5
6					6
7					7
8	31				8
9					9
10					10
11	31				11
12					12
13					13

(d)

	Date	Account Titles and Explanation	Debit	Credit	
1		Closing Entries			1
2	Dec. 31				2
3					3
4					4
5	31				5
6					6
7					7
8					8
9					9
10					10
11					11
12					12
13					13
14					14
15					15
16					16
17	31				17
18					18
19					19
20	31				20
21					21
22					22
23					23

(e)

Loren Foelske Wholesale Company Post-Closing Trial Balance December 31, 2005	Debit	Credit
1		
2		
3		
4		
5		
6		
7		
8		
9		
10		
11		
12		
13		
14		
15		

General Journal

	Date	Account Titles and Explanation	Debit	Credit	
1	July 1				1
2					2
3					3
4	3				4
5					5
6					6
7					7
8					8
9					9
10	9				10
11					11
12					12
13					13
14	12				14
15					15
16					16
17					17
18	17				18
19					19
20					20
21					21
22					22
23					23
24	18				24
25					25
26					26
27					27
28					28
29					29
30	20				30
31					31
32					32
33	21				33
34					34
35					35
36					36
37					37
38					38
39					39
40					40

General Journal

	Date	Account Titles and Explanation	Debit	Credit	
1	July 22				1
2					2
3					3
4					4
5					5
6					6
7	30				7
8					8
9					9
10	31				10
11					11
12					12
13					13
14					14
15					15
16					16
17					17
18					18
19					19
20					20
21					21
22					22
23					23
24					24
25					25
26					26
27					27
28					28
29					29
30					30
31					31
32					32
33					33
34					34
35					35
36					36
37					37
38					38
39					39
40					40

(a)   General Journal   J1

	Date	Account Titles and Explanation	Ref.	Debit	Credit	
1	Apr. 2					1
2						2
3						3
4	4					4
5						5
6						6
7						7
8						8
9						9
10	5					10
11						11
12						12
13	6					13
14						14
15						15
16	11					16
17						17
18						18
19						19
20	13					20
21						21
22						22
23						23
24	14					24
25						25
26						26
27	16					27
28						28
29						29
30	18					30
31						31
32						32
33	20					33
34						34
35						35
36	23					36
37						37
38						38
39						39
40						40

(a) (Continued)

General Journal   J1

	Date	Account Titles and Explanation	Ref	Debit	Credit	
1	Apr. 26					1
2						2
3						3
4	27					4
5						5
6						6
7						7
8	29					8
9						9
10						10
11						11
12						12
13						13
14	30					14
15						15
16						16
17						17
18						18
19						19
20						20

(b)

Cash   No. 101

Date	Explanation	Ref.	Debit	Credit	Balance
May 1	Balance	√			9 0 0 0

Accounts Receivable   No. 112

Date	Explanation	Ref.	Debit	Credit	Balance

(b) (Continued)

Merchandise Inventory   No. 120

Date	Explanation	Ref.	Debit	Credit	Balance

Accounts Payable   No. 201

Date	Explanation	Ref.	Debit	Credit	Balance

O. Shmi, Capital   No. 301

Date	Explanation	Ref.	Debit	Credit	Balance
Apr. 1	Balance	√			9 0 0 0

Sales   No. 401

Date	Explanation	Ref.	Debit	Credit	Balance

Sales Returns and Allowances   No. 412

Date	Explanation	Ref.	Debit	Credit	Balance

(b) (Continued)

Sales Discounts   No. 414

Date	Explanation	Ref.	Debit	Credit	Balance

Cost of Goods Sold   No. 505

Date	Explanation	Ref.	Debit	Credit	Balance

Freight-out   No. 644

Date	Explanation	Ref.	Debit	Credit	Balance

(c)

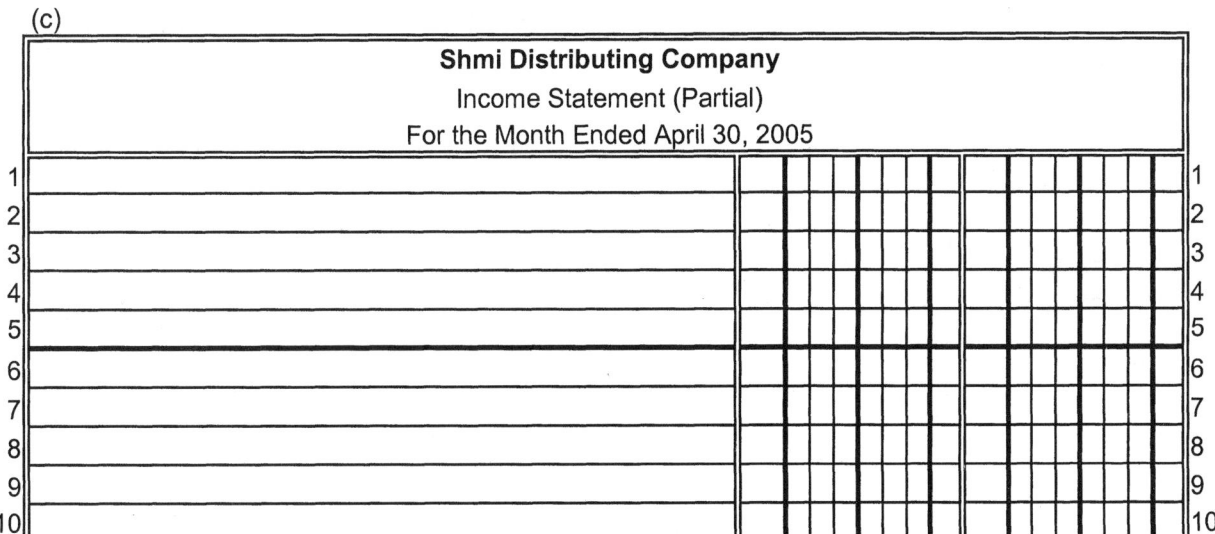

Shmi Distributing Company		
Income Statement (Partial)		
For the Month Ended April 30, 2005		

(a)

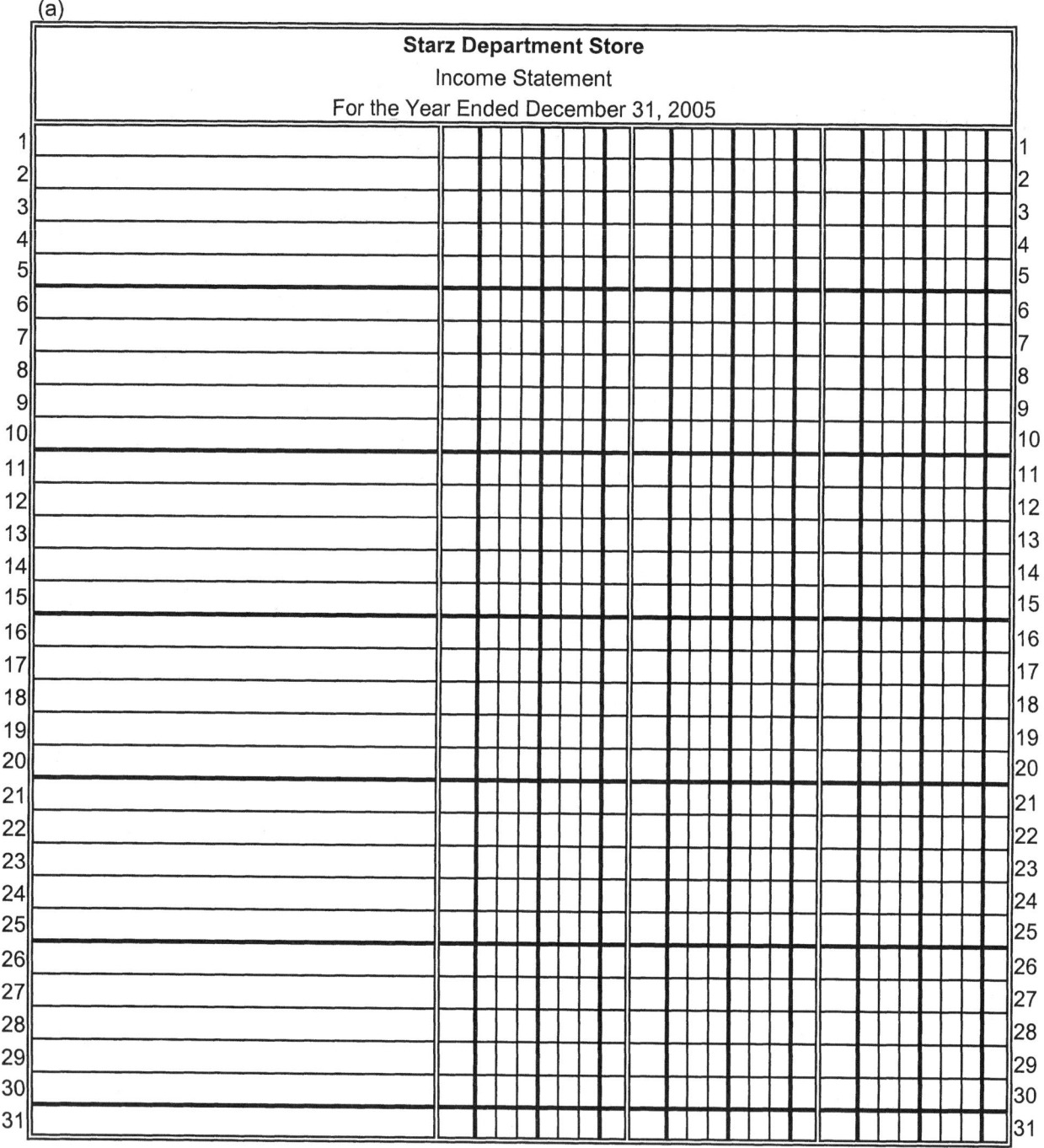

Starz Department Store
Income Statement
For the Year Ended December 31, 2005

Starz Department Store
Owner's Equity Statement
For the Year Ended December 31, 2005

(a) (Continued)

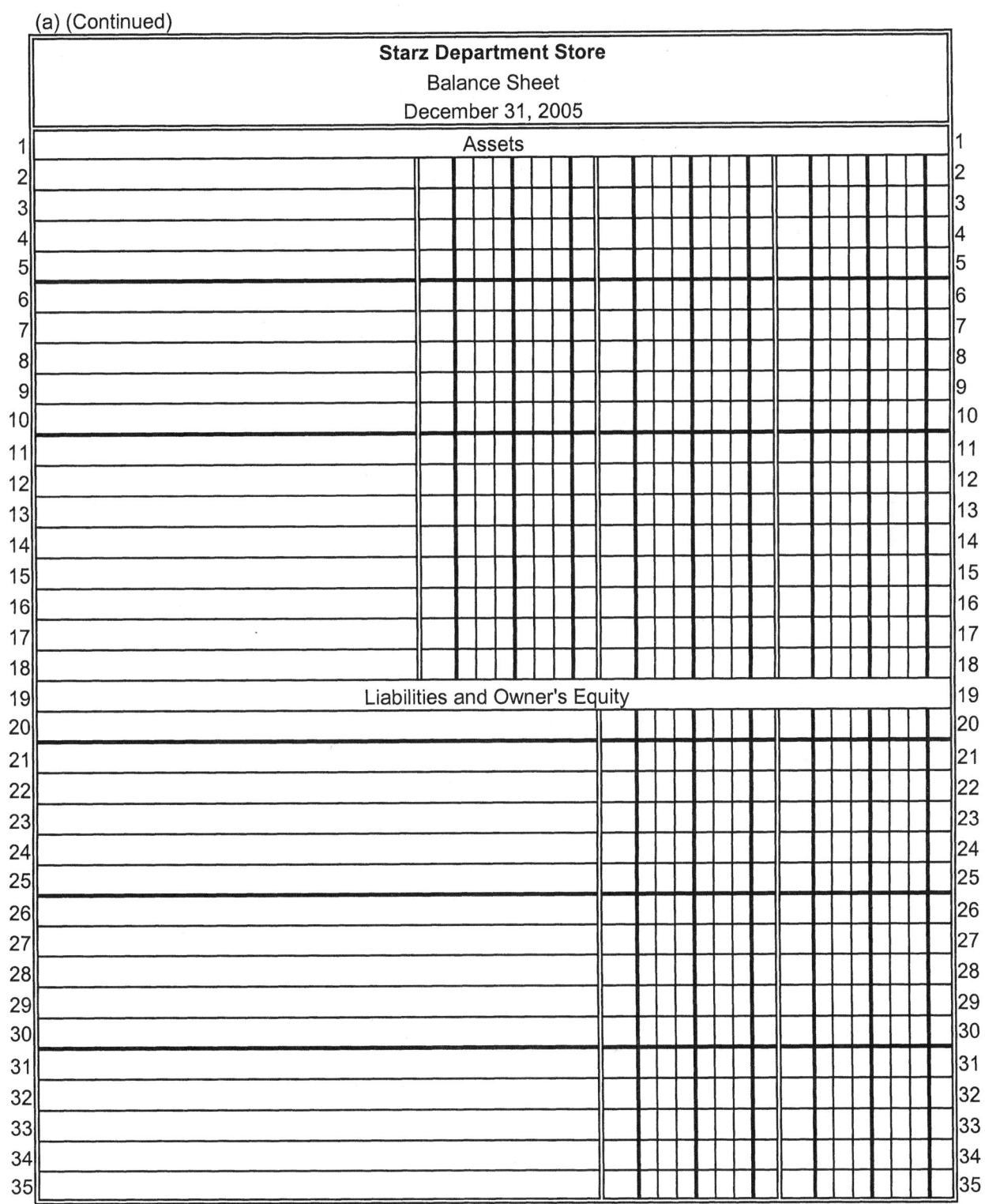

Starz Department Store

Balance Sheet

December 31, 2005

Assets

Liabilities and Owner's Equity

(b)

General Journal

	Date	Account Titles and Explanation	Debit	Credit	
1		Adjusting Entries			1
2	Dec. 31				2
3					3
4					4
5	31				5
6					6
7					7
8	31				8
9					9
10					10
11	31				11
12					12
13					13
14	31				14
15					15
16					16
17	31				17
18					18
19					19
20	31				20
21					21
22					22
23					23
24					24
25					25

(c)   General Journal

	Date	Account Titles and Explanation	Debit	Credit	
1		Closing Entries			1
2	Dec. 31				2
3					3
4					4
5					5
6	31				6
7					7
8					8
9					9
10					10
11					11
12					12
13					13
14					14
15					15
16					16
17					17
18					18
19	31				19
20					20
21					21
22	31				22
23					23
24					24
25					25
26					26
27					27
28					28
29					29
30					30
31					31
32					32
33					33
34					34
35					35

(a) General Journal J1

	Date	Account Titles and Explanation	Ref.	Debit	Credit	
1	Apr. 4					1
2						2
3						3
4	6					4
5						5
6						6
7	8					7
8						8
9						9
10						10
11						11
12						12
13	10					13
14						14
15						15
16	11					16
17						17
18						18
19	13					19
20						20
21						21
22						22
23	14					23
24						24
25						25
26	15					26
27						27
28						28
29	17					29
30						30
31						31
32	18					32
33						33
34						34
35						35
36						36
37						37
38						38
39						39
40						40
41						41

(a) (Continued) General Journal J1

	Date	Account Titles and Explanation	Ref.	Debit	Credit	
1	Apr. 20					1
2						2
3						3
4	21					4
5						5
6						6
7						7
8	27					8
9						9
10						10
11	30					11
12						12
13						13
14						14
15						15
16						16
17						17
18						18
19						19
20						20
21						21
22						22
23						23
24						24
25						25
26						26
27						27
28						28
29						29
30						30
31						31
32						32
33						33
34						34
35						35
36						36
37						37
38						38
39						39
40						40
41						41

(b)

Cash   No. 101

Date	Explanation	Ref.	Debit	Credit	Balance
Apr 1	Balance	√			2 5 0 0

Accounts Receivable   No. 112

Date	Explanation	Ref.	Debit	Credit	Balance

Merchandise Inventory   No. 120

Date	Explanation	Ref.	Debit	Credit	Balance
Apr 1	Balance	√			1 7 0 0

Accounts Payable   No. 201

Date	Explanation	Ref.	Debit	Credit	Balance

(b) (Continued)

J. Ackbar, Capital   No. 301

Date	Explanation	Ref.	Debit	Credit	Balance
Apr 1	Balance	√			4 2 0 0

Sales   No. 401

Date	Explanation	Ref.	Debit	Credit	Balance

Sales Returns and Allowances   No. 412

Date	Explanation	Ref.	Debit	Credit	Balance

Cost of Goods Sold   No. 505

Date	Explanation	Ref.	Debit	Credit	Balance

(c)

Ackbar's Tennis Shop
Trial Balance
April 30, 2005

	Debit	Credit
1		
2		
3		
4		
5		
6		
7		
8		
9		
10		

High-Point Department Store							
Income Statement (Partial)							
For the Year Ended December 31, 2005							

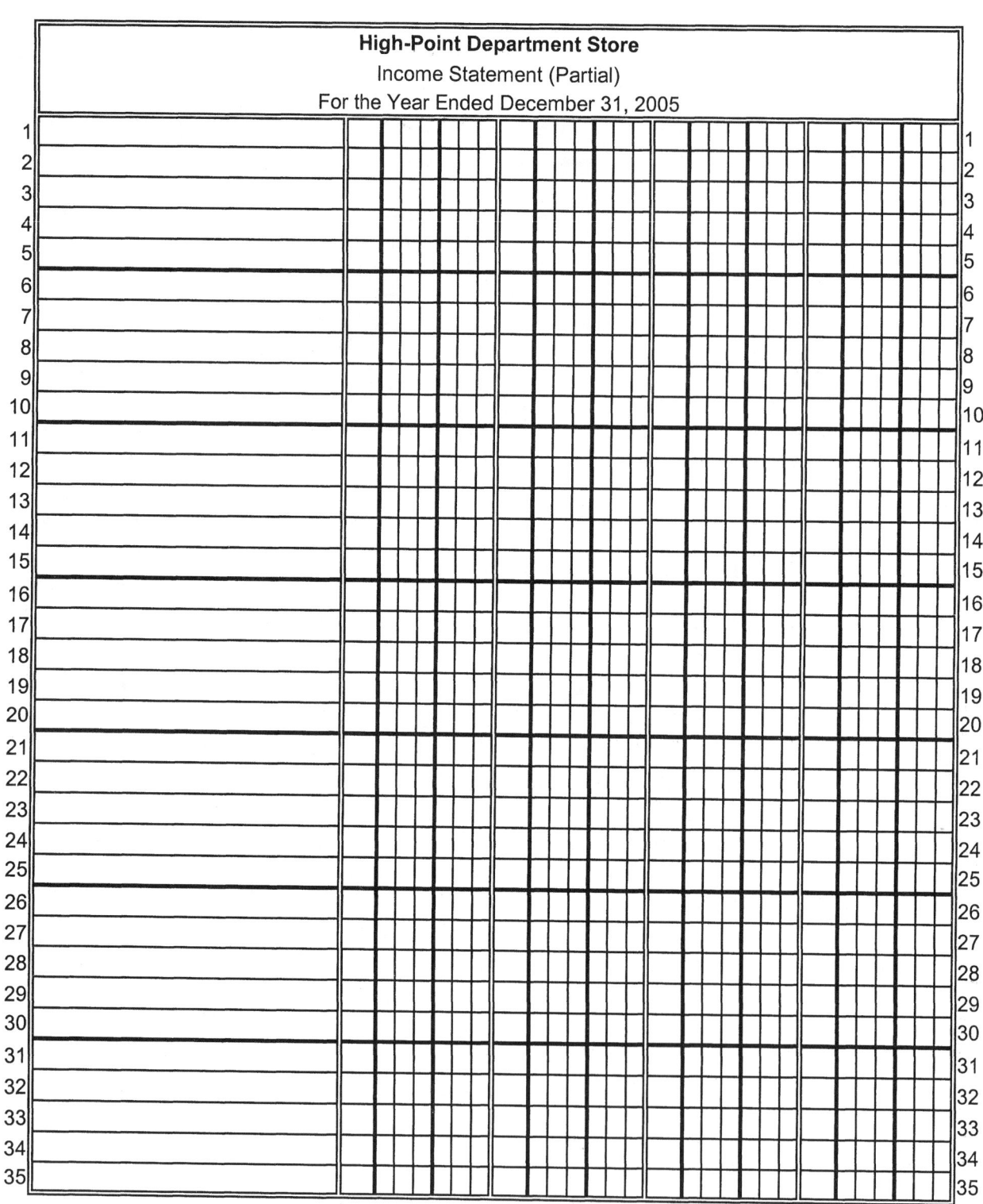

(a)	2004	2005	2006
1 Cost of goods sold:			
2			
3			
4			
5			
6			
7			
8 (b)			
9 Sales			
10			
11			
12			
13 (c)			
14 Beginning accounts payable			
15			
16			
17			
18			
19 (d)			
20 Gross profit rate			
21			

(a)   General Journal

	Date	Account Titles and Explanation	Debit	Credit	
1	Apr. 4				1
2					2
3					3
4	6				4
5					5
6					6
7	8				7
8					8
9					9
10	10				10
11					11
12					12
13	11				13
14					14
15					15
16	13				16
17					17
18					18
19					19
20	14				20
21					21
22					22
23	15				23
24					24
25					25
26	17				26
27					27
28					28
29	18				29
30					30
31					31
32					32
33					33
34					34
35					35
36					36
37					37
38					38
39					39
40					40

(a) (Continued)   General Journal

	Date	Account Titles and Explanation	Debit	Credit	
1	Apr. 20				1
2					2
3					3
4	21				4
5					5
6					6
7					7
8	27				8
9					9
10					10
11	30				11
12					12
13					13
14					14
15					15
16					16
17					17
18					18
19					19
20					20
21					21
22					22
23					23
24					24
25					25
26					26
27					27
28					28
29					29
30					30

(b)

Cash	Sales Returns and Allowances

	Purchases

Accounts Receivable	

	Purchase Returns and Allowances

Merchandise Inventory	

	Purchase Discount

Accounts Payable	

	Freight-in

Althea Gibson, Capital	

Sales	

(c)

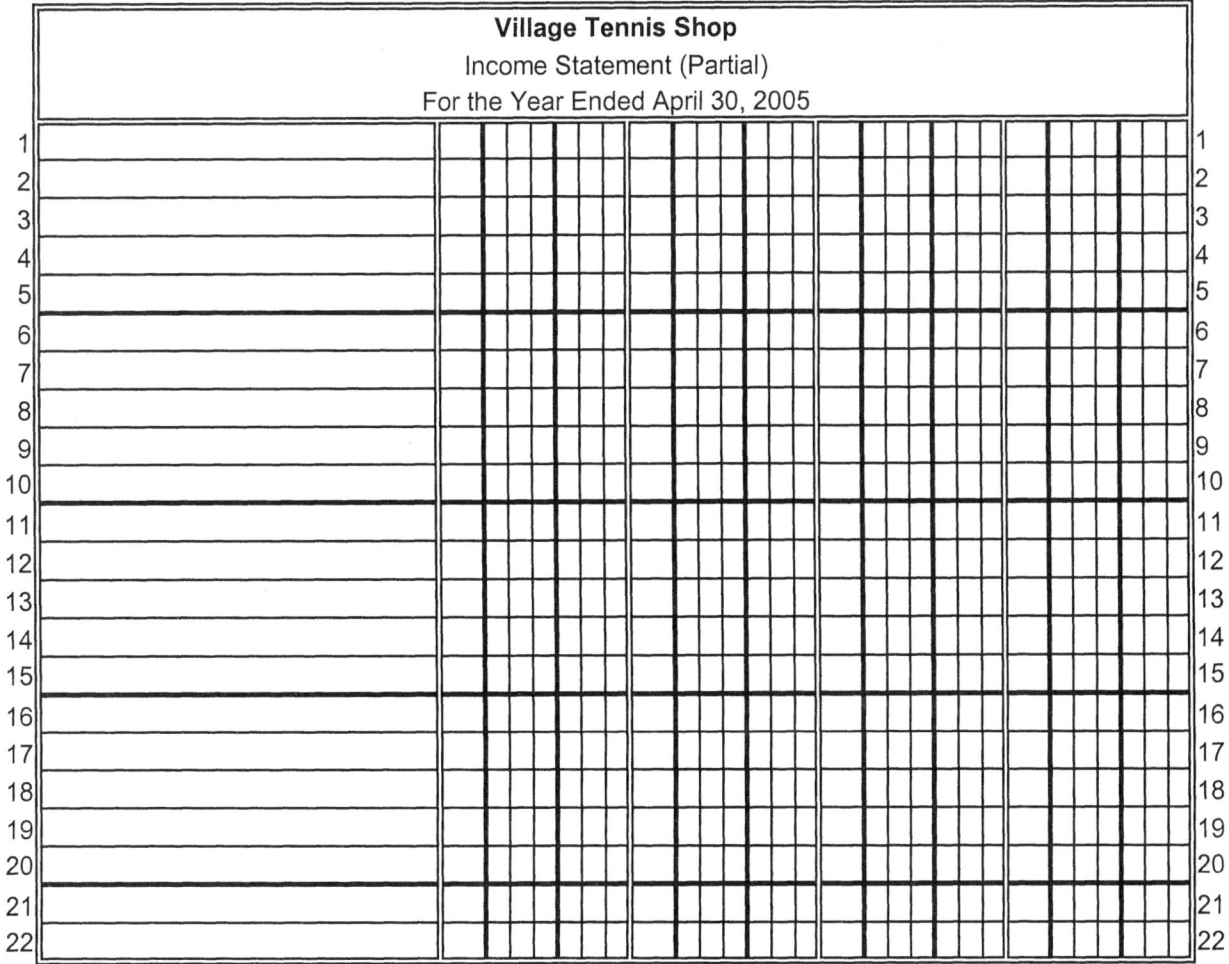

Village Tennis Shop
Trial Balance
April 30, 2005

	Debit	Credit
1		
2		
3		
4		
5		
6		
7		
8		
9		
10		
11		
12		
13		

Village Tennis Shop
Income Statement (Partial)
For the Year Ended April 30, 2005

PROBLEM 5 – 8B
See Appendix

(b)

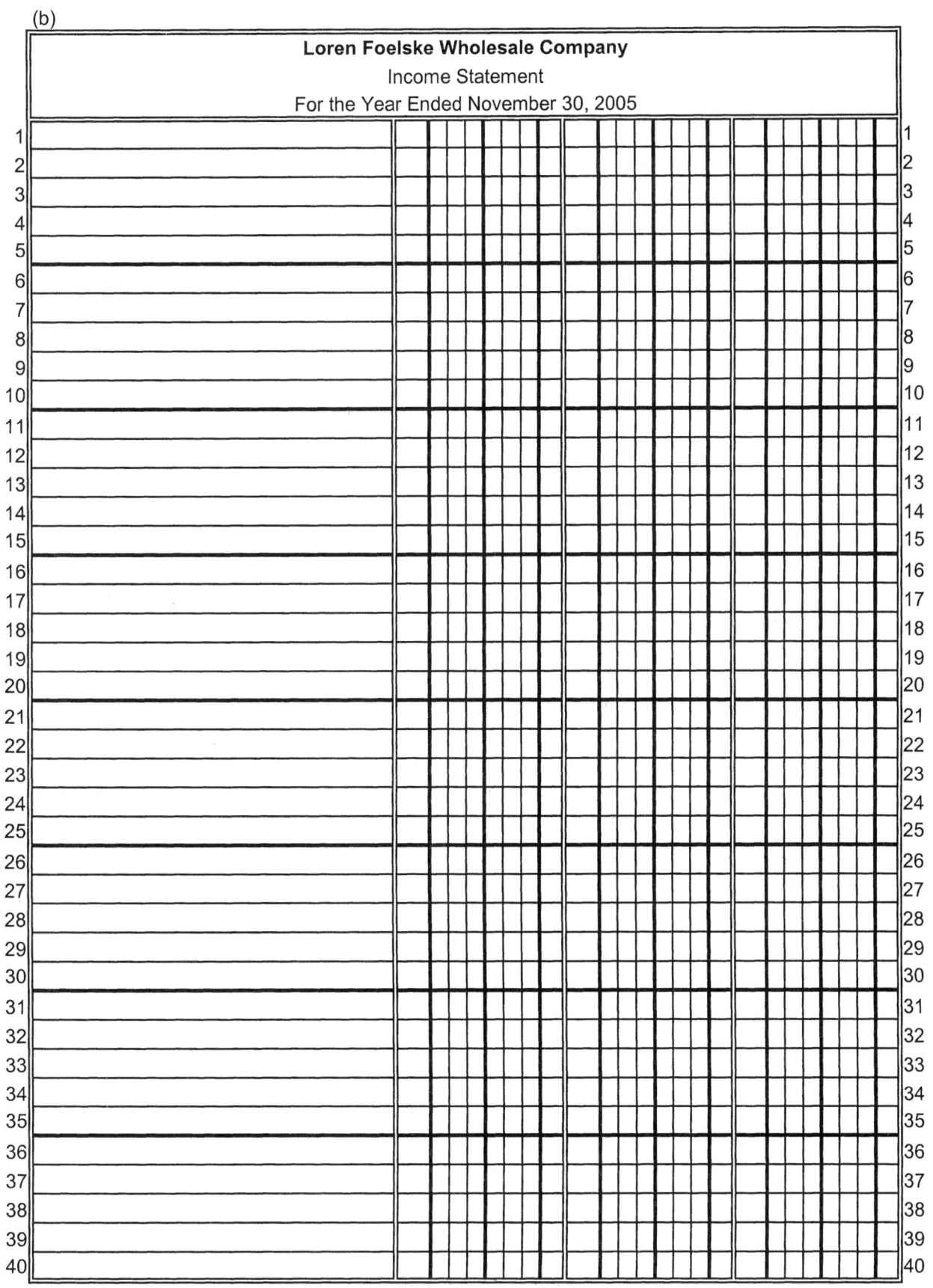

Loren Foelske Wholesale Company

Income Statement

For the Year Ended November 30, 2005

(b) (Continued)

	Kevin Poorten Fashion Center
	Owner's Equity Statement
	For the Year Ended November 30, 2005

1									1
2									2
3									3
4									4
5									5

	Kevin Poorten Fashion Center
	Balance Sheet
	November 30, 2005

	Assets					
1						1
2						2
3						3
4						4
5						5
6						6
7						7
8						8
9						9
10						10
11						11
12						12
13						13
14						14
15						15
16						16
17	Liabilities and Owner's Equity					17
18						18
19						19
20						20
21						21
22						22
23						23
24						24
25						25
26						26
27						27
28						28
29						29
30						30

(c)   General Journal

	Date	Account Titles and Explanation	Debit	Credit	
1		Adjusting Entries			1
2	Nov. 30				2
3					3
4					4
5	30				5
6					6
7					7
8	30				8
9					9
10					10
11	30				11
12					12
13					13
14	30				14
15					15

(d)

	Date	Account Titles and Explanation	Debit	Credit	
1		Closing Entries			1
2	Nov. 30				2
3					3
4					4
5	30				5
6					6
7					7
8					8
9					9
10					10
11					11
12					12
13					13
14					14
15					15
16					16
17					17
18					18
19	30				19
20					20
21					21
22	30				22
23					23

(e)

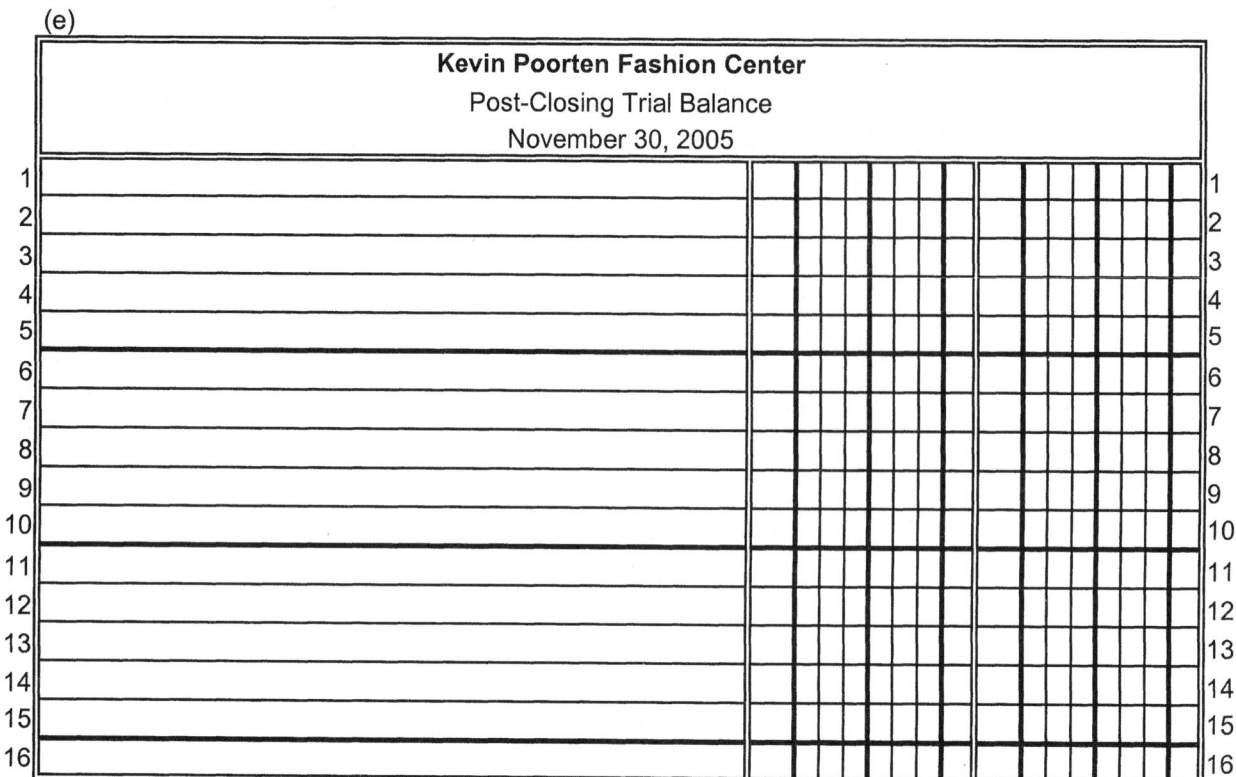

Kevin Poorten Fashion Center				
Post-Closing Trial Balance				
November 30, 2005				
1				
2				
3				
4				
5				
6				
7				
8				
9				
10				
11				
12				
13				
14				
15				
16				

		2001		2002
1 (a) (1) Percentage change in sales:					1
2					2
3					3
4					4
5					5
6					6
7					7
8					8
9 (2) Percentage change in net income:					9
10					10
11					11
12					12
13					13
14					14
15					15
16					16
17					17
18 (b) Gross profit rate:					18
19					19
20					20
21					21
22					22
23					23
24					24
25					25
26					26
27					27
28					28
29					29
30 (c) Percentage of net income to sales:					30
31					31
32					32
33					33
34					34
35 Comment:					35
36					36
37					37
38					38
39					39
40					40

	PepsiCo		Coca-Cola
(a)			
(1) 2002 Gross profit			
(2) 2002 Gross profit rate			
(3) 2002 Operating Income			
(4) Percentage change in			
operating income, 2001			
to 2002			
(b)			

		Carrefour/ Promodes (French francs)		Wal-Mart (Dollars)	
1	(a) Greoss profit rate				1
2					2
3					3
4					4
5					5
6					6
7	(b) Operating expense to sales ratio				7
8					8
9					9
10					10
11					11
12					12
13					13
14					14
15					15
16	(c)				16
17					17
18					18
19					19
20					20
21					21
22					22
23					23
24					24
25					25
26					26
27					27
28					28
29					29
30					30
31					31
32					32

1	1
2	2
3	3
4	4
5	5
6	6
7	7
8	8
9	9
10	10
11	11
12	12
13	13
14	14
15	15
16	16
17	17
18	18
19	19
20	20
21	21
22	22
23	23
24	24
25	25
26	26
27	27
28	28
29	29
30	30
31	31
32	32
33	33
34	34
35	35
36	36
37	37
38	38
39	39
40	40

(a) (1)

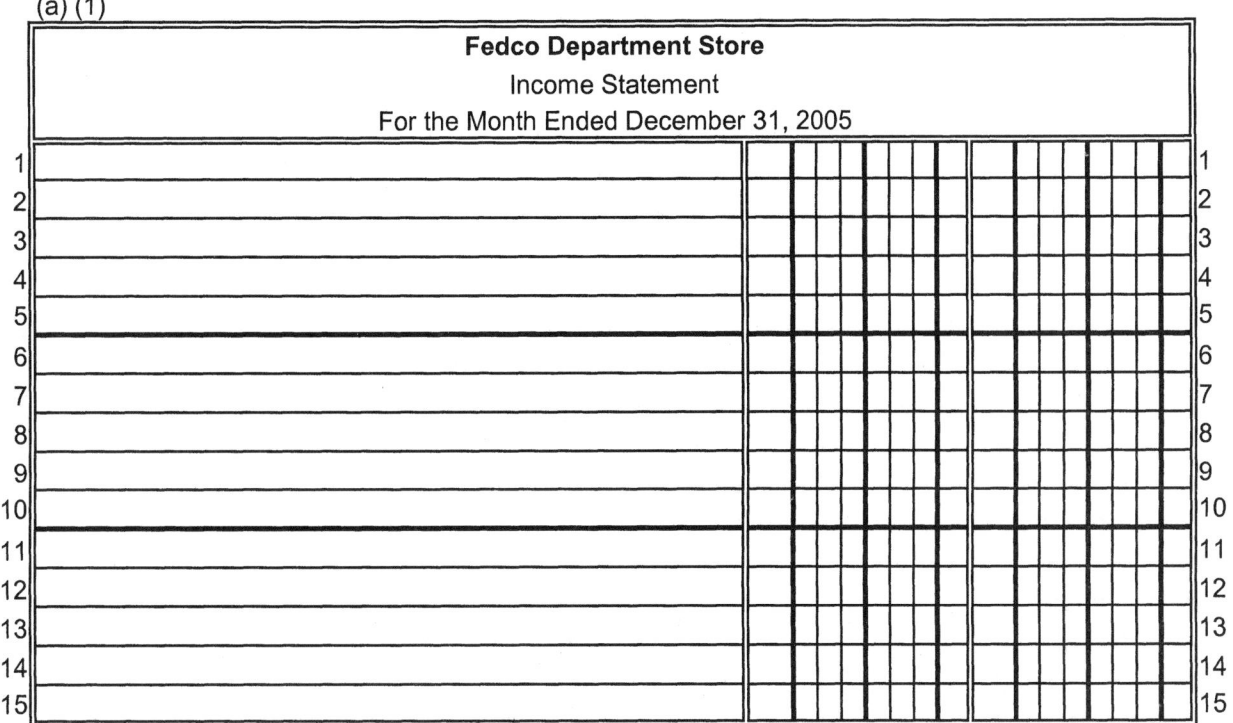

Fedco Department Store

Income Statement

For the Month Ended December 31, 2005

(2)

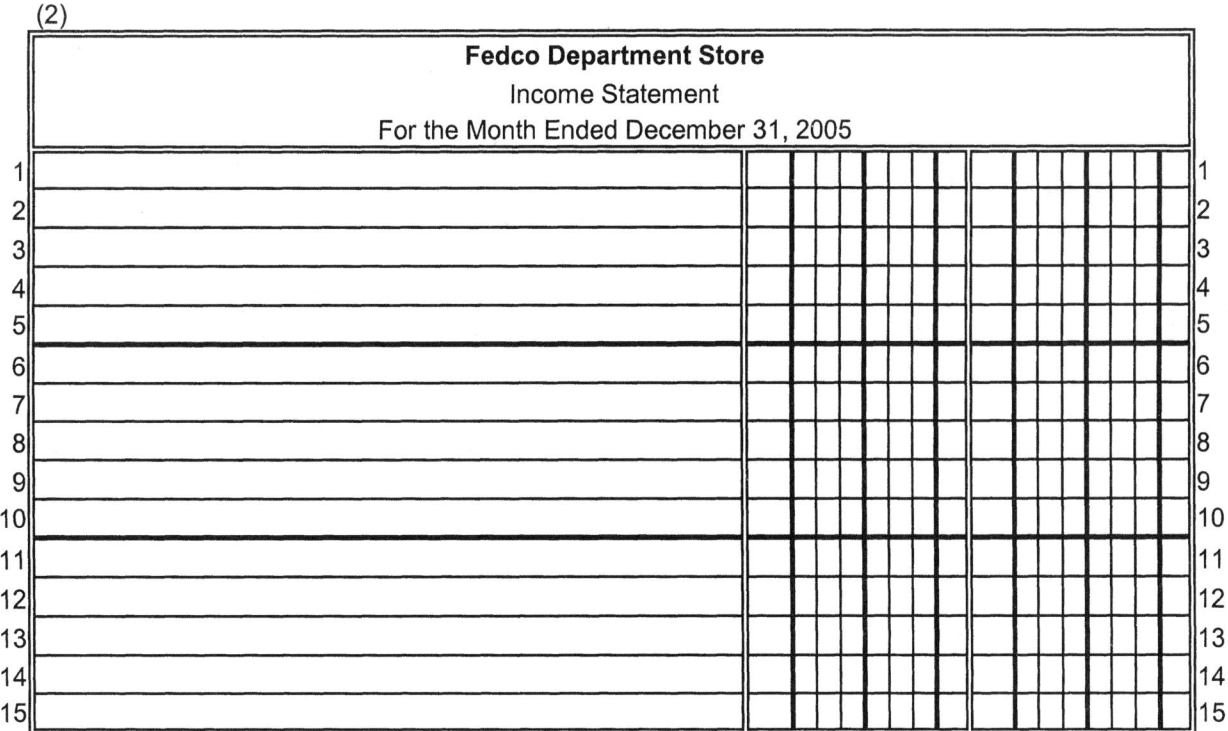

Fedco Department Store

Income Statement

For the Month Ended December 31, 2005

(b)

(c)

Fedco Department Store

Income Statement

For the Year Ended December 31, 2005

(a) & (b)

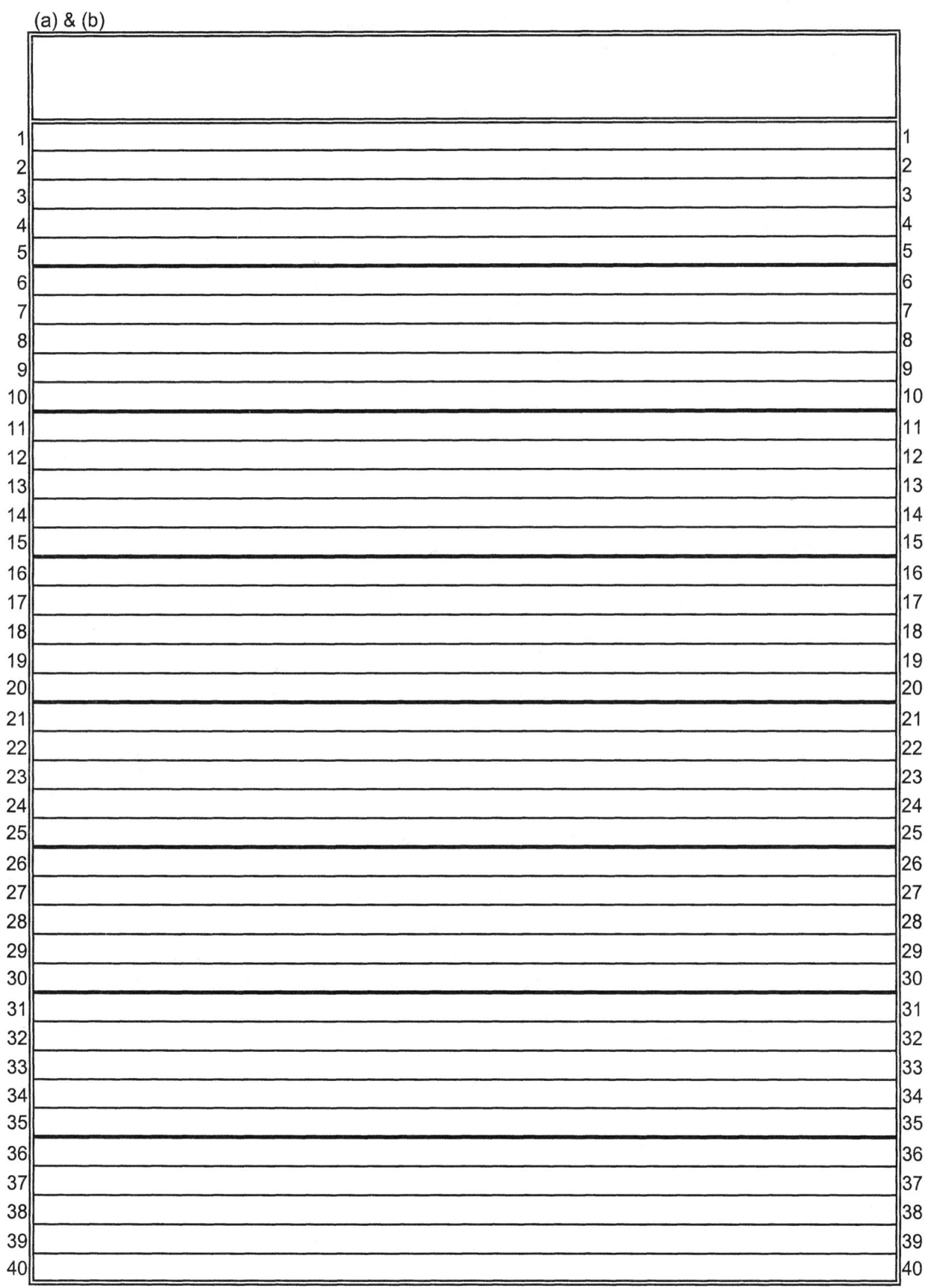

(a)

1	1
2	2
3	3
4	4
5	5
6	6
7	7

(b)

8	8
9	9
10	10
11	11
12	12
13	13
14	14
15	15

(c)

16	16
17	17
18	18
19	19
20	20
21	21
22	22
23	23
24	24
25	25
26	26
27	27
28	28
29	29
30	30
31	31
32	32
33	33
34	34
35	35
36	36
37	37
38	38
39	39
40	40

	#1										
1	(a)										1
2											2
3											3
4	(b)										4
5											5
6											6
7	(c)										7
8											8
9											9
10	(d)										10
11											11
12											12
13											13
14											14
15	#2										15
16											16
17											17
18											18
19											19
20											20

	#3	(a) FIFO			(b) LIFO			
21		Units	Unit Cost	Total	Units	Unit Cost	Total	21
22								22
23								23
24								24
25	Ending inventory			Ending inventory				25
26								26

	#4		Units	Unit Cost	Total	
27			Units	Unit Cost	Total	27
28						28
29						29
30						30
31						31
32						32
33	Average cost per unit					33
34						34
35	Ending inventory					35
36						36
37						37
38						38
39						39
40						40

#5

1	(a)
2	(b)
3	(c)
4	
5	(d)
6	
7	
8	

#6 Cost of goods sold under:

		LIFO	FIFO
10	Purchases		
11			
12			
13	Cost of goods available for sale		
14	Less: Ending inventory		
15	Cost of goods sold		

#7

Inventory categories:	Cost	Market	LCM
Cameras			
Camcorders			
VCRs			
Total valuation			

#8

#9

1	Inventory turnover:	1
2		2
3		3
4		4
5	Days in inventory:	5
6		6
7		7
8		8

#10

(1)   FIFO Method

Date	Purchases	Sales	Balance
	Product E2-D2		

(2)   LIFO Method

Date	Purchases	Sales	Balance

(3)   Average Cost

Date	Purchases	Sales	Balance

#11

		At Cost	At Retail
1	(1)		
2			
3			
4			
5	(2)		
6			
7			
8			
9	**#12**	At Cost	At Retail
10			
11			
12			
13			
14	Cost-to-retail ratio:		
15			
16	Estimated cost of ending inventory:		
17			
18			
19			
20			
21			
22			
23			
24			
25			

Name

Section

Date

#1

1	Ending Inventory - physical count	1
2		2
3		3
4		4
5		5
6		6
7		7
8		8
9		9
10		10
11		11
12		12
13		13
14	**#2**	14
15	Ending inventory - as reported	15
16		16
17		17
18		18
19		19
20		20
21		21
22		22
23		23
24		24
25		25
26		26
27		27
28		28
29		29
30		30
31		31
32		32
33		33
34		34
35		35
36		36
37		37
38		38
39		39
40		40

1	(a)		1
2			2
3			3
4			4
5			5
6	(b)		6
7			7
8			8
9			9
10			10
11			11
12			12
13			13
14			14
15			15
16	(c)		16
17			17
18			18
19			19
20			20
21			21
22			22
23			23
24			24
25			25

(a)

FIFO

	Date	Units	Unit Cost	Total Cost
1				
2				
3				
4				
5				
6				
7				
8				

Proof:

	Date	Units	Unit Cost	Total Cost

LIFO

Proof:

	Date	Units	Unit Cost	Total Cost

(b)

	FIFO					
1						
2						
3						
4						
5						
6						
7						
8						

Proof:

	Date	Units	Unit Cost	Total Cost
10				
11				
12				
13				
14				
15				

	LIFO		
16			
17			
18			
19			

Proof:

	Date	Units	Unit Cost	Total Cost
21				
22				
23				
24				
25				
26				
27				

(a) (1)	FIFO		
(2)	LIFO		
(b)			
(c)			

#7

	Cost of Goods Available for Sale	÷	Total Units Avaialable for Sale	=	Weighted Average Unit Cost	
1	(a)					1
2						2
3	Ending inventory					3
4	Cost of goods sold					4
5						5
6	(b)					6
7						7
8						8
9						9
10	(c)					10
11						11
12						12

#8

		Cost	Market		Lower of Cost or Market	
1	Cameras					1
2	Minolta					2
3	Canon					3
4	Total					4
5	Light Meters					5
6	Vivitar					6
7	Kodak					7
8	Total					8
9	Total inventory					9
10						10

#9

		2005	2006	
1				1
2				2
3				3
4				4
5				5
6				6
7				7
8				8

(a)	2005	2006	
1			1
2			2
3			3
4			4
5			5
6			6
7			7
8			8
9			9
10			10
11			11
12			12
13 (b)			13
14			14
15			15
16			16
17			17
18			18
19			19
20			20
21 (c)			21
22			22
23			23
24			24
25			25
26			26
27			27
28			28
29			29
30			30
31			31
32			32
33			33
34			34
35			35
36			36
37			37
38			38
39			39
40			40

#11

	2003	2004	2005
Inventory turnover ratio			
Days in inventory			
Gross profit rate			

(1)

	FIFO		
Date	Purchases	Sales	Balance

(2)

	LIFO		
Date	Purchases	Sales	Balance

(3)

	Average Cost		
Date	Purchases	Sales	Balance

(a)

| 1 | Cost of goods available for sale: | | | | | 1 |

FIFO

Date	Purchases	Sales	Balance

Ending inventory   Cost of goods sold

LIFO

Date	Purchases	Sales	Balance

Ending inventory   Cost of goods sold

(a) (Continued)

	Average Cost		
Date	Purchases	Cost of Goods Sold	Balance
Ending inventory		Cost of goods sold	

(b)

(c)

(a)

FIFO			
Date	Purchases	Sales	Balance

LIFO			
Date	Purchases	Sales	Balance

(a) (Continued)

	Average Cost		
Date	Purchases	Sales	Balance

(b)

		Periodic	Perpetual
Ending inventory FIFO			
Ending inventory LIFO			

(c)

#15

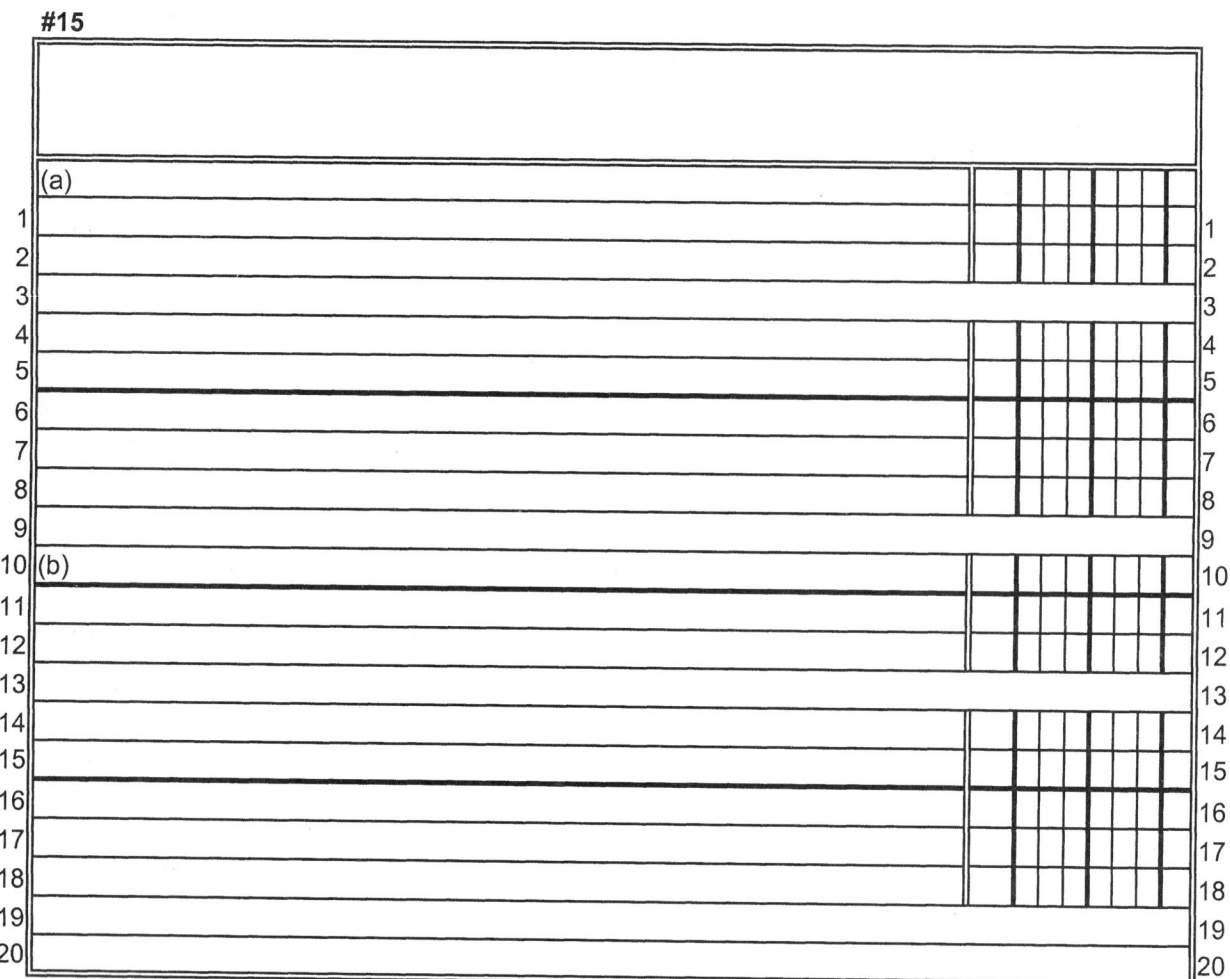

(a)

(b)

#16

	Women's Department		Men's Department	
	Cost	Retail	Cost	Retail
Beginning inventory				
Goods purchased				
Goods avail. for sale				
Net sales				
Ending inv. at retail				
Cost/retail ratio				
Est. cost of ending inventory				

(a)	
1	1
2	2
3	3
4	4
5 (b)	5
6	6
7	7
8	8
9	9
10 (c)	10
11	11
12	12
13	13
14	14
15 (d)	15
16	16
17	17
18	18
19	19
20 (e)	20
21	21
22	22
23	23
24	24
25 (f)	25
26	26
27	27
28	28
29	29
30	30
31	31
32	32
33	33
34	34
35	35
36	36
37	37
38	38
39	39

(a)

COST OF GOODS AVAILABLE FOR SALE				
Date	Explanation	Units	Unit Cost	Total Cost
Oct 1				
3				
9				
19				
25				

(b)

FIFO							
(1) Ending Inventory					(2) Cost of Goods Sold		
Date	Units	x	Unit Cost	=	Total Cost		

Proof of Cost of Goods Sold						
Date	Units	x	Unit Cost	=	Total Cost	

LIFO							
(1) Ending Inventory					(2) Cost of Goods Sold		
Date	Units	x	Unit Cost	=	Total Cost		

(b) (Continued) and (c)

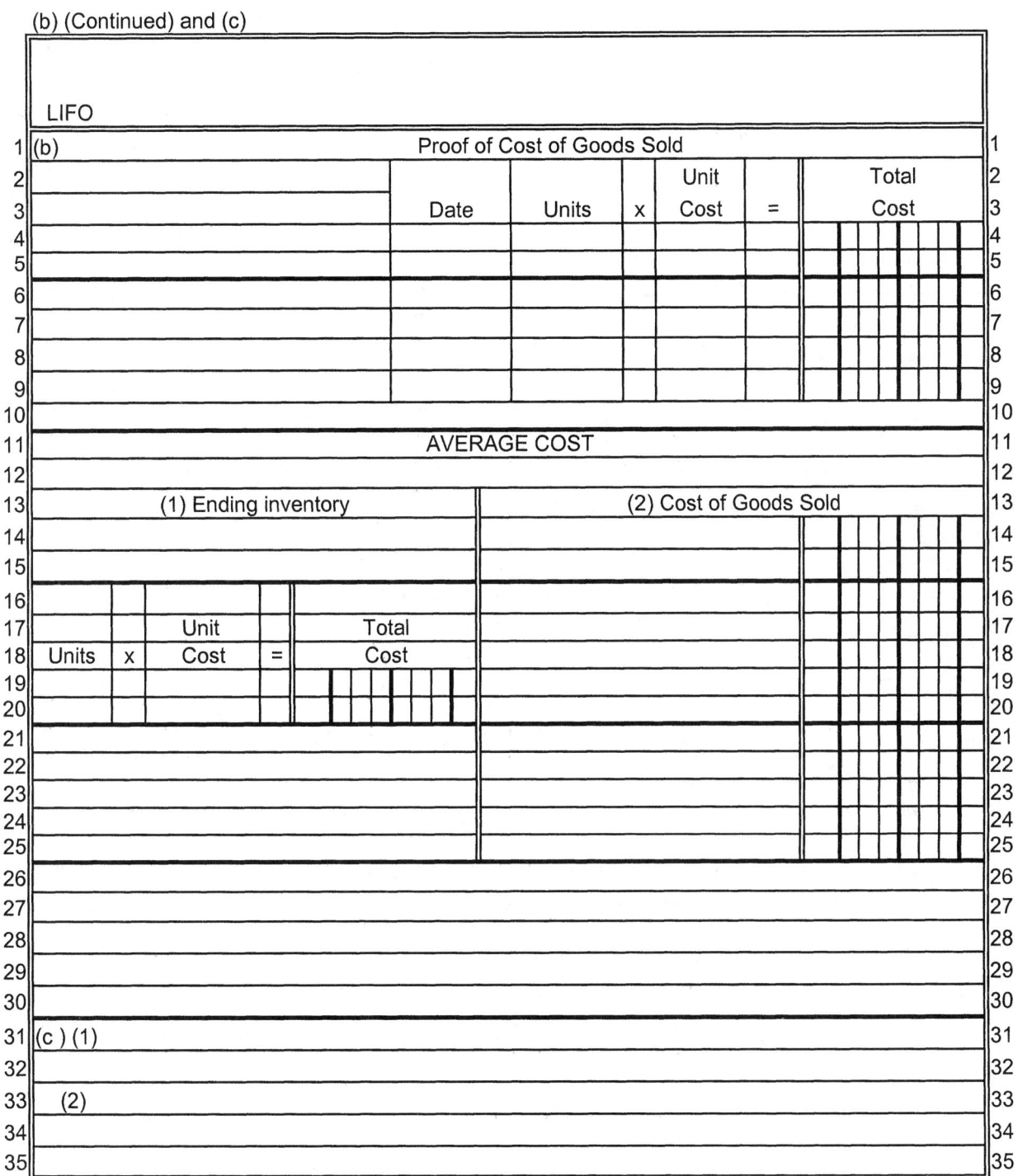

LIFO

(b)   Proof of Cost of Goods Sold

	Date	Units	x	Unit Cost	=	Total Cost

AVERAGE COST

(1) Ending inventory					(2) Cost of Goods Sold	
Units	x	Unit Cost	=	Total Cost		

(c) (1)

(2)

(a)

	Date	Explanation	Units	Unit Cost	Total Cost	
1	Oct 1					1
2	3					2
3	9					3
4	19					4
5	25					5
6						6
7						7

COST OF GOODS AVAILABLE FOR SALE

(b)

FIFO

	(1) Ending Inventory					(2) Cost of Goods Sold		
	Date	Units	x	Unit Cost	=	Total Cost		
5	Jan. 1							
6	Mar. 15							
7	July 20							
8	Sept. 4							
9	Dec. 2							

Proof of Cost of Goods Sold

	Date	Units	x	Unit Cost	=	Total Cost	
13							
14							
15							
16							
17							
18							

LIFO

	(1) Ending Inventory					(2) Cost of Goods Sold		
	Date	Units	x	Unit Cost	=	Total Cost		
23								
24								
25								
26								
27								

(b) (Continued) and (c)

LIFO

(b) Proof of Cost of Goods Sold

	Date	Units	x	Unit Cost	=	Total Cost

AVERAGE COST

(1) Ending inventory					(2) Cost of Goods Sold	

Units	x	Unit Cost	=	Total Cost		

Proof of Cost of Goods Sold

Units	x	Unit Cost	=	Total Cost		

(c) (1)

  (2)

(a)

Red Robin Inc.		
Condensed Income Statements		
For the Year Ended December 31, 2005		
	FIFO	LIFO
1		
2		
3		
4		
5		
6		
7		
8		
9		
10		
11		
12		
13		
14		
15		
16		
17		
18		

(b) (1)

(2)

(3)

(4)

(5)

(a)

	Date	Explanation	Units	Unit Cost	Total Cost
		COST OF GOODS AVAILABLE FOR SALE			
1	June 1				
2	4				
3	18				
4	18				
5	28				
6					
7					

Ending Inventory in Units		Sales Revenue			
Explanation	Units	Date	Units	Unit Price	Total Sales

(1)

LIFO

(i) Ending Inventory						(ii) Cost of Goods Sold	
Date	Units	x	Unit Cost	=	Total Cost		

(iii) Gross Profit		(iv) Gross Profit Rate	

(2)

	FIFO						
	(i) Ending Inventory						
Date	Units	x	Unit Cost	=	Total Cost		

(iii) Gross Profit		(iv) Gross Profit Rate	

(3)

Average Cost			
Weighted average cost per unit:			
(i) Ending Inventory		(ii) Cost of Goods Sold	
(iii) Gross Profit		(iv) Gross Profit Rate	

(b)

(a)

Gas Gusslers Income Statement (Partial) For the Period Ended March 31,			
	Specific Identification	FIFO	LIFO
1			
2			
3			
4			
5			
6			
7			
8			
9			
10			
11			
12			
13			
14			

Specific identification ending inventory consists of:

	Units	Unit Cost	Total Cost
17			
18			
19			
20			
21			

FIFO ending inventory consists of:

23			
24			
25			

LIFO ending inventory consists of:

27			
28			
29			
30			
31			
32			
33			
34			

(b)

(a)

Creek Co. Condensed Income Statement For the Year Ended December 31, 2005	FIFO	LIFO
1		
2		
3		
4		
5		
6		
7		
8		
9		
10		
11		
12		
13		

(b)

(1)

(2)

(3)

(4)

(5)

(a)

1	Cost of goods available for sale:
2	Inventory
3	Purchases:
4	
5	
6	
7	
8	
9	
10	Sales:
11	
12	
13	
14	
15	

(1) LIFO

Date	Purchases	Sales	Balance

(i)	Cost of Goods Sold:	
(ii)	Ending Inventory:	
(iii)	Gross Profit:	

(a) (Continued)

(2) FIFO

Date	Purchases	Sales	Balance

(i)   Cost of Goods Sold:

(ii)   Ending Inventory:

(iii) Gross Profit:

(3) Average Cost

Date	Purchases	Sales	Balance

(i)   Cost of Goods Sold:

(ii)   Ending Inventory:

(iii) Gross Profit:

(b)

	LIFO	FIFO	Weighted Average
1			
2			
3			
4			
5			
6			
7			
8			
9			
10			
11			
12			
13			
14			
15			
16			
17			
18			
19			
20			
21			
22			
23			
24			
25			
26			
27			
28			
29			
30			
31			
32			
33			
34			
35			
36			
37			
38			
39			
40			

(a)

(1) FIFO			
Date	Purchases	Sales	Balance

(2) Average Cost			
Date	Purchases	Sales	Balance

(3) LIFO			
Date	Purchases	Sales	Balance

(b)

	November
(a)	
Net sales	
1	
2	
3	
4	
5	
6	
7	
8	
9	
10	
11	
12	
13	
14 Gross profit rate	
15	
16	
17 (b)	
18 Net sales	
19	
20	
21	
22	
23	
24	
25	
26	
27	
28	
29	
30	
31	
32	
33	
34	
35	
36	
37	
38	
39	

(a)	Hardcovers		Paperbacks	
	Cost	Retail	Cost	Retail
Beginning inventory				
Purchases				
Freight-in				
Purchase discounts				
Goods avail. for sale				
Net sales				
Ending inventory				
Cost-to-retail ratio:				
Hardcovers:				
Paperbacks:				
Estimated ending inventory at cost:				
Hardcovers:				
Paperbacks:				
(b) Hardcovers:				
Paperbacks:				

(a)

1
2
3
4
5 (b)
6
7
8
9
10 (c)
11
12
13
14
15 (d)
16
17
18
19
20 (e)
21
22
23
24
25 (f)
26
27
28
29
30 (g)
31
32
33
34
35
36
37
38
39

(a)

	COST OF GOODS AVAILABLE FOR SALE				
Date	Explanation	Units	Unit Cost	Total Cost	
1	Oct 1					1
2	3					2
3	9					3
4	19					4
5	25					5
6						6
7						7

(b)

	FIFO					
	(1) Ending Inventory				(2) Cost of Goods Sold	
Date	Units	x	Unit Cost	=	Total Cost	

Proof of Cost of Goods Sold

Date	Units	x	Unit Cost	=	Total Cost	

	LIFO					
	(1) Ending Inventory				(2) Cost of Goods Sold	
Date	Units	x	Unit Cost	=	Total Cost	

(b) (Continued) and (c)

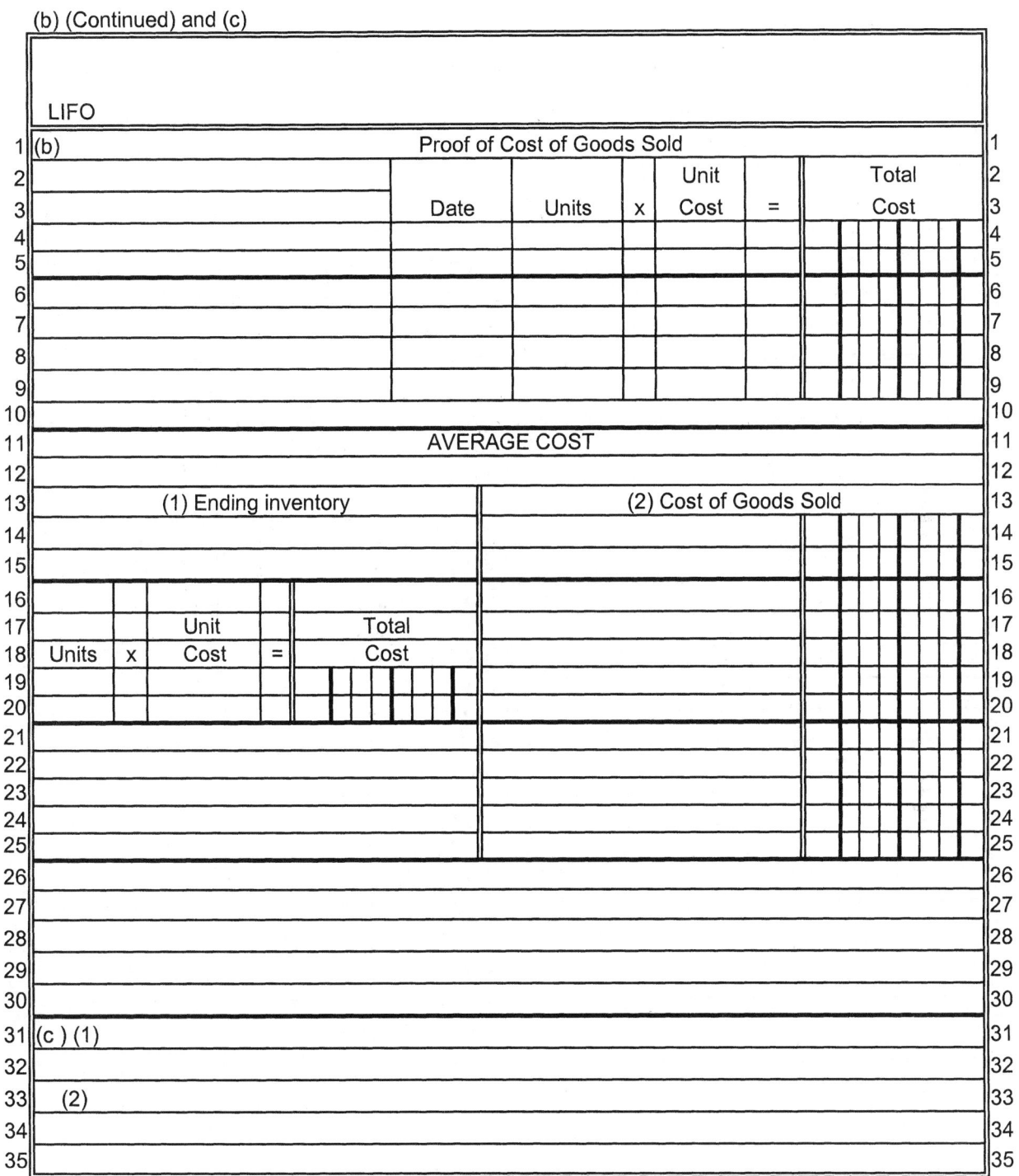

LIFO

	(b)	Proof of Cost of Goods Sold						
			Date	Units	x	Unit Cost	=	Total Cost
1								
2								
3								

AVERAGE COST

(1) Ending inventory				(2) Cost of Goods Sold	
Units	x	Unit Cost	=	Total Cost	

(c) (1)

   (2)

(a)

		COST OF GOODS AVAILABLE FOR SALE				
	Date	Explanation	Units	Unit Cost	Total Cost	
1	Oct 1					1
2	3					2
3	9					3
4	19					4
5	25					5
6						6
7						7

(b)

				FIFO				
1								1
2	(1) Ending Inventory					(2) Cost of Goods Sold		2
3				Unit		Total		3
4	Date	Units	x	Cost	=	Cost		4
5	Jan. 1							5
6	Mar. 15							6
7	July 20							7
8	Sept. 4							8
9	Dec. 2							9
10	Proof of Cost of Goods Sold							10
11				Unit		Total		11
12	Date	Units	x	Cost	=	Cost		12
13								13
14								14
15								15
16								16
17								17
18								18
19	LIFO							19
20	(1) Ending Inventory					(2) Cost of Goods Sold		20
21				Unit		Total		21
22	Date	Units	x	Cost	=	Cost		22
23								23
24								24
25								25
26								26
27								27

(b) (Continued) and (c)

	LIFO						
(b)	Proof of Cost of Goods Sold						
	Date	Units	x	Unit Cost	=	Total Cost	

AVERAGE COST

(1) Ending inventory				(2) Cost of Goods Sold	
Units	x	Unit Cost	=	Total Cost	

Proof of Cost of Goods Sold

Units	x	Unit Cost	=	Total Cost

(c) (1)

(2)

(a)

Gilbert Co. Condensed Income Statement For the Year Ended December 31, 2005	FIFO	LIFO	
1			1
2			2
3			3
4			4
5			5
6			6
7			7
8			8
9			9
10			10
11			11
12			12
13			13
14			14
15			15
16			16
17			17
18			18

19 (b) (1)

20

21

22

23 (2)

24

25

26

27 (3)

28

29

30

31 (4)

32

33

34 (5)

35

36

37

38

39

40

(a)

		COST OF GOODS AVAILABLE FOR SALE			
	Date	Explanation	Units	Unit Cost	Total Cost
1	Oct. 1				
2	9				
3	17				
4	25				
5					
6					
7					

	Ending Inventory in Units		Sales Revenue			
	Explanation	Units	Date	Units	Unit Price	Total Sales
3						
4						
5						
6						
7						
8						

(1)

	LIFO					
	(i) Ending Inventory				(ii) Cost of Goods Sold	
	Date	Units	x	Unit Cost	=	Total Cost		

(iii) Gross Profit   (iv) Gross Profit Rate

(2)

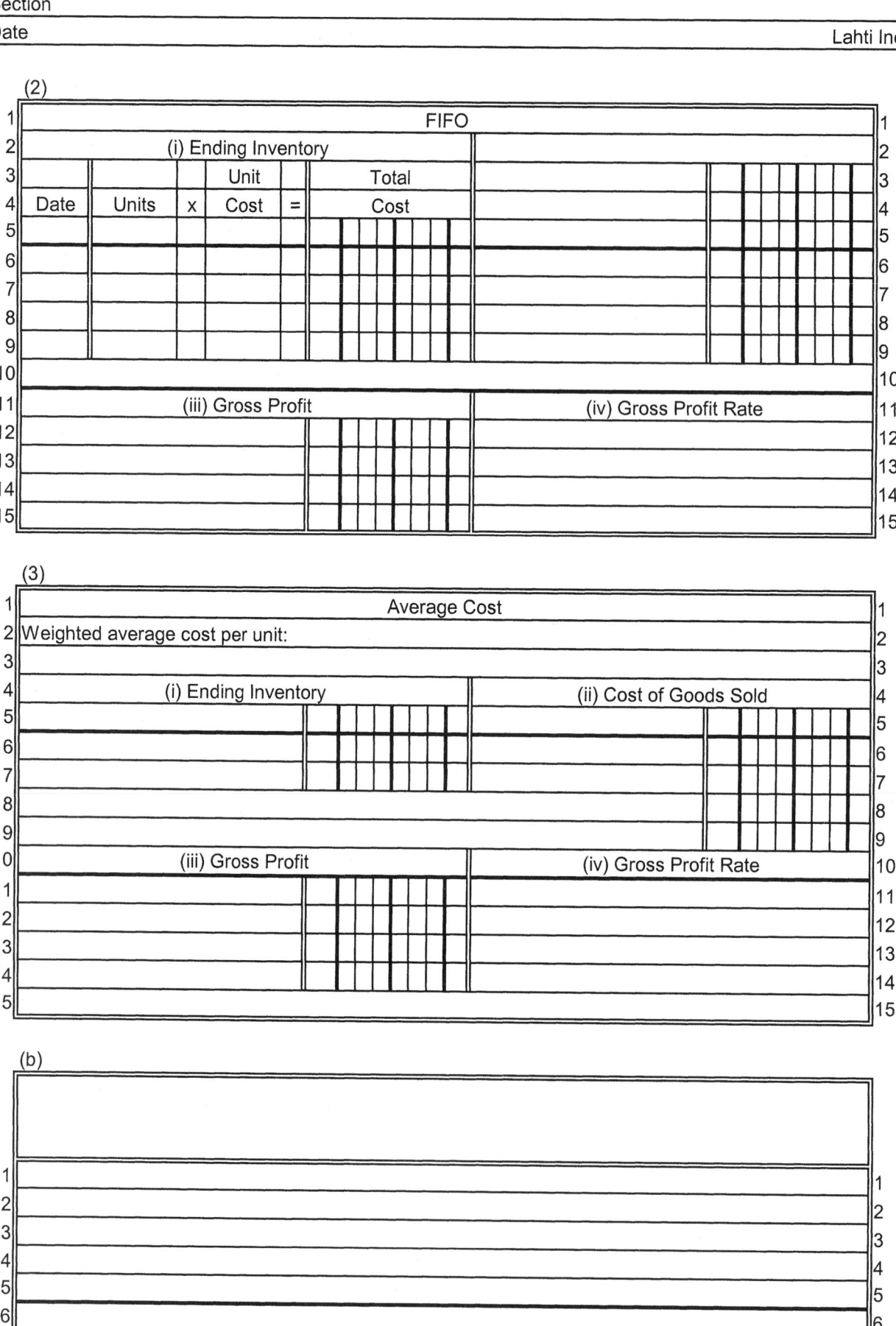

FIFO						
(i) Ending Inventory						
			Unit		Total	
Date	Units	x	Cost	=	Cost	
(iii) Gross Profit					(iv) Gross Profit Rate	

(3)

Average Cost		
Weighted average cost per unit:		
(i) Ending Inventory		(ii) Cost of Goods Sold
(iii) Gross Profit		(iv) Gross Profit Rate

(b)

(a)   (1) Maximize gross profit:

Sale Date	Cost of Goods Sold		Sales Revenue	

(2) Minimize gross profit:

Sale Date	Cost of Goods Sold		Sales Revenue	

(b) FIFO

Cost of Goods Available for Sale:

Date	Explanation		

Ending inventory:

Cost of goods sold:

Gross profit:

(c)   LIFO

(d)

(a)

	Zwick Inc. Condensed Income Statement For the Year Ended December 31, 2005	FIFO	LIFO
1			
2			
3			
4			
5			
6			
7			
8			
9			
10			
11			
12			
13			
14			
15	(b)		
16	(1)		
17			
18			
19			
20	(2)		
21			
22			
23			
24	(3)		
25			
26			
27			
28	(4)		
29			
30			
31	(5)		
32			
33			
34			
35			
36			
37			
38			
39			

(a)

1	Cost of goods available for sale:	
2	Inventory	
3	Purchases:	
4	January 2	
5	January 9	
6	January 10 return	
7	January 23	
8		
9		
10	Sales:	
11	January 6	
12	January 9 return	
13	January 10 return	
14	January 30	
15		

(1) LIFO

Date	Purchases	Sales	Balance

(i)	Cost of Goods Sold:	
(ii)	Ending Inventory:	
(iii)	Gross Profit:	

(a) (Continued)

(2) FIFO

Date	Purchases	Sales	Balance

(i)   Cost of Goods Sold:

(ii) Ending Inventory:

(iii) Gross Profit:

(3) Average Cost

Date	Purchases	Sales	Balance

(i)   Cost of Goods Sold:

(ii) Ending Inventory:

(iii) Gross Profit:

(b)

	LIFO	FIFO	Weighted Average	
1				1
2				2
3				3
4				4
5				5
6				6
7				7
8				8
9				9
10				10
11				11
12				12
13				13
14				14
15				15
16				16
17				17
18				18
19				19
20				20
21				21
22				22
23				23
24				24
25				25
26				26
27				27
28				28
29				29
30				30
31				31
32				32
33				33
34				34
35				35
36				36
37				37
38				38
39				39
40				40

(a)

		(1) FIFO		
Date	Purchases	Sales	Balance	

		(2) Average Cost		
Date	Purchases	Sales	Balance	

		(3) LIFO		
Date	Purchases	Sales	Balance	

(b)　(1)

(2)

	February
(a)	
Net sales	
Gross profit rate	

(b)	
Net sales	

(a)	Sporting Goods		Jewelry and Cosmetics		
	Cost	Retail	Cost	Retail	
1 Beginning inventory					1
2 Purchases					2
3 Purchase returns					3
4 Purchase discounts					4
5 Freight-in					5
6 Goods avail. for sale					6
7 Net sales					7
8 Ending inventory					8
9 at retail					9
10					10
11 Cost-to-retail ratio:					11
12 Sporting goods:					12
13 Jewelry and cosmetics:					13
14					14
15 Estimated ending inventory at cost:					15
16 Sporting goods:					16
17 Jewelry and cosmetics:					17
18					18
19					19
20 (b) Sporting goods:					20
21					21
22 Jewelry and cosmetics:					22
23					23
24					24
25					25

	December 28, 2002	December 29, 2001
1 (a) Inventory (in millions)		
2		
3		
4		
5		
6 (b) Dollar changes in inventories between 2001 and 2002:		
7		
8		
9 Percent change in inventories between 2001 and 2002:		
10		
11		
12 2002 inventory as a percent of current assets:		
13		
14		
15		
16 (c)		
17		
18		
19		
20		
21		

	2002	2001	2000
22 (d) PepsiCo (in millions)			
23			
24 Cost of goods sold			
25			
26			
27 2002 cost of goods sold as a percent of sales:			
28			
29			
30			
31			
32			
33			
34			
35			

(a)	PepsiCo	Coca-Cola
Inventory turnover ratio:		
Average days to sell		
inventory:		

(b)

(a)		

(b)	Fuji (millions of yen)	Kodak (millions of dollars)
Inventory turnover		
Average days in inventory		
(c)		

(d)

	Fuji		Kodak	
	(millions of yen)	%	(millions of $)	%
Finished goods				
Work in process				
Raw materials				
Total				

(a)	
(b)	
(c)	
(d)	

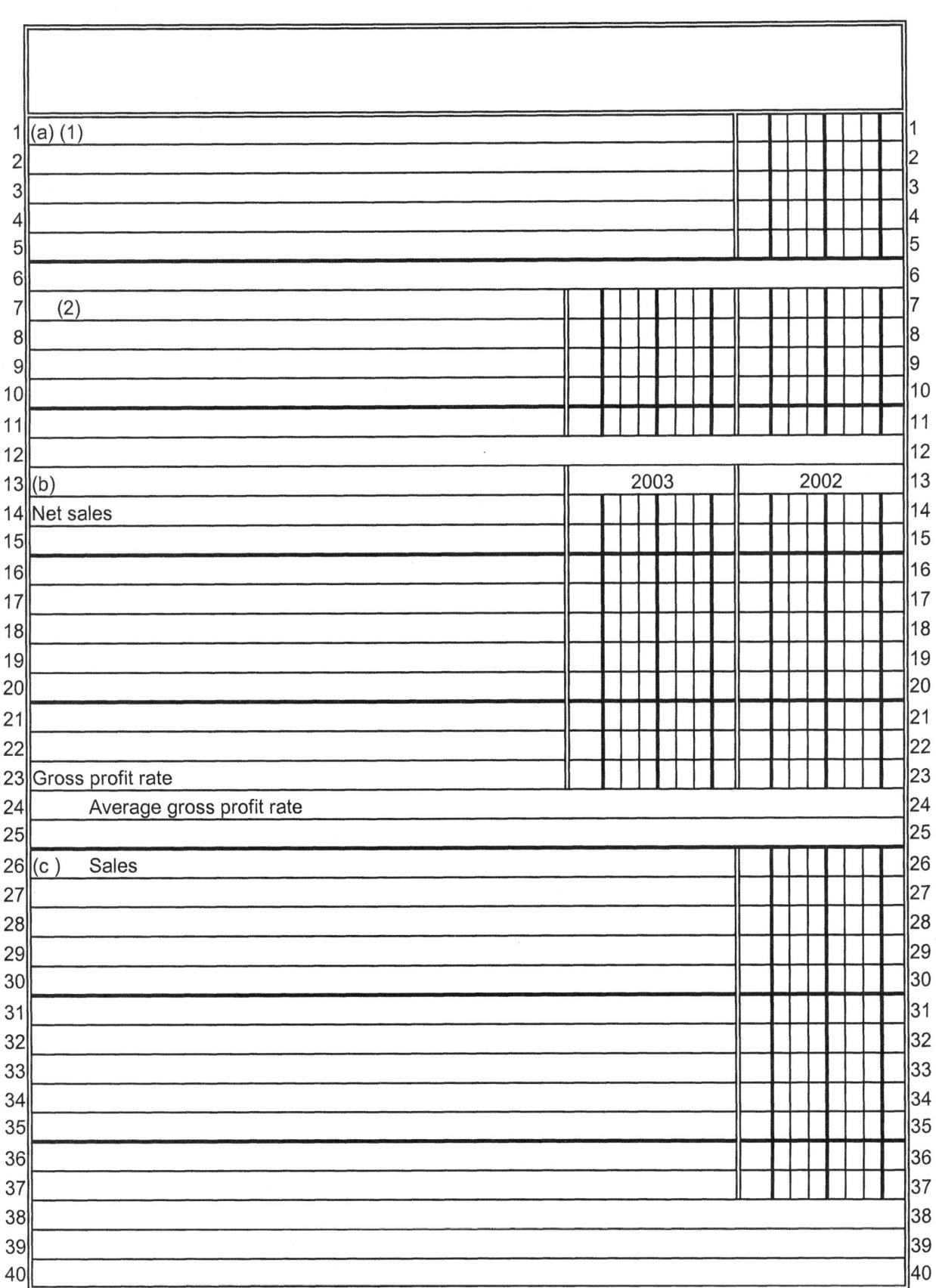

	2003	2002

(a) (1)

(2)

(b)

Net sales

Gross profit rate

    Average gross profit rate

(c)   Sales

1		1
2		2
3		3
4		4
5		5
6		6
7		7
8		8
9		9
10		10
11		11
12		12
13		13
14		14
15		15
16		16
17		17
18		18
19		19
20		20
21		21
22		22
23		23
24		24
25		25
26		26
27		27
28		28
29		29
30		30
31		31
32		32
33		33
34		34
35		35
36		36
37		37
38		38
39		39
40		40

1	(a)	1
2		2
3		3
4		4
5		5
6		6
7		7
8		8
9		9
10		10
11	(b)	11
12		12
13		13
14		14
15		15
16	(c)	16
17		17
18		18
19		19
20		20
21		21
22		22
23		23
24		24
25		25
26		26
27		27
28		28
29		29
30		30
31		31
32		32
33		33
34		34
35		35
36		36
37		37
38		38
39		39
40		40

1	#1	1
2	1.	2
3	2.	3
4	3.	4
5		5
6	#2	6
7	1. 3.	7
8	2. 4.	8
9		9

#3

Accounts Receivable Subsidiary Ledger
Duffy Co.

Date	Explanation	Ref.	Debit	Credit	Balance

Hanson Co.

Date	Explanation	Ref.	Debit	Credit	Balance

Lewis Co.

Date	Explanation	Ref.	Debit	Credit	Balance

General Ledger
Accounts Receivable

Date	Explanation	Ref.	Debit	Credit	Balance

#4		
1	1.	3.
2	2.	4.
3		
4	**#5**	
5	1.	4.
6	2.	5.
7	3.	6.
8		
9	**#6**	
10	1.	3.
11	2.	4.
12		
13	**#7**	
14	1.	3.
15	2.	4.
16		
17		
18	**#8**	
19	1.	
20		
21	2.	
22		
23	3.	
24		
25	4.	
26		
27	**#9**	
28	1.	
29		
30	2.	
31		
32	3.	
33		
34	4.	
35		
36	5.	
37		
38		
39		
40		

Name

Section

Date

#1

1	(a)
2	
3	
4	(b)
5	
6	
7	(c)
8	
9	
10	
11	(d)
12	
13	
14	
15	

#2

(a) & (b)   *General Ledger*

Accounts Receivable

Date	Explanation	Ref.	Debit	Credit	Balance
9/1	Balance	√			1 1 9 6 0

Accounts Receivable Subsidiary Ledger

Jana

Date	Explanation	Ref.	Debit	Credit	Balance
9/1	Balance	√			2 4 4 0

Kingston

Date	Explanation	Ref.	Debit	Credit	Balance
9/1	Balance	√			2 6 4 0

Iman

Date	Explanation	Ref.	Debit	Credit	Balance

Cavanaugh

Date	Explanation	Ref.	Debit	Credit	Balance
9/1	Balance	√			2 0 6 0

Bickford

Date	Explanation	Ref.	Debit	Credit	Balance
9/1	Balance	√			4 8 2 0

#3 (c)

Welter Company Schedule of Customers As of September 30, 2005	
1	
2	
3	
4	
5	
6	
7	
8	
9	
10	
11	
12	

#4 (a) & (b)

Sing Tao Company
Sales Journal
S1

	Date	Account Debited	Invoice No.	Ref.	Accounts Receiv. Dr. Sales Cr.	COGS Dr. Merchandise Inventory Cr.	
1	2005						1
2							2
3							3
4							4
5							5

Sing Tao Company
Purchases Journal
P1

	Date	Account Credited	Terms	Ref	Merchandise Inventory (Dr.) Acc. Pay (Cr.)	
1	2005					1
2						2
3						3
4						4
5						5

#5 (a) & (b)

Svenska Co.

Cash Receipts Journal

Date	Account Credited	Ref.	Cash Dr.	Sales Discounts Dr.	Accounts Receivable Cr.	Sales Cr.	Other Accounts Cr.	COGS Dr. Merch Inv Cr.
2005								

Svenska Co.

Cash Payments Journal

Date	Check Number	Account Debited	Ref	Other Accounts Dr.	Accounts Payable Dr.	Cash Cr.
2005						

#6

	(a) Journal	(b) Journal Columns	
1	1.		1
2			2
3	2.		3
4			4
5	3.		5
6			6
7	4.		7
8			8
9	5.		9
10			10
11	6.		11
12			12
13	7.		13
14			14
15	8.		15
16			16
17	9.		17
18			18
19	10.		19
20			20

(a)

	Date	Account Titles	Debit	Credit	
1	Mar 2				1
2					2
3					3
4	5				4
5					5
6					6
7	7				7
8					8
9					9
10					10
11					11
12					12

(b)

1		1
2		2
3		3
4		4
5		5
6		6
7		7
8		8
9		9
10		10
11		11
12		12
13		13
14		14
15		15
16		16
17		17
18		18
19		19
20		20
21		21
22		22
23		23

#8

1	1.
2	2.
3	3.
4	4.
5	5.
6	6.
7	7.
8	8.
9	9.
10	10.
11	11.
12	12.
13	13.
14	

#9

1	(a)
2	
3	
4	
5	
6	
7	
8	(b)
9	
10	
11	
12	
13	
14	
15	
16	
17	
18	
19	
20	
21	

#10 (a)

		Purchases Journal		
				P1
	Date	Account Credited	Ref.	Merchandise Inventory (Dr.) Acc. Pay. (Cr.)
1	July 3			
2	12			
3	14			
4	17			
5	20			
6	21			
7	29			
8				
9				

(b)

General Journal

	Date	Account Titles	Ref	Debit	Credit
1	July 1				
2					
3					
4					
5	15				
6					
7					
8					
9	18				
10					
11					
12	25				
13					

 # 11

1		
2		
3		
4		
5		
6		

(a)

Cash Receipts Journal

CR1

Date	Account Credited	Ref.	Cash Dr.	Sales Discounts Dr.	Accounts Receivable Cr.	Sales Cr.	Other Accounts Cr.	COGS Dr. Merch Inv Cr.
1								
2								
3								
4								
5								
6								
7								
8								
9								
10								
11								
12								
13								
14								
15								
16								
17								

(b)

General Ledger

Accounts Receivable   No. 112

Date	Explanation	Ref	Debit	Credit	Balance
June 1	Balance	√			8 3 0 0

Accounts Receivable Subsidiary Ledger

Bernard & Son

Date	Explanation	Ref	Debit	Credit	Balance
June 1	Balance	√			3 5 0 0

Farley & Co.

Date	Explanation	Ref	Debit	Credit	Balance
June 1	Balance	√			1 9 0 0

Grinnell Bros.

Date	Explanation	Ref	Debit	Credit	Balance
June 1	Balance	√			1 6 0 0

Maquoketa Co.

Date	Explanation	Ref	Debit	Credit	Balance
June 1	Balance	√			1 3 0 0

(c)

1	1
2	2
3	3

Congo Company

(a)

Cash Payments Journal

CP1

Date	Ck. No.	Account Debited	Ref.	Other Accounts Dr.	Accounts Payable Dr.	Merchandise Inventory Cr.	Cash Cr.
1							
2							
3							
4							
5							
6							
7							
8							
9							
10							
11							
12							
13							
14							
15							
16							
17							
18							
19							
20							

(b)

General Ledger

Accounts Payable   No. 201

Date	Explanation	Ref	Debit	Credit	Balance
Nov. 1	Balance	√			9 7 5 0

Accounts Payable Subsidiary Ledger

A. Hess & Co.

Date	Explanation	Ref	Debit	Credit	Balance
Nov. 1	Balance	√			4 5 0 0

C. Pillsbury

Date	Explanation	Ref	Debit	Credit	Balance
Nov. 1	Balance	√			2 3 5 0

G. Saeman

Date	Explanation	Ref	Debit	Credit	Balance
Nov. 1	Balance	√			1 0 0 0

Wex Bros.

Date	Explanation	Ref	Debit	Credit	Balance
Nov. 1	Balance	√			1 9 0 0

(c)

1	Accounts payable balance:		1
2			2
3			3
4	Subsidiary account balances:		4
5			5
6			6
7			7
8			8
9			9
10			10

(a)

		Purchases Journal				P1
	Date	Account Credited (Debited)	Ref.	Other Accounts Dr.	Merchandise Inventory Dr.	Accounts Payable Cr.
1						
2						
3						
4						
5						
6						
7						
8						
9						
10						
11						
12						
13						
14						
15						
16						
17						
18						

		Sales Journal			S1
	Date	Account Debited	Ref.	Accounts Receiv. Dr. Sales Cr.	COGS Dr. Merchandise Inventory Cr.
1					
2					
3					
4					
5					
6					
7					
8					
9					
10					

(a) (Continued)

General Journal   G1

	Date	Account Titles and Explanation	Ref.	Debit	Credit	
1						1
2						2
3						3
4						4
5						5
6						6
7						7
8						8
9						9
10						10
11						11
12						12

(b)

General Ledger

Accounts Receivable   No. 112

Date	Explanation	Ref.	Debit	Credit	Balance

Merchandise Inventory   No. 120

Date	Explanation	Ref.	Debit	Credit	Balance

Supplies   No. 126

Date	Explanation	Ref.	Debit	Credit	Balance

Equipment   No. 157

Date	Explanation	Ref.	Debit	Credit	Balance

(b)(Continued)

Accounts Payable   No. 201

Date	Explanation	Ref.	Debit	Credit	Balance

Sales   No. 401

Date	Explanation	Ref.	Debit	Credit	Balance

Sales Returns and Allowances   No. 412

Date	Explanation	Ref.	Debit	Credit	Balance

Cost of Goods Sold   No. 505

Date	Explanation	Ref.	Debit	Credit	Balance

Advertising Expense   No. 610

Date	Explanation	Ref.	Debit	Credit	Balance

(b)(Continued)

Accounts Receivable Subsidiary Ledger

Ellie Company

Date	Explanation	Ref.	Debit	Credit	Balance

Cornelis Bros.

Date	Explanation	Ref.	Debit	Credit	Balance

Jan Company

Date	Explanation	Ref.	Debit	Credit	Balance

(b)(Continued)   *Accounts Payable Subsidiary Ledger*

Ruden Freight

Date	Explanation	Ref.	Debit	Credit	Balance

Van Houk Company

Date	Explanation	Ref.	Debit	Credit	Balance

Sandvoort Supply

Date	Explanation	Ref.	Debit	Credit	Balance

Tulip Company

Date	Explanation	Ref.	Debit	Credit	Balance

Zeider Company

Date	Explanation	Ref.	Debit	Credit	Balance

Amster Advertising

Date	Explanation	Ref.	Debit	Credit	Balance

(c)

1	Accounts receivable balance:	
2		
3		
4		
5		
6	Subsidiary account balances:	
7		
8		
9		
10		
11		
12		
13		
14		
15		
16		
17	Accounts payable balance:	
18		
19		
20		
21	Subsidiary account balances:	
22		
23		
24		
25		
26		
27		
28		
29		
30		
31		
32		
33		
34		
35		
36		
37		
38		
39		
40		

(a), (b), & (c)

Sales Journal

S1

	Date	Account Debited	Invoice No.	Ref.	Accounts Receivable Dr. Sales Cr.	COGS Dr. Merchandise Inventory Cr.	
1							1
2							2
3							3
4							4
5							5
6							6
7							7

Purchases Journal

P1

	Date	Account Credited	Ref.	Merchandise Inventory (Dr.) Acc. Pay (Cr.)	
1					1
2					2
3					3
4					4
5					5
6					6
7					7
8					8

General Journal

G1

	Date	Account Titles and Explanation	Ref.	Debit	Credit	
1	Oct 13					1
2						2
3						3
4	25					4
5						5
6						6

(a), (b), (c) (Continued)

Cash Receipts Journal

CR1

Date	Account Credited	Ref.	Cash Dr.	Sales Discounts Dr.	Accounts Receivable Cr.	Sales Cr.	Other Accounts Cr.	COGS Dr. Merch Inv Cr.
1								
2								
3								
4								
5								
6								
7								
8								
9								
10								

Cash Payments Journal

CP1

Date	Account Debited	Ref.	Other Accounts Dr.	Accounts Payable Dr.	Merchandise Inventory Cr.	Cash Cr.
1						
2						
3						
4						
5						
6						
7						
8						
9						
10						
11						

(b)

Purchases Journal

P1

Date	Account Credited	Ref.	Merchandise Inventory (Dr) Acc Pay (Cr)
1			
2			
3			
4			
5			
6			
7			

Cash Payments Journal

CP1

Date	Account Debited	Ref.	Other Accounts Dr.	Accounts Payable Dr.	Merchandise Inventory Cr.	Cash Cr.
1						
2						
3						
4						
5						
6						
7						
8						
9						
10						

(a), (d), & (g)

General Ledger

Cash   No. 101

Date	Explanation	Ref.	Debit	Credit	Balance

Accounts Receivable   No. 112

Date	Explanation	Ref.	Debit	Credit	Balance

Merchandise Inventory   No. 120

Date	Explanation	Ref.	Debit	Credit	Balance

Supplies   No. 126

Date	Explanation	Ref.	Debit	Credit	Balance

Equipment   No. 157

Date	Explanation	Ref.	Debit	Credit	Balance

Accumulated Depreciation - Equipment   No. 158

Date	Explanation	Ref.	Debit	Credit	Balance

(a), (d) and (g) (Continued)

Accounts Payable   No. 201

Date	Explanation	Ref.	Debit	Credit	Balance

A. Zamtel, Capital   No. 301

Date	Explanation	Ref.	Debit	Credit	Balance

A. Zamtel, Drawing   No. 306

Date	Explanation	Ref.	Debit	Credit	Balance

Sales   No. 401

Date	Explanation	Ref.	Debit	Credit	Balance

Sales Discounts   No. 414

Date	Explanation	Ref.	Debit	Credit	Balance

Cost of Goods Sold   No. 505

Date	Explanation	Ref.	Debit	Credit	Balance

Supplies Expense   No. 631

Date	Explanation	Ref.	Debit	Credit	Balance

Depreciation Expense   No. 711

Date	Explanation	Ref.	Debit	Credit	Balance

(c)

Accounts Receivable Subsidiary Ledger

S. Appel

Date	Explanation	Ref.	Debit	Credit	Balance

F. Catt

Date	Explanation	Ref.	Debit	Credit	Balance

C. Boyd

Date	Explanation	Ref.	Debit	Credit	Balance

M. Dogg

Date	Explanation	Ref.	Debit	Credit	Balance

Accounts Payable Subsidiary Ledger

G. Reedy

Date	Explanation	Ref.	Debit	Credit	Balance

J. Zea

Date	Explanation	Ref.	Debit	Credit	Balance

P. Kneiser

Date	Explanation	Ref.	Debit	Credit	Balance

(c) (Continued)

J. Lakota

Date	Explanation	Ref.	Debit	Credit	Balance

(e)

	Zamtel Co. Trial Balance February 28, 2005		
		Debit	Credit
1	Cash			1
2	Accounts Receivable			2
3	Merchandise Inventory			3
4	Supplies			4
5	Equipment			5
6	Accounts Payable			6
7	A. Zamtel, Capital			7
8	A. Zamtel, Drawing			8
9	Sales			9
10	Sales Discounts			10
11	Cost of Goods Sold			11
12				12
13				13

(f)

1	Accounts receivable control account:		1
2			2
3	Accounts receivable subsidiary accounts:		3
4			4
5			5
6			6
7			7
8	Accounts payable control account:		8
9			9
10	Accounts payable subsidiary accounts:		10
11			11
12			12
13			13

(g)

		General Journal				G1
	Date	Account Titles and Explanation	Ref.	Debit	Credit	
1	Feb 28					1
2						2
3						3
4						4
5						5
6	28					6
7						7
8						8
9						9
10						10

(h)

Zamtel Co.
Adjusted Trial Balance
February 28, 2005

		Debit	Credit	
1	Cash			1
2	Accounts Receivable			2
3	Merchandise Inventory			3
4	Supplies			4
5	Equipment			5
6	Accumulated Depreciation - Equipment			6
7	Accounts Payable			7
8	A. Zamtel, Capital			8
9	A. Zamtel, Drawing			9
10	Sales			10
11	Sales Discounts			11
12	Cost of Goods Sold			12
13	Supplies Expense			13
14	Depreciation Expense			14
15				15
16				16
17				17
18				18
19				19
20				20
21				21

Problem 7-6A

Bedazzle Co.

(b) & (c)

Cash Receipts Journal

CR1

Date	Account Credited	Ref.	Cash Dr.	Sales Discounts Dr.	Accounts Receivable Cr.	Sales Cr.	Other Accounts Cr.	COGS Dr. Merch Inv Cr.
1								
2								
3								
4								
5								
6								

Cash Payments Journal

CP1

Date	Account Debited	Ref.	Other Accounts Dr.	Accounts Payable Dr.	Merchandise Inventory Cr.	Cash Cr.
1						
2						
3						
4						
5						
6						
7						
8						

(b) & (c) (Continued)

Sales Journal   S1

	Date	Account Debited	Ref.	Accounts Receivable Dr. Sales Cr.	COGS Dr. Merchandise Inventory Cr.	
1						1
2						2
3						3
4						4
5						5

Purchases Journal   P1

	Date	Account Credited	Ref.	Merchandise Inventory Dr. Acc. Pay. Cr.	
1					1
2					2
3					3
4					4
5					5

General Journal   G1

	Date	Account Titles and Explanation	Ref.	Debit	Credit	
1	Jan 14					1
2						2
3						3
4						4
5	20					5
6						6
7						7
8						8
9	30					9
10						10
11						11
12						12
13						13

Section

(a) and (c)

Cash   No. 101

Date	Explanation	Ref.	Debit	Credit	Balance
Jan. 1	Balance	√			41500

Accounts Receivable   No. 112

Date	Explanation	Ref.	Debit	Credit	Balance
Jan. 1	Balance	√			15000

Notes Receivable   No. 115

Date	Explanation	Ref.	Debit	Credit	Balance
Jan. 1	Balance	√			45000

Merchandise Inventory   No. 120

Date	Explanation	Ref.	Debit	Credit	Balance
Jan. 1	Balance	√			23000

Equipment   No. 157

Date	Explanation	Ref.	Debit	Credit	Balance
Jan. 1	Balance	√			6450

Accumulated Depreciation - Equipment   No. 158

Date	Explanation	Ref.	Debit	Credit	Balance
Jan. 1	Balance	√			1500

(a) and (c) (Continued)

Notes Payable   No. 200

Date	Explanation	Ref.	Debit	Credit	Balance

Accounts Payable   No. 201

Date	Explanation	Ref.	Debit	Credit	Balance
Jan. 1	Balance	√			4 3 0 0

B. Dazzle, Capital   No. 301

Date	Explanation	Ref.	Debit	Credit	Balance
Jan. 1	Balance	√			8 6 4 5 0

Sales   No. 401

Date	Explanation	Ref.	Debit	Credit	Balance

Sales Returns and Allowances   No. 412

Date	Explanation	Ref.	Debit	Credit	Balance

Sales Discounts   No. 414

Date	Explanation	Ref.	Debit	Credit	Balance

Cost of Goods Sold   No. 505

Date	Explanation	Ref.	Debit	Credit	Balance

(a) and (c) (Continued)

Sales Salaries Expense   No. 726

Date	Explanation	Ref.	Debit	Credit	Balance

Office Salaries Expense   No. 727

Date	Explanation	Ref.	Debit	Credit	Balance

Rent Expense   No. 729

Date	Explanation	Ref.	Debit	Credit	Balance

Accounts Receivable Subsidiary Ledger

J. Balton

Date	Explanation	Ref.	Debit	Credit	Balance
Jan. 1	Balance	√			2 5 0 0

F. Cone

Date	Explanation	Ref.	Debit	Credit	Balance
Jan. 1	Balance	√			7 5 0 0

T. Dudley

Date	Explanation	Ref.	Debit	Credit	Balance
Jan. 1	Balance	√			5 0 0 0

M. Sanford

Date	Explanation	Ref.	Debit	Credit	Balance

(a) and (c) (Continued)

Accounts Payable Subsidiary Ledger

G. Louis

Date	Explanation	Ref.	Debit	Credit	Balance

J. Feeney

Date	Explanation	Ref.	Debit	Credit	Balance
Jan. 1	Balance	√			1 0 0 0 0

D. Goodman

Date	Explanation	Ref.	Debit	Credit	Balance
Jan. 1	Balance	√			1 8 0 0 0

K. Hollis

Date	Explanation	Ref.	Debit	Credit	Balance
Jan. 1	Balance	√			1 5 0 0 0

E. Westphal

Date	Explanation	Ref.	Debit	Credit	Balance

(d)

Bedazzle Co. Trial Balance January 31, 2005	Debit	Credit
1 Cash		
2 Accounts Receivable		
3 Notes Receivable		
4 Merchandise Inventory		
5 Equipment		
6 Accumulated Depreciation - Equipment		
7 Notes Payable		
8 Accounts Payable		
9 B. Dazzle, Capital		
10 Sales		
11 Sales Returns and Allowances		
12 Sales Discounts		
13 Cost of Goods Sold		
14 Sales Salaries Expense		
15 Office Salaries Expense		
16 Rent Expense		
17		
18		

(e)

1 Accounts receivable subsidiary ledger:		
2		
3		
4		
5		
6		
7 Account receivable control:		
8		
9 Accounts payable subsidiary ledger:		
10		
11		
12		
13		
14		
15 Accounts payable control:		
16		

(a)

Cash Receipts Journal

CR1

Date	Account Credited	Ref.	Cash Dr.	Sales Discounts Dr.	Accounts Receivable Cr.	Sales Cr.	Other Accounts Cr.	COGS Dr. Merch Inv Cr.	
									1
									2
									3
									4
									5
									6
									7
									8
									9
									10
									11
									12
									13
									14
									15
									16
									17

(b)

General Ledger

Accounts Receivable No. 112

Date	Explanation	Ref	Debit	Credit	Balance
Apr. 1	Balance	√			7 0 5 0

Accounts Receivable Subsidiary Ledger

Naper

Date	Explanation	Ref	Debit	Credit	Balance
Apr. 1	Balance	√			1 5 5 0

Chelsea

Date	Explanation	Ref	Debit	Credit	Balance
Apr. 1	Balance	√			1 2 0 0

Finlandia Co.

Date	Explanation	Ref	Debit	Credit	Balance
Apr. 1	Balance	√			2 9 0 0

Baez

Date	Explanation	Ref	Debit	Credit	Balance
Apr. 1	Balance	√			1 4 0 0

(c)

1	Accounts receivable balance:	1
2		2
3		3
4	Subsidiary account balances:	4
5		5
6		6
7		7
8		8
9		9
10		10

Name _____   Problem 7-2B

Section _____

Date _____   Mann Company

(a)

Cash Payments Journal   CP1

Date	Ck. No.	Account Debited	Ref.	Other Accounts Dr.	Accounts Payable Dr.	Merchandise Inventory Cr.	Cash Cr.
1							
2							
3							
4							
5							
6							
7							
8							
9							
10							
11							
12							
13							
14							
15							
16							
17							
18							
19							
20							

(b)

General Ledger

Accounts Payable   No. 201

Date	Explanation	Ref	Debit	Credit	Balance
Oct. 1	Balance	√			9700

Accounts Payable Subsidiary Ledger

Bovary Co.

Date	Explanation	Ref	Debit	Credit	Balance
Oct. 1	Balance	√			1700

Magic Co.

Date	Explanation	Ref	Debit	Credit	Balance
Oct. 1	Balance	√			2500

Pyron

Date	Explanation	Ref	Debit	Credit	Balance
Oct. 1	Balance	√			1800

Tess Co.

Date	Explanation	Ref	Debit	Credit	Balance
Oct. 1	Balance	√			3700

(c)

1	Accounts payable balance:	
2		
3		
4	Subsidiary account balances:	
5		
6		
7		
8		
9		
10		

(a)

	Purchases Journal					P1
Date	Account Credited (Debited)	Ref.	Other Accounts Dr.	Merchandise Inventory Dr.	Accounts Payable Cr.	
1						1
2						2
3						3
4						4
5						5
6						6
7						7
8						8
9						9
10						10
11						11
12						12
13						13
14						14
15						15
16						16
17						17
18						18

	Sales Journal				S1
Date	Account Debited	Ref.	Accounts Receiv. Dr. Sales Cr.	COGS Dr. Merchandise Inventory Cr.	
1					1
2					2
3					3
4					4
5					5
6					6
7					7
8					8
9					9
10					10

(a) (Continued)

General Journal

G1

	Date	Account Titles and Explanation	Ref.	Debit	Credit	
1	July 8					1
2						2
3						3
4						4
5						5
6	22					6
7						7
8						8
9						9
10						10
11						11
12						12

(b)

General Ledger

Accounts Receivable

No. 112

Date	Explanation	Ref.	Debit	Credit	Balance

Merchandise Inventory

No. 120

Date	Explanation	Ref.	Debit	Credit	Balance

Supplies

No. 126

Date	Explanation	Ref.	Debit	Credit	Balance

Equipment

No. 157

Date	Explanation	Ref.	Debit	Credit	Balance

(b)(Continued)

Accounts Payable   No. 201

Date	Explanation	Ref.	Debit	Credit	Balance

Sales   No. 401

Date	Explanation	Ref.	Debit	Credit	Balance

Sales Returns and Allowances   No. 412

Date	Explanation	Ref.	Debit	Credit	Balance

Cost of Goods Sold   No. 505

Date	Explanation	Ref.	Debit	Credit	Balance

Advertising Expense   No. 610

Date	Explanation	Ref.	Debit	Credit	Balance

(b)(Continued)

Accounts Receivable Subsidiary Ledger

Wayne Bros.

Date	Explanation	Ref.	Debit	Credit	Balance

Marion Company

Date	Explanation	Ref.	Debit	Credit	Balance

Rowen Company

Date	Explanation	Ref.	Debit	Credit	Balance

Haddad Company

Date	Explanation	Ref.	Debit	Credit	Balance

(b)(Continued)　　　*Accounts Payable Subsidiary Ledger*

Boyd Supply

Date	Explanation	Ref.	Debit	Credit	Balance

Wayward Shipping

Date	Explanation	Ref.	Debit	Credit	Balance

Gucci Company

Date	Explanation	Ref.	Debit	Credit	Balance

Lee Company

Date	Explanation	Ref.	Debit	Credit	Balance

Lynda Advertisements

Date	Explanation	Ref.	Debit	Credit	Balance

Anton Company

Date	Explanation	Ref.	Debit	Credit	Balance

(c)

1	Accounts receivable balance:	
2		
3		
4		
5		
6	Subsidiary account balances:	
7		
8		
9		
10		
11		
12		
13		
14		
15		
16		
17	Accounts payable balance:	
18		
19		
20		
21	Subsidiary account balances:	
22		
23		
24		
25		
26		
27		
28		
29		
30		
31		
32		
33		
34		
35		
36		
37		
38		
39		
40		

(a), (b), & (c)

		Sales Journal				S1

	Date	Account Debited	Invoice No.	Ref.	Accounts Receivable Dr. Sales Cr.	COGS Dr. Merchandise Inventory Cr.	
1							1
2							2
3							3
4							4
5							5
6							6
7							7

		Purchases Journal		P1

	Date	Account Credited	Ref.	Merchandise Inventory (Dr.) Acc. Pay (Cr.)	
1					1
2					2
3					3
4					4
5					5
6					6
7					7
8					8

		General Journal			G1

	Date	Account Titles and Explanation	Ref.	Debit	Credit	
1	Jan. 5					1
2						2
3						3
4	19					4
5						5
6						6

(a), (b), (c) (Continued)

Cash Receipts Journal

CR1

Date	Account Credited	Ref.	Cash Dr.	Sales Discounts Dr.	Accounts Receivable Cr.	Sales Cr.	Other Accounts Cr.	COGS Dr. Merch Inv Cr.
1								
2								
3								
4								
5								
6								
7								
8								
9								
10								
11								
12								
13								
14								
15								

(a), (b), (c) (Continued)

Cash Payments Journal

CP1

Date	Account Debited	Ref.	Other Accounts Dr.	Accounts Payable Dr.	Merchandise Inventory Cr.	Cash Cr.	
							1
							2
							3
							4
							5
							6
							7
							8
							9
							10
							11
							12
							13
							14
							15

(a), (d) & (g)

Cash   No. 101

Date	Explanation	Ref.	Debit	Credit	Balance

Accounts Receivable   No. 112

Date	Explanation	Ref.	Debit	Credit	Balance

Merchandise Inventory   No. 120

Date	Explanation	Ref.	Debit	Credit	Balance

Store Supplies   No. 127

Date	Explanation	Ref.	Debit	Credit	Balance

Prepaid Rent   No. 131

Date	Explanation	Ref.	Debit	Credit	Balance

Accounts Payable   No. 201

Date	Explanation	Ref.	Debit	Credit	Balance

Scott, Capital   No. 301

Date	Explanation	Ref.	Debit	Credit	Balance

(a), (d) & (g) (Continued)

Scott, Drawing
No. 306

Date	Explanation	Ref.	Debit	Credit	Balance

Sales
No. 401

Date	Explanation	Ref.	Debit	Credit	Balance

Sales Discounts
No. 414

Date	Explanation	Ref.	Debit	Credit	Balance

Cost of Goods Sold
No. 505

Date	Explanation	Ref.	Debit	Credit	Balance

Supplies Expense
No. 631

Date	Explanation	Ref.	Debit	Credit	Balance

Rent Expense
No. 729

Date	Explanation	Ref.	Debit	Credit	Balance

(b)

Sales Journal
S1

	Date	Account Debited	Ref.	Accounts Receivable Dr. Sales Cr.	COGS Dr. Merchandise Inventory Cr.	
1						1
2						2
3						3
4						4
5						5
6						6
7						7

Problem 7-5B Continued

Scott Co.

(a), (b), (c) (Continued)

Cash Receipts Journal

CR1

Date	Account Credited	Ref.	Cash Dr.	Sales Discounts Dr.	Accounts Receivable Cr.	Sales Cr.	Other Accounts Cr.	COGS Dr. Merch. Inv. Cr.
1								
2								
3								
4								
5								
6								
7								
8								
9								
10								
11								
12								
13								
14								
15								

(c)

Accounts Payable Subsidiary Ledger

C. Sleepy

Date	Explanation	Ref.	Debit	Credit	Balance

A. Doc

Date	Explanation	Ref.	Debit	Credit	Balance

M. Sneezy

Date	Explanation	Ref.	Debit	Credit	Balance

G. Bashful

Date	Explanation	Ref.	Debit	Credit	Balance

J. Happy

Date	Explanation	Ref.	Debit	Credit	Balance

(c) (Continued)

Accounts Receivable Subsidiary Ledger

Dopey Co.

Date	Explanation	Ref.	Debit	Credit	Balance

H. Prince

Date	Explanation	Ref.	Debit	Credit	Balance

W. Queen

Date	Explanation	Ref.	Debit	Credit	Balance

S. Beauty

Date	Explanation	Ref.	Debit	Credit	Balance

(e)

Scott Co. Trial Balance July 31, 2005	Debit	Credit
1		
2		
3		
4		
5		
6		
7		
8		
9		
10		
11		
12		
13		
14		
15		

(f)

1	Accounts payable balance:	1
2		2
3	Subsidiary accounts balance:	3
4		4
5		5
6		6
7		7
8	Accounts receivable balance:	8
9		9
10	Subsidiary accounts balance:	10
11		11
12		12

(g)

		General Journal			G1

	Date	Account Titles and Explanation	Ref.	Debit	Credit	
1	July 31					1
2						2
3						3
4	31					4
5						5
6						6

(h)

Scott Co. Adjusted Trial Balance July 31, 2005	Debit	Credit
1 Cash		
2 Accounts Receivable		
3 Merchandise Inventory		
4 Store Supplies		
5 Prepaid Rent		
6 Accounts Payable		
7 Scott, Capital		
8 Scott, Drawing		
9 Sales		
10 Sales Discounts		
11 Cost of Goods Sold		
12 Supplies Expense		
13 Rent Expense		
14		
15		
16		

(a)

| | | Sales Journal | | | | S1 |

	Date	Account Debited	Invoice No.	Ref.	Accounts Receiv. Dr. Sales Cr.	
1						1
2						2
3						3
4						4
5						5
6						6
7						7
8						8
9						9
10						10
11						11
12						12

Purchases Journal — P1

	Date	Account Credited	Terms	Ref.	Purchases Dr. Acc. Pay Cr.	
1						1
2						2
3						3
4						4
5						5
6						6
7						7
8						8
9						9
10						10
11						11
12						12

(a) (Continued)

Cash Receipts Journal

CR1

Date	Explanation	Account Credited	Ref.	Cash Dr.	Accounts Receivable Cr.	Sales Cr.	Other Accounts Cr.
1							
2							
3							
4							
5							
6							
7							
8							
9							
10							
11							
12							
13							
14							
15							

Comprehensive Problem: Chapters 3 to 7 Continued

Raymond Company

(a) (Continued)

Cash Payments Journal CR1

Date	Explanation	Cash Cr.	Accounts Payable Dr.	Office Supplies Dr.	Accounts Debited	Ref.	Other Accounts Dr.
1							
2							
3							
4							
5							
6							
7							
8							
9							
10							
11							
12							
13							
14							
15							

Name _____

Section _____

Date _____ Raymond Company

(a) and (e)

General Journal   G1

	Date	Account Titles and Explanation	Ref	Debit	Credit	
1						1
2						2
3						3
4						4
5						5
6						6
7						7
8						8
9						9
10						10
11						11
12						12
13						13
14						14
15						15
16						16
17						17
18						18
19						19
20						20
21						21
22						22
23						23
24						24
25						25
26						26
27						27
28						28
29						29
30						30
31						31
32						32
33						33
34						34
35						35
36						36
37						37
38						38
39						39
40						40

(a) and (e)

General Journal   G1

	Date	Account Titles and Explanation	Ref	Debit	Credit	
1						1
2						2
3						3
4						4
5						5
6						6
7						7
8						8
9						9
10						10
11						11
12						12
13						13
14						14
15						15
16						16
17						17
18						18
19						19
20						20
21						21
22						22
23						23
24						24
25						25
26						26
27						27
28						28
29						29
30						30
31						31
32						32
33						33
34						34
35						35
36						36
37						37
38						38
39						39
40						40

(b) and (e)

General Ledger

Cash   No. 101

Date	Explanation	Ref.	Debit	Credit	Balance
Jan. 1	Balance	√			3 3 7 5 0

Accounts Receivable   No. 112

Date	Explanation	Ref.	Debit	Credit	Balance
Jan. 1	Balance	√			1 3 0 0 0

Notes Receivable   No. 115

Date	Explanation	Ref.	Debit	Credit	Balance
Jan. 1	Balance	√			3 9 0 0 0

Merchandise Inventory   No. 120

Date	Explanation	Ref.	Debit	Credit	Balance
Jan. 1	Balance	√			2 0 0 0 0

Office Supplies   No. 125

Date	Explanation	Ref.	Debit	Credit	Balance
Jan. 1	Balance	√			1 0 0 0

Prepaid Insurance   No. 130

Date	Explanation	Ref.	Debit	Credit	Balance
Jan. 1	Balance	√			2 0 0 0

(b) and (e) (Continued)

Equipment   No. 157

Date	Explanation	Ref.	Debit	Credit	Balance
Jan. 1	Balance	√			6 4 5 0

Accumulated Depreciation - Equipment   No. 158

Date	Explanation	Ref.	Debit	Credit	Balance
Jan. 1	Balance	√			1 5 0 0

Notes Payable   No. 200

Date	Explanation	Ref.	Debit	Credit	Balance
	Balance				

Accounts Payable   No. 201

Date	Explanation	Ref.	Debit	Credit	Balance
Jan. 1	Balance	√			3 5 0 0 0

Interest Payable   No. 230

Date	Explanation	Ref.	Debit	Credit	Balance

I. Raymond, Capital   No. 301

Date	Explanation	Ref.	Debit	Credit	Balance
Jan. 1	Balance	√			7 8 7 0 0

I. Raymond, Drawing   No. 306

Date	Explanation	Ref.	Debit	Credit	Balance

(b) and (e) (Continued)

Income Summary   No. 350

Date	Explanation	Ref.	Debit	Credit	Balance

Sales   No. 401

Date	Explanation	Ref.	Debit	Credit	Balance

Sales Returns and Allowances   No. 412

Date	Explanation	Ref.	Debit	Credit	Balance

Purchases   No. 510

Date	Explanation	Ref.	Debit	Credit	Balance

Purchase Returns and Allowances   No. 512

Date	Explanation	Ref.	Debit	Credit	Balance

Freight-in   No. 516

Date	Explanation	Ref.	Debit	Credit	Balance

Sales Salaries Expense   No. 627

Date	Explanation	Ref.	Debit	Credit	Balance

(b) and (e) (Continued)

Depreciation Expense   No. 711

Date	Explanation	Ref.	Debit	Credit	Balance

Interest Expense   No. 718

Date	Explanation	Ref.	Debit	Credit	Balance

Insurance Expense   No. 722

Date	Explanation	Ref.	Debit	Credit	Balance

Office Salaries Expense   No. 727

Date	Explanation	Ref.	Debit	Credit	Balance

Office Supplies Expense   No. 728

Date	Explanation	Ref.	Debit	Credit	Balance

Rent Expense   No. 729

Date	Explanation	Ref.	Debit	Credit	Balance

(b) and (e) (Continued)

Accounts Receivable Subsidiary Ledger

R. Draves

Date	Explanation	Ref.	Debit	Credit	Balance
Jan. 1	Balance	√			1500

J. Ebel

Date	Explanation	Ref.	Debit	Credit	Balance

B. Jacovetti

Date	Explanation	Ref.	Debit	Credit	Balance
Jan. 1	Balance	√			7500

S. Kysely

Date	Explanation	Ref.	Debit	Credit	Balance
Jan. 1	Balance	√			4000

B. Soto

Date	Explanation	Ref.	Debit	Credit	Balance

(b) and (e) (Continued)

Accounts Payable Subsidiary Ledger

D. Laux

Date	Explanation	Ref.	Debit	Credit	Balance

S. Liazuk

Date	Explanation	Ref.	Debit	Credit	Balance
Jan. 1	Balance	√			9 0 0 0

R. Mikush

Date	Explanation	Ref.	Debit	Credit	Balance
Jan. 1	Balance	√			1 5 0 0 0

D. Nguyen

Date	Explanation	Ref.	Debit	Credit	Balance
Jan. 1	Balance	√			1 1 0 0 0

S. Welz

Date	Explanation	Ref.	Debit	Credit	Balance

COMPREHENSIVE PROBLEM: CHAPTERS 3 TO 7
RAYMOND COMPANY
See Appendix

(d)

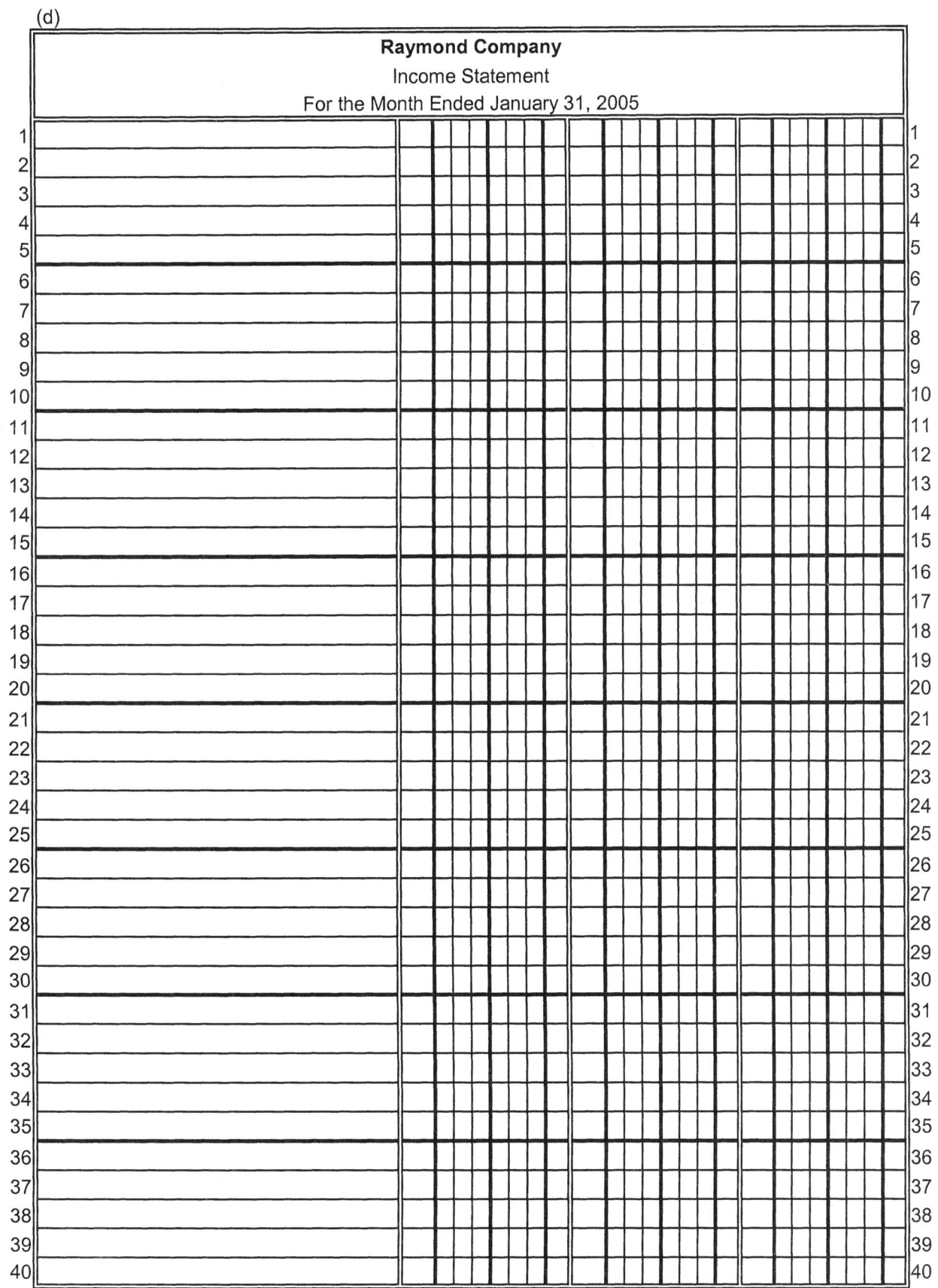

Raymond Company

Income Statement

For the Month Ended January 31, 2005

(d) (Continued)

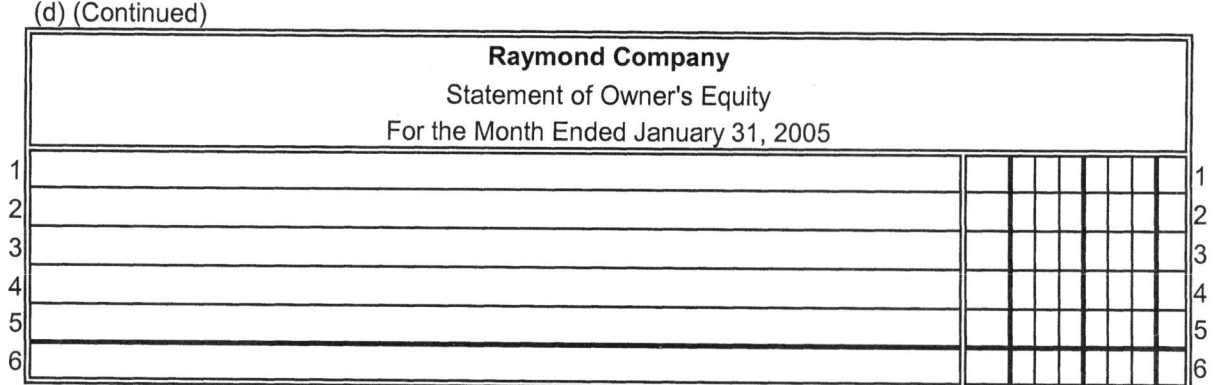

Raymond Company

Statement of Owner's Equity

For the Month Ended January 31, 2005

1		1
2		2
3		3
4		4
5		5
6		6

Raymond Company

Balance Sheet

January 31, 2005

	Assets	
1		1
2		2
3		3
4		4
5		5
6		6
7		7
8		8
9		9
10		10
11		11
12		12
13		13
14		14
15		15
16	Liabilities and Owner's Equity	16
17		17
18		18
19		19
20		20
21		21
22		22
23		23
24		24
25		25
26		26
27		27
28		28
29		29
30		30

(f)

Raymond Company Post-Closing Trial Balance January 31, 2005	Debit	Credit
1 Cash		
2 Notes Receivable		
3 Accounts Receivable		
4 Merchandise Inventory		
5 Office Supplies		
6 Prepaid Insurance		
7 Equipment		
8 Accumulated Depreciation - Equipment		
9 Notes Payable		
10 Accounts Payable		
11 Interest Payable		
12 I. Raymond, Capital		
13		
14		

1 Accounts Receivable balance:		
2		
3 Subsidiary account balances:		
4		
5		
6		
7		
8		
9		
10 Accounts Payable balance:		
11		
12 Subsidiary account balances:		
13		
14		
15		
16		
17		

Sales Journal

S1

	Date	Account Debited	Invoice No.	Ref.	Accounts Receiv. Dr. Sales Cr.	COGS Dr. Merchandise Inventory Cr.	
1							1
2							2
3							3
4							4
5							5
6							6
7							7
8							8
9							9
10							10
11							11
12							12

Purchases Journal

P1

	Date	Account Credited	Terms	Ref.	Merchandise Inventory (Dr.) Acc. Pay (Cr.)	
1						1
2						2
3						3
4						4
5						5
6						6
7						7
8						8
9						9
10						10
11						11
12						12

(a) (Continued)

Cash Receipts Journal

CR1

Date	Account Credited	Ref.	Cash Dr.	Sales Discounts Dr.	Accounts Receivable Cr.	Sales Cr.	Other Accounts Cr.	COGS Dr. Inventory Cr.
1								
2								
3								
4								
5								
6								
7								
8								
9								
10								
11								
12								
13								
14								
15								

(a) (Continued)

Cash Payments Journal

CP1

Date	Account Debited	Ref.	Other Accounts Dr.	Accounts Payable Dr.	Office Supplies Dr.	Merchandise Inventory Cr.	Cash Cr.
1							
2							
3							
4							
5							
6							
7							
8							
9							
10							
11							
12							
13							
14							
15							

(a) and (e)

General Journal   G1

	Date	Account Titles and Explanation	Ref	Debit	Credit	
1						1
2						2
3						3
4						4
5						5
6						6
7						7
8						8
9						9
10						10
11						11
12						12
13						13
14						14
15						15
16						16
17						17
18						18
19						19
20						20
21						21
22						22
23						23
24						24
25						25
26						26
27						27
28						28
29						29
30						30
31						31
32						32
33						33
34						34
35						35
36						36
37						37
38						38
39						39
40						40

(a) and (e) (Continued)

General Journal
G1

	Date	Account Titles and Explanation	Ref	Debit	Credit	
1						1
2						2
3						3
4						4
5						5
6						6
7						7
8						8
9						9
10						10
11						11
12						12
13						13
14						14
15						15
16						16
17						17
18						18
19						19
20						20
21						21
22						22
23						23
24						24
25						25
26						26
27						27
28						28
29						29
30						30
31						31
32						32
33						33
34						34
35						35
36						36
37						37
38						38
39						39
40						40

(b) and (e)

General Ledger

Cash
No. 101

Date	Explanation	Ref.	Debit	Credit	Balance
Jan. 1	Balance	√			3 5 7 5 0

Accounts Receivable
No. 112

Date	Explanation	Ref.	Debit	Credit	Balance
Jan. 1	Balance	√			1 3 0 0 0

Notes Receivable
No. 115

Date	Explanation	Ref.	Debit	Credit	Balance
Jan. 1	Balance	√			3 9 0 0 0

Merchandise Inventory
No. 120

Date	Explanation	Ref.	Debit	Credit	Balance
Jan. 1	Balance	√			1 8 0 0 0

Office Supplies
No. 125

Date	Explanation	Ref.	Debit	Credit	Balance
Jan. 1	Balance	√			1 0 0 0

Prepaid Insurance
No. 130

Date	Explanation	Ref.	Debit	Credit	Balance
Jan. 1	Balance	√			2 0 0 0

(b) and (e) (Continued)

Equipment   No. 157

Date	Explanation	Ref.	Debit	Credit	Balance
Jan. 1	Balance	√			6450

Accumulated Depreciation - Equipment   No. 158

Date	Explanation	Ref.	Debit	Credit	Balance
Jan. 1	Balance	√			1500

Notes Payable   No. 200

Date	Explanation	Ref.	Debit	Credit	Balance

Accounts Payable   No. 201

Date	Explanation	Ref.	Debit	Credit	Balance
Jan. 1	Balance	√			35000

Interest Payable   No. 230

Date	Explanation	Ref.	Debit	Credit	Balance

M.Cedzo, Capital   No. 301

Date	Explanation	Ref.	Debit	Credit	Balance
Jan. 1	Balance	√			78700

M. Cedzo, Drawing   No. 306

Date	Explanation	Ref.	Debit	Credit	Balance
					800

(b) and (e) (Continued)

Income Summary — No. 350

Date	Explanation	Ref.	Debit	Credit	Balance

Sales — No. 401

Date	Explanation	Ref.	Debit	Credit	Balance

Sales Returns and Allowances — No. 412

Date	Explanation	Ref.	Debit	Credit	Balance

Sales Discounts — No. 414

Date	Explanation	Ref.	Debit	Credit	Balance

Cost of Goods Sold — No. 505

Date	Explanation	Ref.	Debit	Credit	Balance

Sales Salaries Expense — No. 627

Date	Explanation	Ref.	Debit	Credit	Balance

Depreciation Expense — No. 711

Date	Explanation	Ref.	Debit	Credit	Balance

(b) and (e) (Continued)

Interest Expense   No. 718

Date	Explanation	Ref.	Debit	Credit	Balance

Insurance Expense   No. 722

Date	Explanation	Ref.	Debit	Credit	Balance

Office Salaries Expense   No. 727

Date	Explanation	Ref.	Debit	Credit	Balance

Office Supplies Expense   No. 728

Date	Explanation	Ref.	Debit	Credit	Balance

Rent Expense   No. 729

Date	Explanation	Ref.	Debit	Credit	Balance

(b) and (e) (Continued)

Accounts Receivable Subsidiary Ledger

R. Dvorak

Date	Explanation	Ref.	Debit	Credit	Balance
Jan. 1	Balance	√			1500

J. Eppler

Date	Explanation	Ref.	Debit	Credit	Balance

B. Garcia

Date	Explanation	Ref.	Debit	Credit	Balance
Jan. 1	Balance	√			7500

S. LaDew

Date	Explanation	Ref.	Debit	Credit	Balance
Jan. 1	Balance	√			4000

B. Stahre

Date	Explanation	Ref.	Debit	Credit	Balance

(b) and (e) (Continued)

Accounts Payable Subsidiary Ledger

D. Lynch

Date	Explanation	Ref.	Debit	Credit	Balance

S. Jung

Date	Explanation	Ref.	Debit	Credit	Balance
Jan. 1	Balance	√			9 0 0 0

R. Moses

Date	Explanation	Ref.	Debit	Credit	Balance
Jan. 1	Balance	√			1 5 0 0 0

D. Norby

Date	Explanation	Ref.	Debit	Credit	Balance
Jan. 1	Balance	√			1 1 0 0 0

S. Wong

Date	Explanation	Ref.	Debit	Credit	Balance

(c)

Cedzo Co.
Work Sheet
For the Month Ended January 31, 2005

Account Titles	Trial Balance		Adjustments		Adjusted Trial Balance		Income Statement		Balance Sheet	
	Dr.	Cr.	Dr.	Cr.	Dr.	Cr.	Dr.	Cr.	Dr.	Cr.
1 Cash										
2 Accounts Receivable										
3 Notes Receivable										
4 Merchandise Inventory										
5 Office Supplies										
6 Prepaid Insurance										
7 Equipment										
8 Accum. Depr. - Equip.										
9 Notes Payable										
10 Accounts Payable										
11 Interest Payable										
12 M. Cedzo, Capital										
13 M. Cedzo, Drawing										
14 Sales										
15 Sales Rtns. and Allow.										
16 Sales Discounts										
17 Cost of Goods Sold										
18 Sales Salaries Exp.										
19 Office Salaries Exp.										
20 Rent Exp.										
21 Totals										
22 Office Supplies Exp.										
23 Insurance Exp.										
24 Depreciation Exp.										
25 Interest Exp.										
26 Totals										
27 Net Income										
28 Totals										
29										

(d)

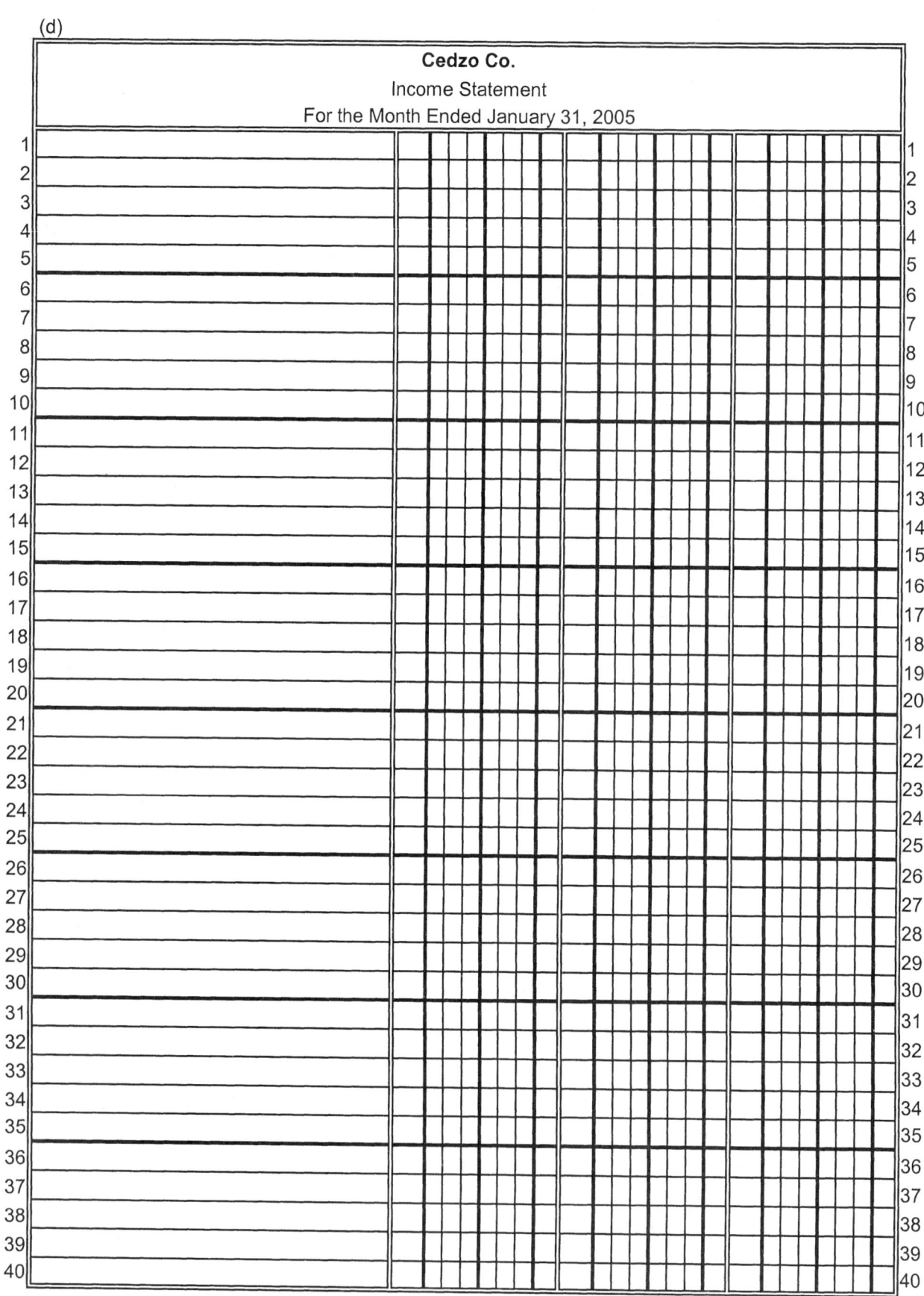

Cedzo Co.

Income Statement

For the Month Ended January 31, 2005

(d) (Continued)

Cedzo Co.

Owner's Equity Statement

For the Month Ended January 31, 2005

1	1
2	2
3	3
4	4
5	5
6	6

Cedzo Co.

Balance Sheet

January 31, 2005

Assets	
1	1
2	2
3	3
4	4
5	5
6	6
7	7
8	8
9	9
10	10
11	11
12	12
13	13
14	14
15	15

Liabilities and Owner's Equity	
16	16
17	17
18	18
19	19
20	20
21	21
22	22
23	23
24	24
25	25
26	26
27	27
28	28
29	29
30	30

(f)

Cedzo Co. Post-Closing Trial Balance January 31, 2005	Debit	Credit
1. Cash		
2. Notes Receivable		
3. Accounts Receivable		
4. Merchandise Inventory		
5. Office Supplies		
6. Prepaid Insurance		
7. Equipment		
8. Accumulated Depreciation - Equipment		
9. Notes Payable		
10. Accounts Payable		
11. Interest Payable		
12. M. Cedzo, Capital		
13.		
14.		
15.		

1. Accounts Receivable balance:		
2.		
3. Subsidiary account balances:		
4.		
5.		
6.		
7.		
8.		
9.		
10. Accounts Payable balance:		
11.		
12. Subsidiary account balances:		
13.		
14.		
15.		
16.		
17.		
18.		
19.		

1	(a)	1
2		2
3		3
4		4
5		5
6		6
7		7
8		8
9		9
10		10
11		11
12		12
13		13
14		14
15		15
16	(b)	16
17		17
18		18
19		19
20		20
21		21
22		22
23		23
24		24
25		25
26		26
27		27
28		28
29		29
30		30
31		31
32		32
33		33
34		34
35		35
36		36
37		37
38		38
39		39
40		40

(a)

(a) (Continued)

1	1
2	2
3	3
4	4
5	5
6	6
7	7
8	8
9	9
10	10
11	11
12	12
13	13
14	14
15	15
16	16
17	17
18	18
19	19
20	20
21 (b)	21
22	22
23	23
24	24
25	25
26	26
27	27
28	28
29	29
30	30
31	31
32	32
33	33
34	34
35	35
36	36
37	37
38	38
39	39
40	40

1	1
2	2
3	3
4	4
5	5
6	6
7	7
8	8
9	9
10	10
11	11
12	12
13	13
14	14
15	15
16	16
17	17
18	18
19	19
20	20
21	21
22	22
23	23
24	24
25	25
26	26
27	27
28	28
29	29
30	30
31	31
32	32
33	33
34	34
35	35
36	36
37	37
38	38
39	39
40	40

(a)

(b)

(c)

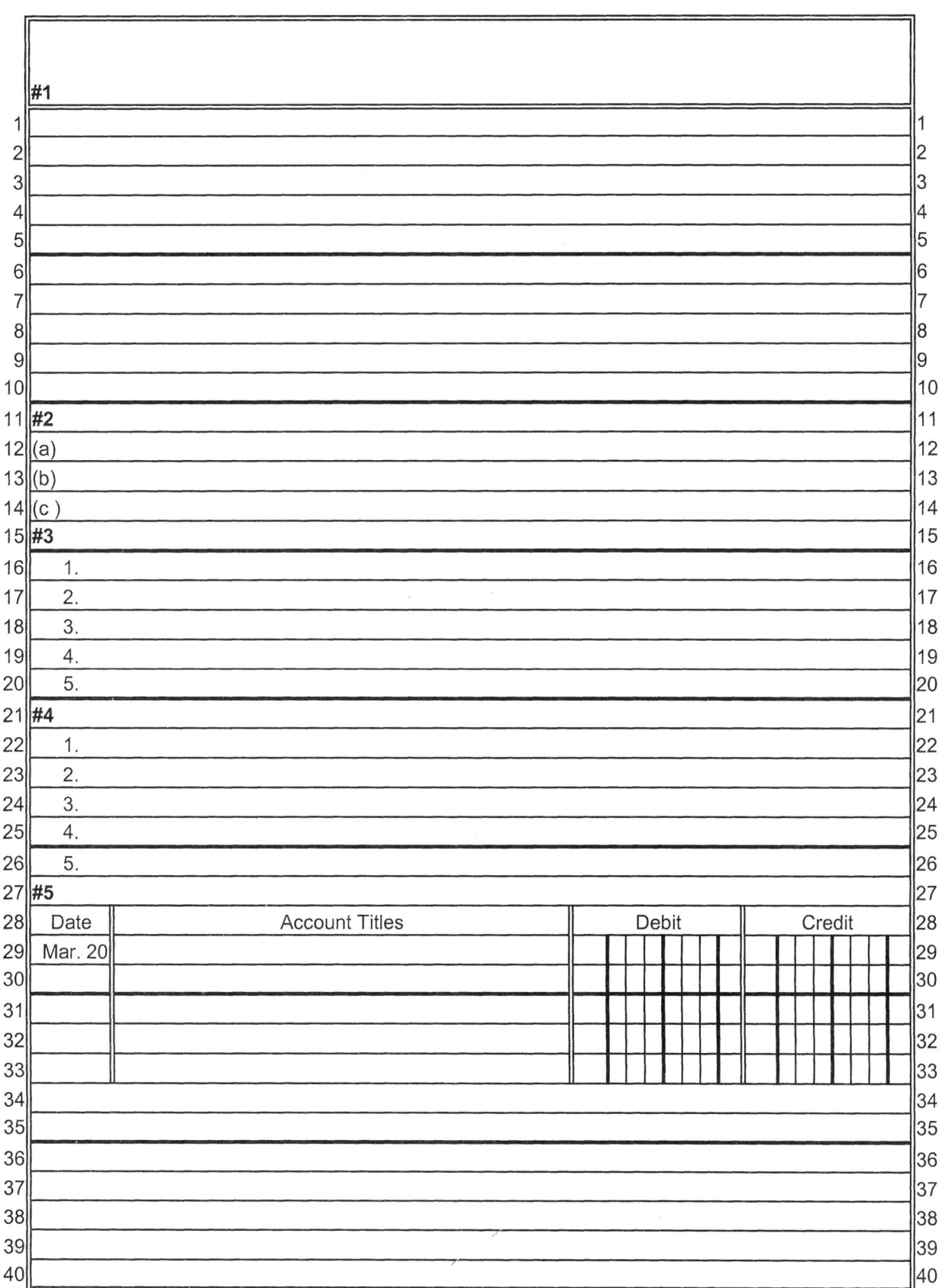

	#1	
1		1
2		2
3		3
4		4
5		5
6		6
7		7
8		8
9		9
10		10
11	#2	11
12	(a)	12
13	(b)	13
14	(c)	14
15	#3	15
16	1.	16
17	2.	17
18	3.	18
19	4.	19
20	5.	20
21	#4	21
22	1.	22
23	2.	23
24	3.	24
25	4.	25
26	5.	26
27	#5	27

	Date	Account Titles	Debit	Credit	
28	Date	Account Titles	Debit	Credit	28
29	Mar. 20				29
30					30
31					31
32					32
33					33
34					34
35					35
36					36
37					37
38					38
39					39
40					40

#6

1   (a)

2

3

4

5   (b)

6

7

8   (c)

9

10

11

12 **#7**

13   (1)

14   (2)

15   (3)

16   (4)

17

18 **#8**

19   (a)

20

21

22   (b)

23

24

25

26 **#9**

27

28

29

30

31

32

33

34

35

36

37

38

39

40

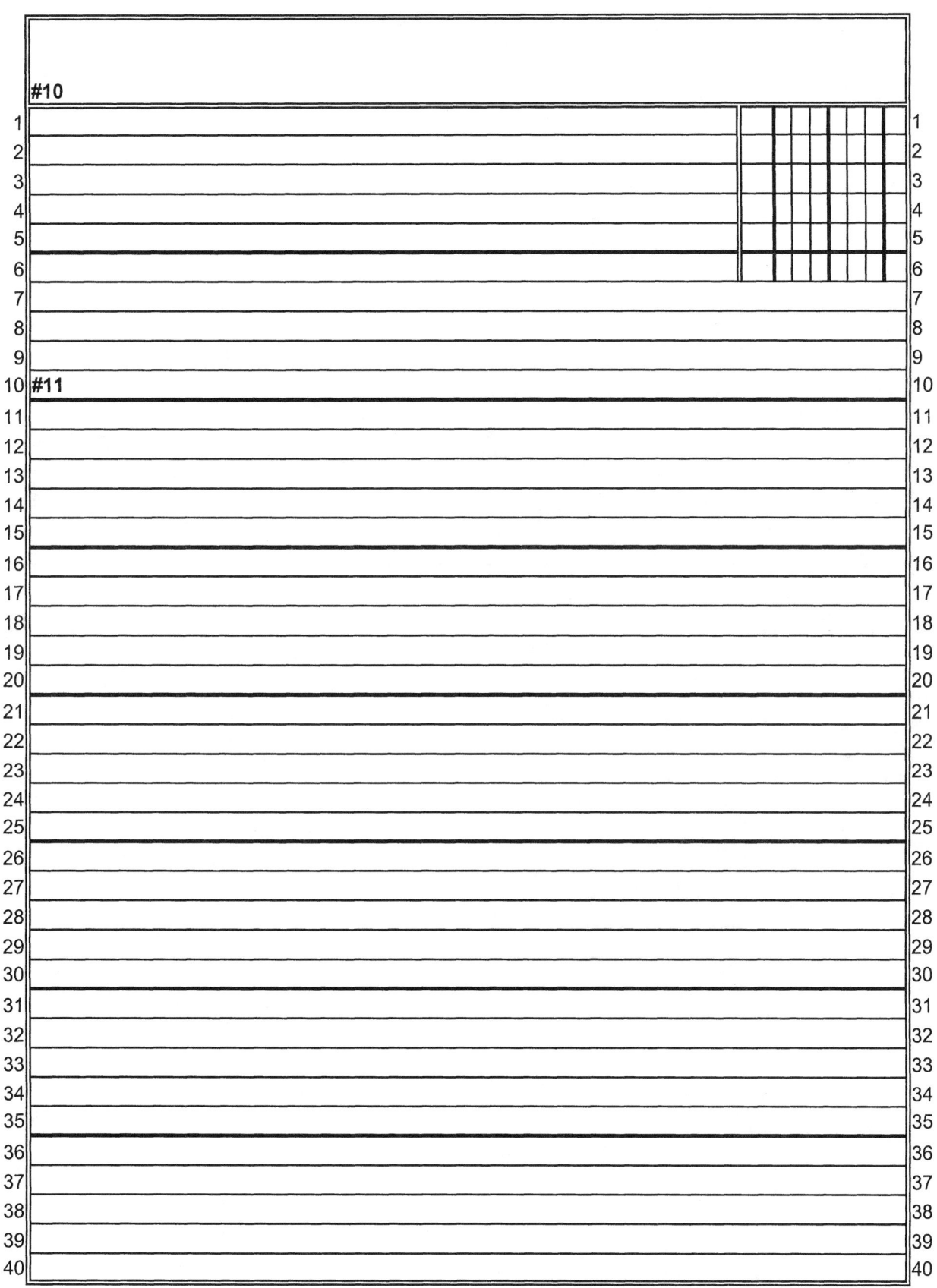

#10

#11

1		1
2		2
3		3
4		4
5		5
6		6
7		7
8		8
9		9
10		10
11		11
12		12
13		13
14		14
15		15
16		16
17		17
18		18
19		19
20		20
21		21
22		22
23		23
24		24
25		25
26		26
27		27
28		28
29		29
30		30
31		31
32		32
33		33
34		34
35		35
36		36
37		37
38		38
39		39
40		40

(a)		(b)
Weakness	Principle Violated	Recommended Change
1.		1
		2
		3
		4
		5
2.		6
		7
		8
		9
		10
3.		11
		12
		13
		14
		15
4.		16
		17
		18
		19
		20
5.		21
		22
		23
		24
		25

Name

Section

Date

Exercise 8-3

Morgan's Boutique

	(a)	(b)
	Weakness	Principle Violated	Suggested Improvement
1.			
2			
3			
4			
5			
2. 6			
7			
8			
9			
10			
3. 11			
12			
13			
14			
15			
4. 16			
17			
18			
19			
20			
5. 21			
22			
23			
24			
25			

Exercise 8-4

Teresa Speck Company

(a)

	Weakness	Suggested Improvement
1.		
2		
3		
4		
5		
6		
7		
8		
9		
10		
11		
12		
13		
14		
15		
16		
17		
18		
19		
20		
21		
22		
23		
24		
25		

(b)

1	1
2	2
3	3
4	4
5	5
6	6
7	7
8	8
9	9
10	10
11	11
12	12
13	13
14	14
15	15
16	16
17	17
18	18
19	19
20	20
21	21
22	22
23	23
24	24
25	25
26	26
27	27
28	28
29	29
30	30
31	31
32	32
33	33
34	34
35	35
36	36
37	37
38	38
39	39
40	40

 # 5

	Date	Account Titles	Debit	Credit	
1	Mar. 1				1
2					2
3					3
4	15				4
5					5
6					6
7					7
8					8
9					9
10					10
11	20				11
12					12

 # 6

(a)

	Lisa Ceja			
	Bank Reconciliation			
	January 31			
1				1
2				2
3				3
4				4
5				5
6				6
7				7
8				8
9				9
10				10
11				11
12				12

(b)

	Date	Account Titles	Debit	Credit	
1					1
2					2
3					3
4					4
5					5
6					6

 # 7

		No.	Amount
1			
2			
3			
4			
5			

 # 8 (a)

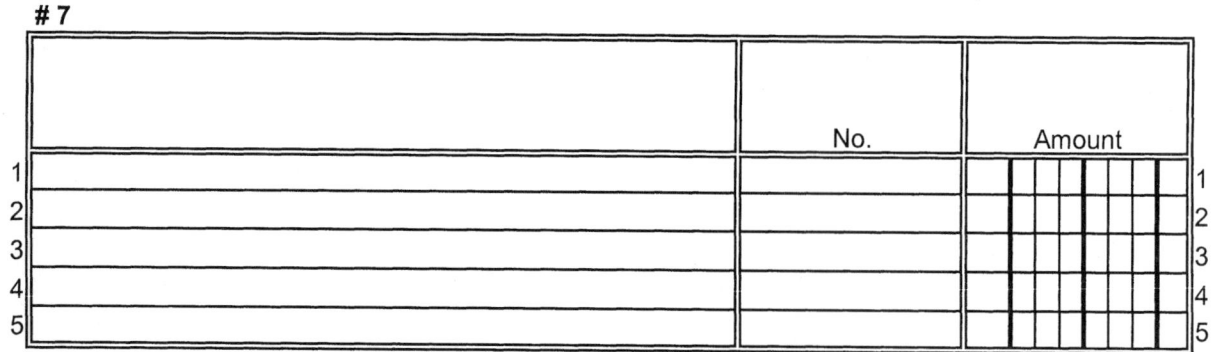

Worthy Video Company

Bank Reconciliation

July 31

1		
2		
3		
4		
5		
6		
7		
8		
9		
10		
11		
12		
13		
14		
15		
16		

(b)

	Date	Account Titles	Debit	Credit
1	July 31			
2				
3				
4				
5				
6	31			
7				
8				
9				
10				

(a)

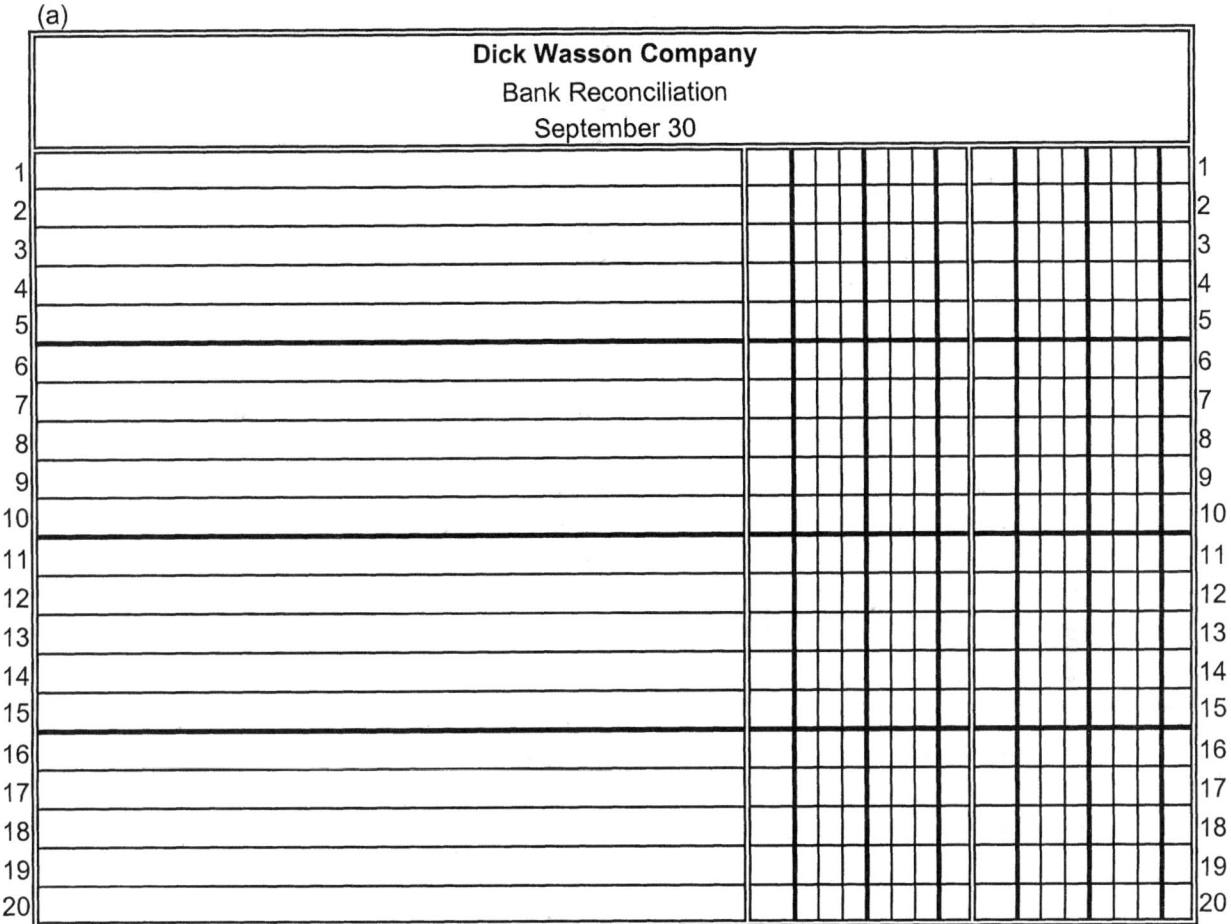

Dick Wasson Company		
Bank Reconciliation		
September 30		
1		
2		
3		
4		
5		
6		
7		
8		
9		
10		
11		
12		
13		
14		
15		
16		
17		
18		
19		
20		

(b)

	Date	Account Titles	Debit	Credit
1	Sept. 30			
2				
3				
4				
5				
6	30			
7				
8				
9	30			
10				
11				
12	30			
13				
14				
15				

	(a)									
1										1
2										2
3										3
4										4
5										5
6										6
7										7
8										8
9										9
10										10
11	(b)									11
12										12
13										13
14										14
15										15
16										16
17										17
18										18
19										19
20										20
21	(c)									21
22										22
23										23
24										24
25										25
26										26
27										27
28										28
29										29
30										30
31	(d)									31
32										32
33										33
34										34
35										35
36										36
37										37
38										38
39										39
40										40

(a)

	Principles	Application to Anita Theater	
1			1
2			2
3			3
4			4
5			5
6			6
7			7
8			8
9			9
10			10
11			11
12			12
13			13
14			14
15			15
16			16
17			17
18			18
19			19
20			20
21			21
22			22
23			23
24			24
25			25

26	(b)	26
27	(1)	27
28		28
29		29
30		30
31		31
32	(2)	32
33		33
34		34
35		35
36		36
37		37
38		38
39		39
40		40

(a)

General Journal

	Date	Account Titles and Explanation	Debit	Credit	
1	July 1				1
2					2
3					3
4	15				4
5					5
6					6
7					7
8					8
9					9
10					10
11	31				11
12					12
13					13
14					14
15					15
16					16
17	Aug. 15				17
18					18
19					19
20					20
21					21
22					22
23					23
24	16				24
25					25
26					26
27	31				27
28					28
29					29
30					30
31					31
32					32
33					33
34					34
35					35
36					36
37					37
38					38
39					39
40					40

(b)

Petty Cash

Date	Explanation	Ref.	Debit	Credit	Balance

(c)

(a)

Agricultural Genetics Company
Bank Reconciliation
May 31, 2005

1		
2		
3		
4		
5		
6		
7		
8		
9		
10		
11		
12		
13		
14		
15		
16		
17		

(b)   General Journal

	Date	Account Titles and Explanation	Debit	Credit
1	May 31			
2				
3				
4				
5				
6	31			
7				
8				
9	31			
10				
11				
12	31			
13				
14				
15	31			
16				
17				

(a)

Mooney Company
Bank Reconciliation
November 30, 2005

1		
2		
3		
4		
5		
6		
7		
8		
9		
10		
11		
12		
13		
14		
15		
16		
17		
18		
19		
20		
21		
22		

(b)   General Journal

	Date	Account Titles and Explanation	Debit	Credit
1	Nov. 30			
2				
3				
4				
5				
6	30			
7				
8				
9	30			
10				
11				
12	30			
13				
14				

Mario Tizani Company		
Bank Reconciliation		
August 31, 2005		

Computations:

Name

Section

Date

Mario Tizani Company

(b)

General Journal

	Date	Account Titles and Explanation	Debit	Credit	
1	Aug. 31				1
2					2
3					3
4					4
5	31				5
6					6
7					7
8	31				8
9					9
10					10
11	31				11
12					12
13					13
14					14
15					15
16					16
17					17
18					18
19					19
20					20

(a)

Stupendous Company		
Bank Reconciliation		
October 31, 2005		

(b)

(c)

Section _____

Date _____ Gore Office Supply Company

	Principles	Application to Cash Disbursements	
1			1
2			2
3			3
4			4
5			5
6			6
7			7
8			8
9			9
10			10
11			11
12			12
13			13
14			14
15			15
16			16
17			17
18			18
19			19
20			20
21			21
22			22
23			23
24			24
25			25
26			26
27			27
28			28
29			29
30			30
31			31
32			32
33			33
34			34
35			35
36			36
37			37
38			38
39			39
40			40

(a)

General Journal

	Date	Account Titles and Explanation	Debit	Credit	
1	July 1				1
2					2
3					3
4	15				4
5					5
6					6
7					7
8					8
9					9
10					10
11	31				11
12					12
13					13
14					14
15					15
16					16
17	Aug. 15				17
18					18
19					19
20					20
21					21
22					22
23					23
24	16				24
25					25
26					26
27	31				27
28					28
29					29
30					30
31					31
32					32
33					33
34					34
35					35
36					36
37					37
38					38
39					39
40					40

(b)

Petty Cash

Date	Explanation	Ref.	Debit	Credit	Balance

(c)

1		1
2		2
3		3
4		4
5		5
6		6
7		7
8		8
9		9
10		10
11		11
12		12
13		13
14		14
15		15

(a)

Terry Duffy Company
Bank Reconciliation
May 31, 2005

(b)

General Journal

	Date	Account Titles and Explanation	Debit	Credit
1	May 31			
6	31			
9	31			
12	31			
15	31			

(a)

Heinisch Company

Bank Reconciliation

December 31, 2005

1		
2		
3		
4		
5		
6		
7		
8		
9		
10		
11		
12		
13		
14		
15		
16		
17		
18		
19		
20		
21		
22		

(b)

General Journal

	Date	Account Titles and Explanation	Debit	Credit
1	Dec. 31			
2				
3				
4				
5				
6	31			
7				
8				
9	31			
10				
11				
12	31			
13				
14				

Cell Ten Company				
Bank Reconciliation				
July 31, 2005				

	1
	2
	3
	4
	5
	6
	7
	8
	9
	10
	11
	12
	13
	14
	15
	16
	17
	18
	19
	20

Computations:

(b)

General Journal

	Date	Account Titles and Explanation	Debit	Credit	
1	July 31				1
2					2
3					3
4					4
5	31				5
6					6
7					7
8	31				8
9					9
10					10
11					11
12					12
13					13
14					14
15					15
16					16
17					17
18					18
19					19
20					20

Name

Section

Date

	1		1
	2		2
	3		3
	4		4
	5		5
	6		6
	7		7
	8		8
	9		9
	10		10
	11		11
	12		12
	13		13
	14		14
	15		15
	16		16
	17		17
	18		18
	19		19
	20		20
	21		21
	22		22
	23		23
	24		24
	25		25
	26		26
	27		27
	28		28
	29		29
	30		30
	31		31
	32		32
	33		33
	34		34
	35		35
	36		36
	37		37
	38		38
	39		39
	40		40

1	1
2	2
3	3
4	4
5	5
6	6
7	7
8	8
9	9
10	10
11	11
12	12
13	13
14	14
15	15
16	16
17	17
18	18
19	19
20	20
21	21
22	22
23	23
24	24
25	25
26	26
27	27
28	28
29	29
30	30
31	31
32	32
33	33
34	34
35	35
36	36
37	37
38	38
39	39
40	40

(a)

(b)

(c)

(d)

Section

(a) (In millions)	PepsiCo	Coca-Cola
(1) Cash and cash equivalents at year-end 2002		
(2) Increase/decrease in cash and cash equivalents from 2001 to 2002		
(3) Cash provided by operating activities during fiscal year 2002		

(b)

(a)

(b)

(c)

(d)

(e)

(a)

(b)

(c)

(d)

(a)

(b)

(c)

Name

Section

Date

Stillwater Company

(a)
Weaknesses

(b)
Suggested Improvement

1
2
3
4
5
6
7
8
9
10
11
12
13
14
15
16
17
18
19
20
21
22
23
24
25
26
27

Name

Section

Date

Stillwater Company

(a)
Weaknesses

(b)
Suggested Improvement

1	
2	
3	
4	
5	
6	
7	
8	
9	
10	
11	
12	
13	
14	
15	
16	
17	
18	
19	
20	
21	
22	
23	
24	

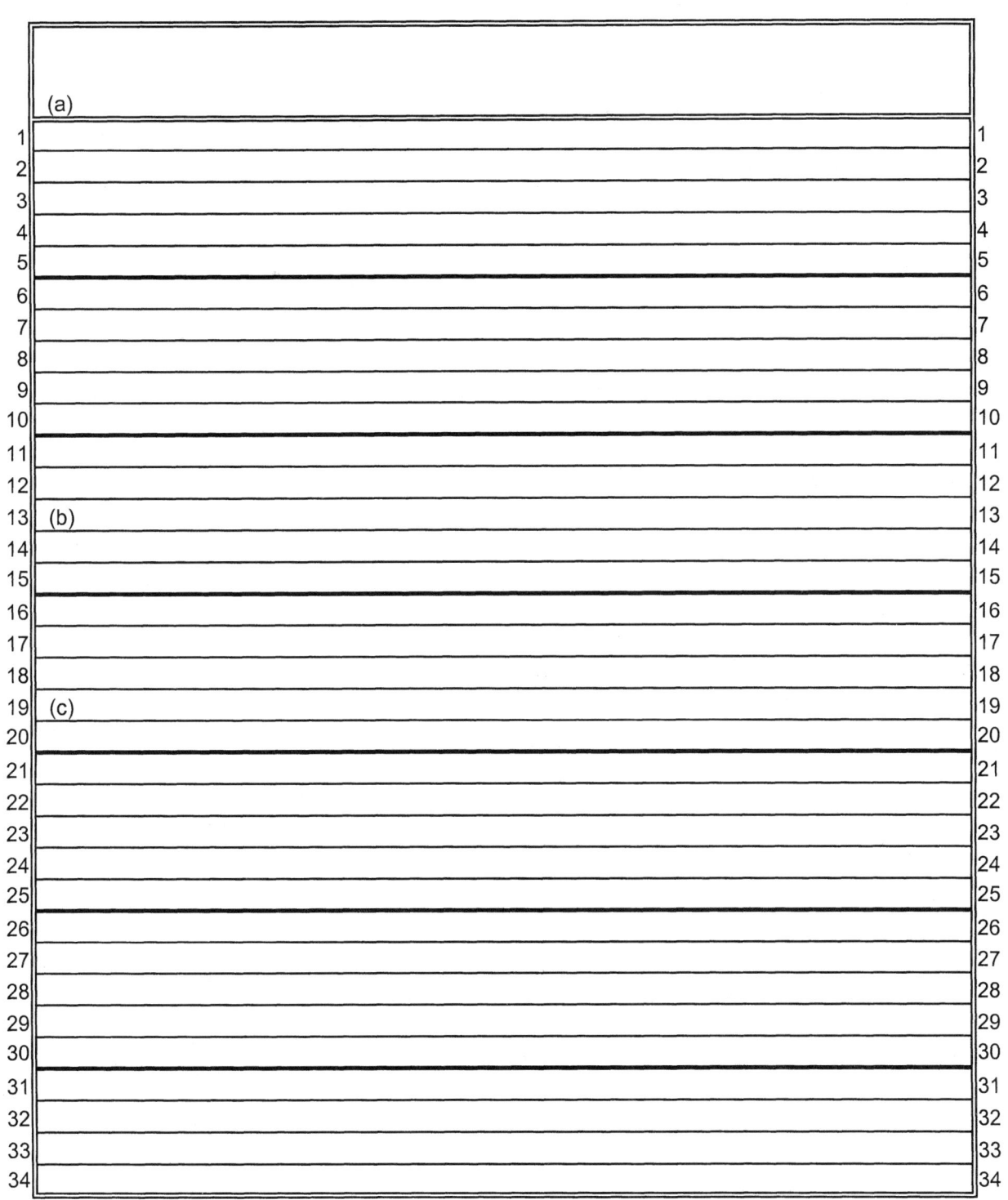

(a)

(b)

(c)

1	1
2	2
3	3
4	4
5	5
6	6
7	7
8	8
9	9
10	10
11	11
12	12
13	13
14	14
15	15
16	16
17	17
18	18
19	19
20	20
21	21
22	22
23	23
24	24
25	25
26	26
27	27
28	28
29	29
30	30
31	31
32	32
33	33
34	34

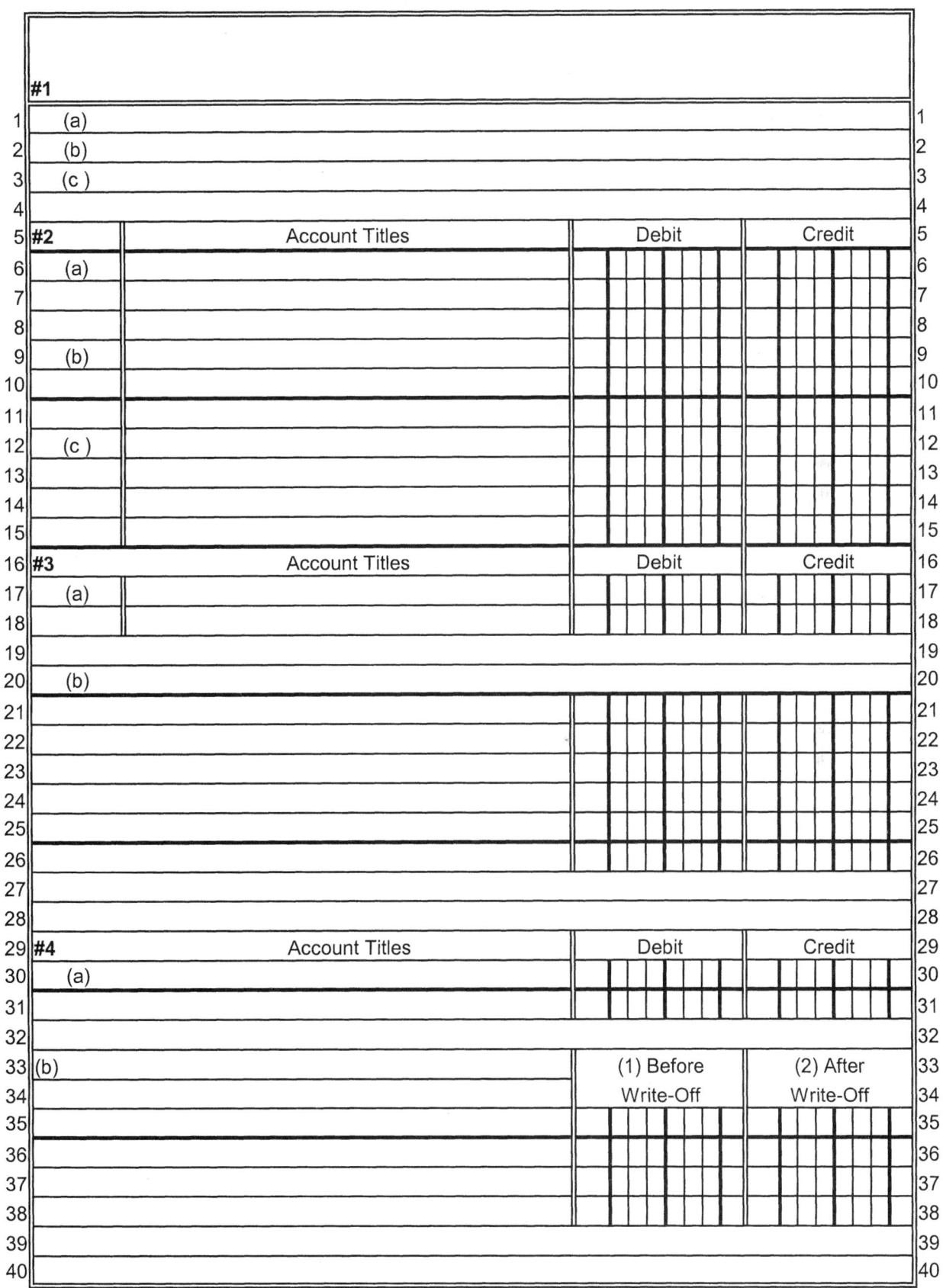

#1			
(a)			
(b)			
(c)			

#2	Account Titles	Debit	Credit
(a)			
(b)			
(c)			

#3	Account Titles	Debit	Credit
(a)			
(b)			

#4	Account Titles	Debit	Credit
(a)			

(b)		(1) Before Write-Off	(2) After Write-Off

#5	Account Titles	Debit	Credit
1			
2			
3			
4			
5			
6			
#6			
7			
8			
9			
10			
#7			
(a)			
13			
14			
15			
(b)			
17			

#8		Interest	Maturity Date
(a)			
(b)			
(c)			

#9		Maturity Date	Annual Interest Rate	Total Interest
(a)				
(b)				
(c)				

#10	Account Titles	Debit	Credit
(a)			
32			
33			
34			
(b)			
36			
37			
38			
39			
40			

#11	Account Titles	Debit	Credit	
1	Date				1
2	Jan. 10				2
3					3
4					4
5					5
6	Feb. 9				6
7					7
8					8
9					9
10					10

11	#12	11
12	Accounts receivable turnover ratio:	12
13		13
14		14
15		15
16	Average collection period for accounts receivable:	16
17		17
18		18
19		19
20		20
21		21
22		22
23		23
24		24
25		25
26		26
27		27
28		28
29		29
30		30
31		31
32		32
33		33
34		34
35		35
36		36
37		37
38		38
39		39
40		40

#1

	Date	Account Titles	Debit	Credit	
1	(a)				1
2	Jan. 6				2
3					3
4					4
5	16				5
6					6
7					7
8					8
9					9
10	(b)				10
11	Jan. 10				11
12					12
13					13
14	Feb. 12				14
15					15
16					16
17	Mar. 10				17
18					18
19					19
20					20
21	**#2**				21
22	(a) (1)				22
23	Dec. 31				23
24					24
25					25
26	(b) (1)				26
27	Dec. 31				27
28					28
29					29
30	(2)				30
31	Dec. 31				31
32					32
33					33
34	(c) (1)				34
35	Dec. 31				35
36					36
37					37
38	(2)				38
39	Dec. 31				39
40					40

#3

(a)

Accounts Receivable	Amount	%	Estimated Uncollectible
1 - 30 days			
30 - 60 days			
60 - 90 days			
Over 90 days			

(b)

Date	Account Titles	Debit	Credit
Mar. 31			

#4

Date	Account Titles	Debit	Credit
2005			
Dec. 31			
2006			
May 11			
2006			
Jan. 12			

#5

	Date	Account Titles	Debit	Credit	
1	(a)				1
2	Mar. 3				2
3					3
4					4
5					5
6					6
7					7
8	(b)				8
9	May 10				9
10					10
11					11
12					12
13					13
14					14
15					15
16	**#6**				16
17	(a)				17
18	Apr. 2				18
19					19
20					20
21	May 3				21
22					22
23					23
24	Jun. 1				24
25					25
26					26
27	(b)				27
28	July 4				28
29					29
30					30
31					31
32					32
33	10				33
34					34
35					35
36					36
37					37
38					38
39					39
40					40

#7

	Date	Account Titles	Debit	Credit	
1	(a)				1
2	Jan. 15				2
3					3
4					4
5	20				5
6					6
7					7
8					8
9	30				9
10					10
11					11
12	Feb. 10				12
13					13
14					14
15	15				15
16					16
17					17
18					18
19	(b)				19
20					20
21					21

#8

	Date	Account Titles	Debit	Credit	
22					22
23	Date	Account Titles	Debit	Credit	23
24	(a)	2005			24
25	Nov. 1				25
26					26
27					27
28	Dec. 11				28
29					29
30					30
31	16				31
32					32
33					33
34	31				34
35					35
36					36
37	(b)	2006			37
38	Nov. 1				38
39					39
40					40
41					41

#9

	Date	Account Titles	Debit	Credit	
1		2005			1
2	May 1				2
3					3
4					4
5	Dec. 31				5
6					6
7					7
8	31				8
9					9
10					10
11					11
12		2006			12
13	May 1				13
14					14
15					15
16					16
17					17
18					18
19					19
20					20
21	**#10**				21
22	(a)				22
23	May 2				23
24					24
25					25
26	(b)				26
27	Nov. 2				27
28					28
29					29
30					30
31	(c)				31
32	Nov. 2				32
33					33
34					34
35					35
36					36
37					37
38					38
39					39
40					40

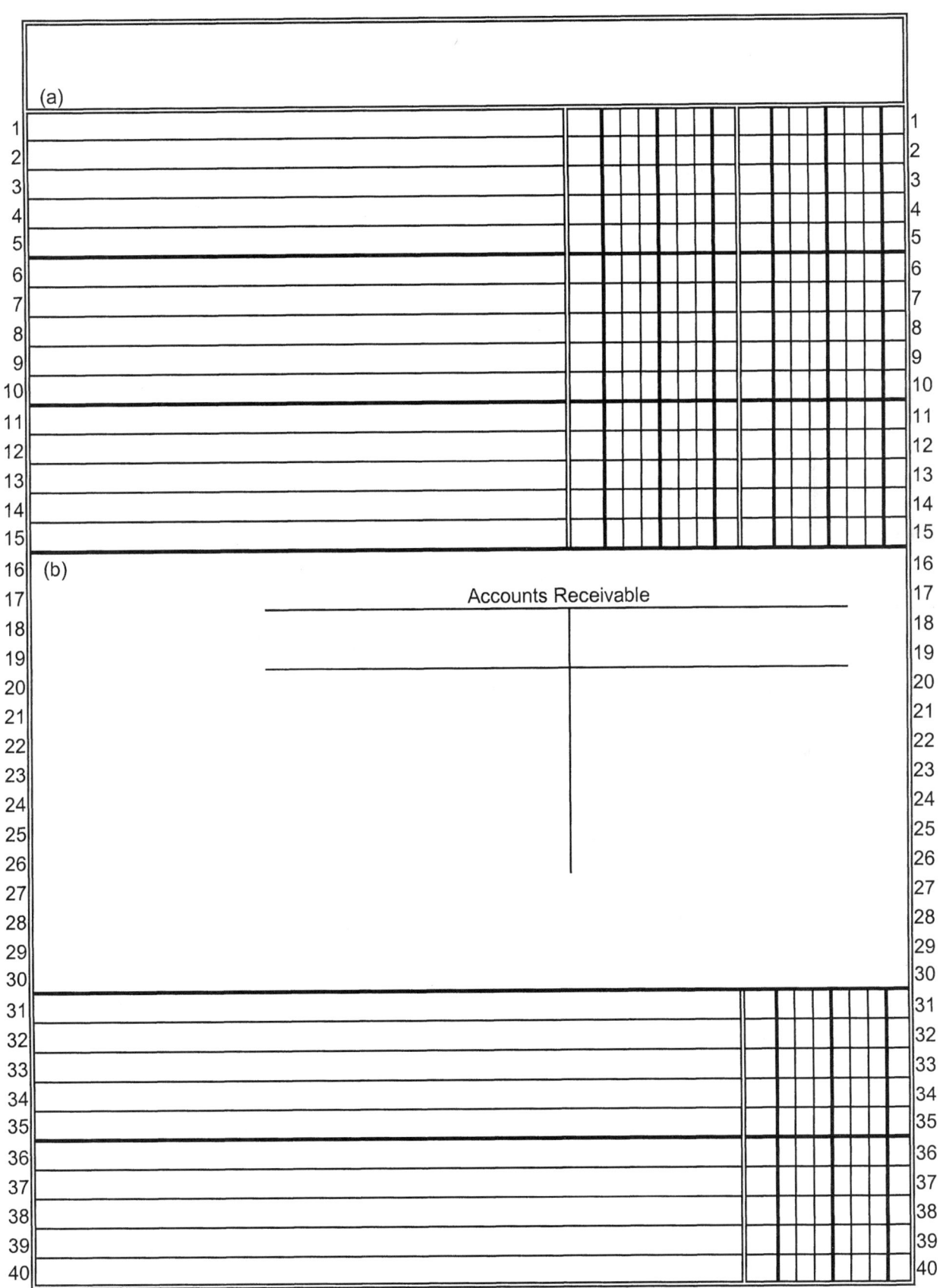

(a)

(b)

Accounts Receivable

		Account Titles and Explanation	Debit	Credit	
1	1.				1
2					2
3					3
4	2.				4
5					5
6					6
7	3.				7
8					8
9					9
10	4.				10
11					11
12					12
13	5.				13
14					14
15					15
16					16
17					17
18					18
19					19
20					20

(b)

ACCOUNTS RECEIVABLE	ALLOWANCE FOR DOUBTFUL ACCOUNTS

(c)

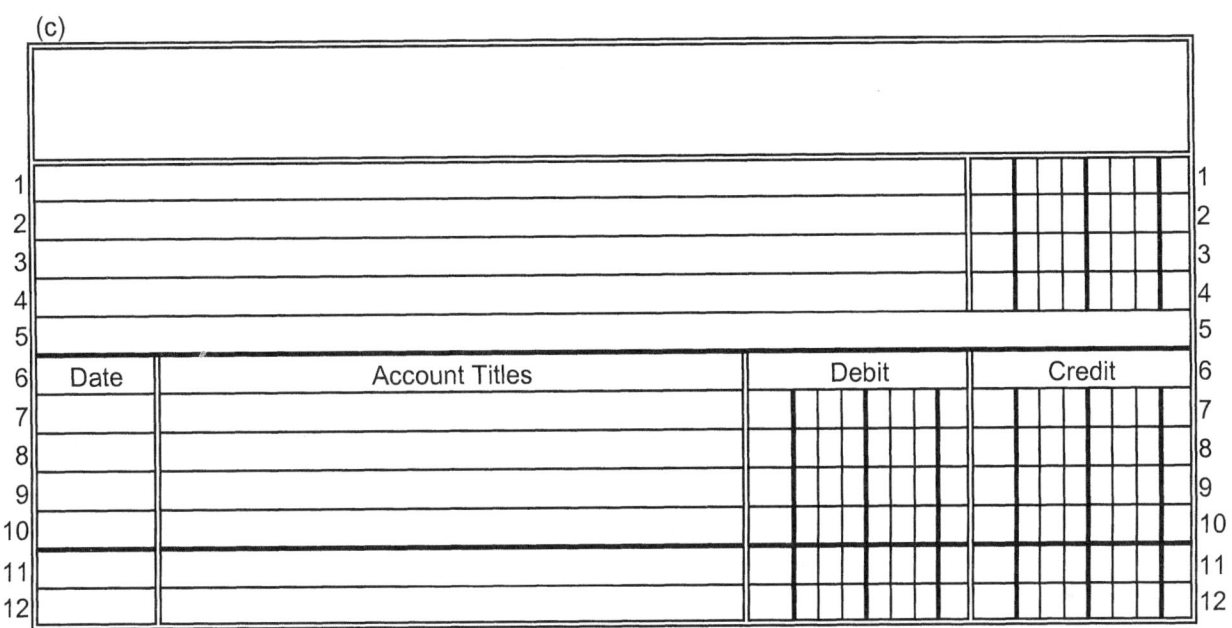

	Date	Account Titles	Debit	Credit	
1					1
2					2
3					3
4					4
5					5
6					6
7					7
8					8
9					9
10					10
11					11
12					12

(d)

(a)

1
2
3
4
5

(b)

6
7
8
9
10

(c)

11
12
13
14
15

(d)

16
17
18
19
20

(e)

21
22
23
24
25
26
27
28
29
30
31
32
33
34
35
36
37
38
39
40

(a), (b), and (c)   General Journal

	Date	Account Titles and Explanation	Debit	Credit	
1	(a)				1
2	Dec. 31				2
3					3
4					4
5					5
6	(b)	(1) 2006			6
7	Mar. 1				7
8					8
9					9
10					10
11		(2)			11
12	May 1				12
13					13
14					14
15	1				15
16					16
17					17
18					18
19	(c)	2006			19
20	Dec. 31				20
21					21
22					22

(a) & (b)

Bad Debt Expense

	Date	Explanation	Ref.	Debit	Credit	Balance	
1							1
2							2
3							3

Allowance for Doubtful Accounts

	Date	Explanation	Ref.	Debit	Credit	Balance	
1							1
2							2
3							3
4							4
5							5
6							6
7							7

Problem 9-4A

Aging Accounts Receivable

(a)

	Total	Number of Days Outstanding				
		0 - 30	31 - 60	61 - 90	91 - 120	Over 120
1 Accounts receivable	$ 260000	$ 100000	$ 60000	$ 50000	$ 300000	$ 200000
2						
3 % uncollectible		1%	5%	7.50%	10%	12%
4						
5 Estimated Bad Debts						

	Date	Account Titles	Debit	Credit	
1	(b)				1
2					2
3					3
4	(c)				4
5					5
6					6
7	(d)				7
8					8
9					9
10					10
11					11
12					12
13					13
14					14
15					15

(e)

1		1
2		2
3		3
4		4
5		5

General Journal

	Date	Account Titles	Debit	Credit	
1	(a) (1)				1
2	Dec. 31				2
3					3
4					4
5					5
6	(2)				6
7	Dec. 31				7
8					8
9					9
10					10
11	(b) (1)				11
12	Dec. 31				12
13					13
14					14
15					15
16	(2)				16
17	Dec. 31				17
18					18
19					19
20	(c)				20
21					21
22					22
23					23
24					24
25	(d)				25
26					26
27					27
28					28
29					29
30					30
31	(e)				31
32	(1)				32
33					33
34					34
35	(2)				35
36					36
37					37

(a)   General Journal

	Date	Account Titles and Explanation	Debit	Credit	
1	July 5				1
2					2
3					3
4	14				4
5					5
6					6
7					7
8	14				8
9					9
10					10
11	15				11
12					12
13					13
14					14
15					15
16	25				16
17					17
18					18
19					19
20					20
21	31				21
22					22
23					23
24					24
25					25
26					26
27					27
28					28
29					29
30					30
31					31
32					32
33					33
34					34
35					35
36					36
37					37
38					38
39					39
40					40

(b)

Notes Receivable

	Date	Explanation	Ref.	Debit	Credit	Balance	
1	July 1	Balance	√			3 0 0 0 0	1
2							2
3							3
4							4

Accounts Receivable

	Date	Explanation	Ref.	Debit	Credit	Balance	
1							1
2							2
3							3
4							4

Interest Receivable

	Date	Explanation	Ref.	Debit	Credit	Balance	
1	July 1	Balance	√			2 4 0	1
2							2
3							3
4							4
5							5

(c)

	Assets		
1			1
2	Current Assets		2
3			3
4			4
5			5
6			6
7			7
8			8

General Journal

	Date	Account Titles and Explanation	Debit	Credit	
1	Jan. 5				1
2					2
3					3
4	Feb. 2				4
5					5
6					6
7	12				7
8					8
9					9
10	26				10
11					11
12					12
13	Apr. 5				13
14					14
15					15
16	12				16
17					17
18					18
19					19
20	June 2				20
21					21
22					22
23					23
24	July 5				24
25					25
26					26
27					27
28	15				28
29					29
30					30
31	Oct. 15				31
32					32
33					33
34					34
35					35
36					36
37					37
38					38
39					39
40					40

		Account Titles and Explanation	Debit	Credit	
1	1.				1
2					2
3					3
4	2.				4
5					5
6					6
7	3.				7
8					8
9					9
10	4.				10
11					11
12					12
13	5.				13
14					14
15					15
16					16
17					17
18					18
19					19
20					20

(b)

ACCOUNTS RECEIVABLE	ALLOWANCE FOR DOUBTFUL ACCOUNTS

(c)

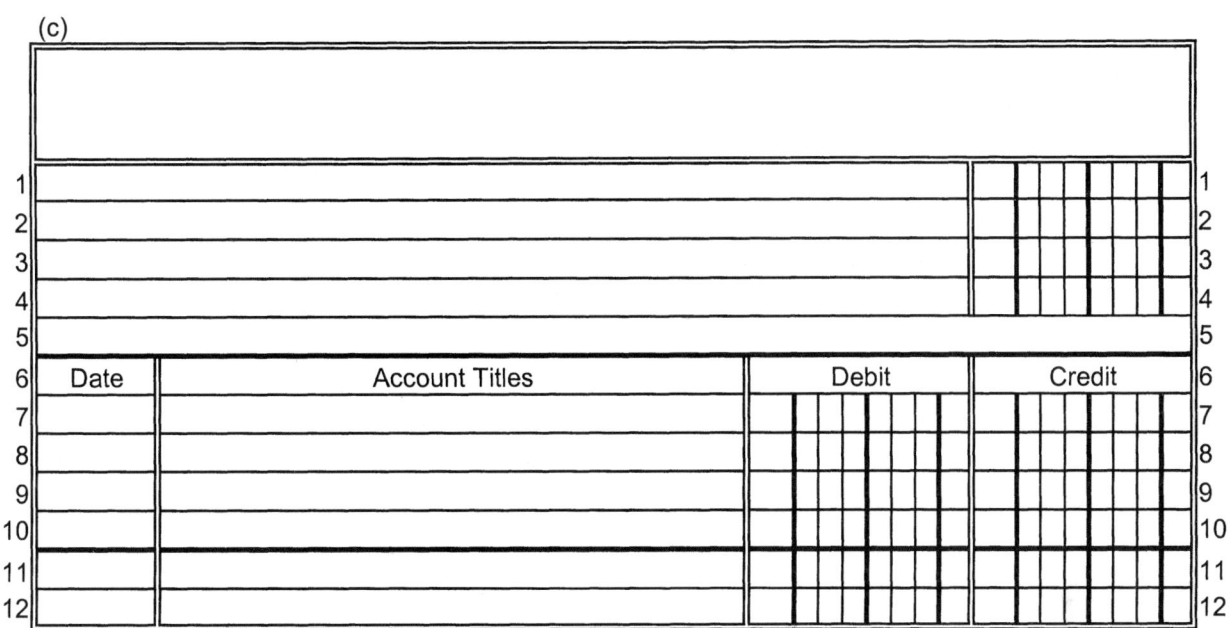

Date	Account Titles	Debit	Credit

(d)

1	(a)
2	
3	
4	
5	
6	(b)
7	
8	
9	
10	
11	(c)
12	
13	
14	
15	
16	(d)
17	
18	
19	
20	
21	(e)
22	
23	
24	
25	
26	
27	
28	
29	
30	
31	
32	
33	
34	
35	
36	
37	
38	
39	
40	

(a), (b), and (c)   General Journal

	Date	Account Titles and Explanation	Debit	Credit	
1	(a)				1
2	Dec. 31				2
3					3
4					4
5					5
6	(b)	(1) 2006			6
7	Mar. 31				7
8					8
9					9
10					10
11		(2)			11
12	May 31				12
13					13
14					14
15	31				15
16					16
17					17
18					18
19	(c)	2006			19
20	Dec. 31				20
21					21
22					22

(a) & (b)

Bad Debt Expense

	Date	Explanation	Ref.	Debit	Credit	Balance	
1							1
2							2
3							3

Allowance for Doubtful Accounts

	Date	Explanation	Ref.	Debit	Credit	Balance	
1							1
2							2
3							3
4							4
5							5
6							6
7							7

(a)

| | Total | Number of Days Outstanding | | | | |
		0 - 30	31 - 60	61 - 90	91 - 120	Over 120
1 Accounts receivable	$ 375000	$ 220000	$ 90000	$ 40000	$ 100000	$ 150000
2						
3 % uncollectible		1%	4%	5%	6%	10%
4						
5 Estimated Bad Debts						

	Date	Account Titles	Debit	Credit	
1	(b)				1
2					2
3					3
4	(c)				4
5					5
6					6
7	(d)				7
8					8
9					9
10					10
11					11
12					12
13					13
14					14
15					15

(e)

1		1
2		2
3		3
4		4
5		5

	Date	Account Titles	Debit	Credit	
1	(a)				1
2					2
3					3
4					4
5					5
6	(b) (1)				6
7	Dec. 31				7
8					8
9					9
10	(2)				10
11	Dec. 31				11
12					12
13					13
14					14
15	(c) (1)				15
16	Dec. 31				16
17					17
18					18
19					19
20	(2)				20
21	Dec. 31				21
22					22
23					23
24					24
25					25
26	(d)				26
27					27
28					28
29					29
30					30
31	(e)				31
32					32
33					33
34					34
35					35
36	(f)				36
37					37
38					38
39					39
40					40

(a)   General Journal

	Date	Account Titles and Explanation	Debit	Credit	
1	Oct. 7				1
2					2
3					3
4	12				4
5					5
6					6
7					7
8	15				8
9					9
10					10
11	15				11
12					12
13					13
14					14
15					15
16	24				16
17					17
18					18
19					19
20					20
21	31				21
22					22
23					23
24					24
25					25
26					26
27					27
28					28
29					29
30					30
31					31
32					32
33					33
34					34
35					35
36					36
37					37
38					38
39					39
40					40

(b)

Notes Receivable

	Date	Explanation	Ref.	Debit	Credit	Balance	
1	Oct 1	Balance	√			2 9 0 0 0	1
2							2
3							3
4							4

Accounts Receivable

	Date	Explanation	Ref.	Debit	Credit	Balance	
1							1
2							2
3							3
4							4

Interest Receivable

	Date	Explanation	Ref.	Debit	Credit	Balance	
1	Oct 1	Balance	√			2 1 0	1
2							2
3							3
4							4
5							5

(c)

	Assets		
1	Assets		1
2	Current Assets		2
3			3
4			4
5			5
6			6
7			7
8			8

General Journal

	Date	Account Titles and Explanation	Debit	Credit	
1	Jan. 5				1
2					2
3					3
4	20				4
5					5
6					6
7					7
8	Feb. 18				8
9					9
10					10
11	Apr. 20				11
12					12
13					13
14					14
15	30				15
16					16
17					17
18					18
19	May 25				19
20					20
21					21
22	Aug. 18				22
23					23
24					24
25					25
26	25				26
27					27
28					28
29					29
30	Sept. 1				30
31					31
32					32
33					33
34					34
35					35
36					36
37					37
38					38
39					39
40					40

(a)

CAF Company Accounts Receivable Aging Schedule May 31, 2005				
	Proportion of Total %	Amount in Category	Probability of Non-Collection %	Estimated Uncollectible Amount
Not yet due				
Less than 30 days past due				
30 to 60 days past due				
61 to 120 days past due				
121 to 180 days past due				
Over 180 days past due				
Totals				

CAF Company Analysis of Allowance for Doubtful Accounts May 31, 2005		
(b)		
Account Titles	Debit	Credit

(c)

	1. Steps to Improve the Accounts Receivable Situation	2. Risks and Costs Involved	
1			1
2			2
3			3
4			4
5			5
6			6
7			7
8			8
9			9
10			10
11			11
12			12
13			13
14			14
15			15
16			16
17			17
18			18
19			19
20			20
21			21
22			22
23			23
24			24
25			25
26			26
27			27
28			28
29			29
30			30
31			31
32			32
33			33
34			34
35			35
36			36
37			37
38			38
39			39
40			40

(a)	PepsiCo	Coca-Cola
(1) Accounts receivable turnover ratio		
(2) Average collection period		

(b)

Name

Section

Date

(a)

(b)

(c)

Name

Section

Date

(a)

1		1
2		2
3		3
4		4
5		5
6		6
7		7
8		8
9		9
10		10
11		11
12		12
13		13
14		14
15		15
16		16
17		17
18		18
19		19
20		20
21		21
22		22
23		23
24		24
25		25
26		26
27		27
28		28
29		29
30		30
31		31
32		32
33		33
34		34
35		35

(a) (Continued)

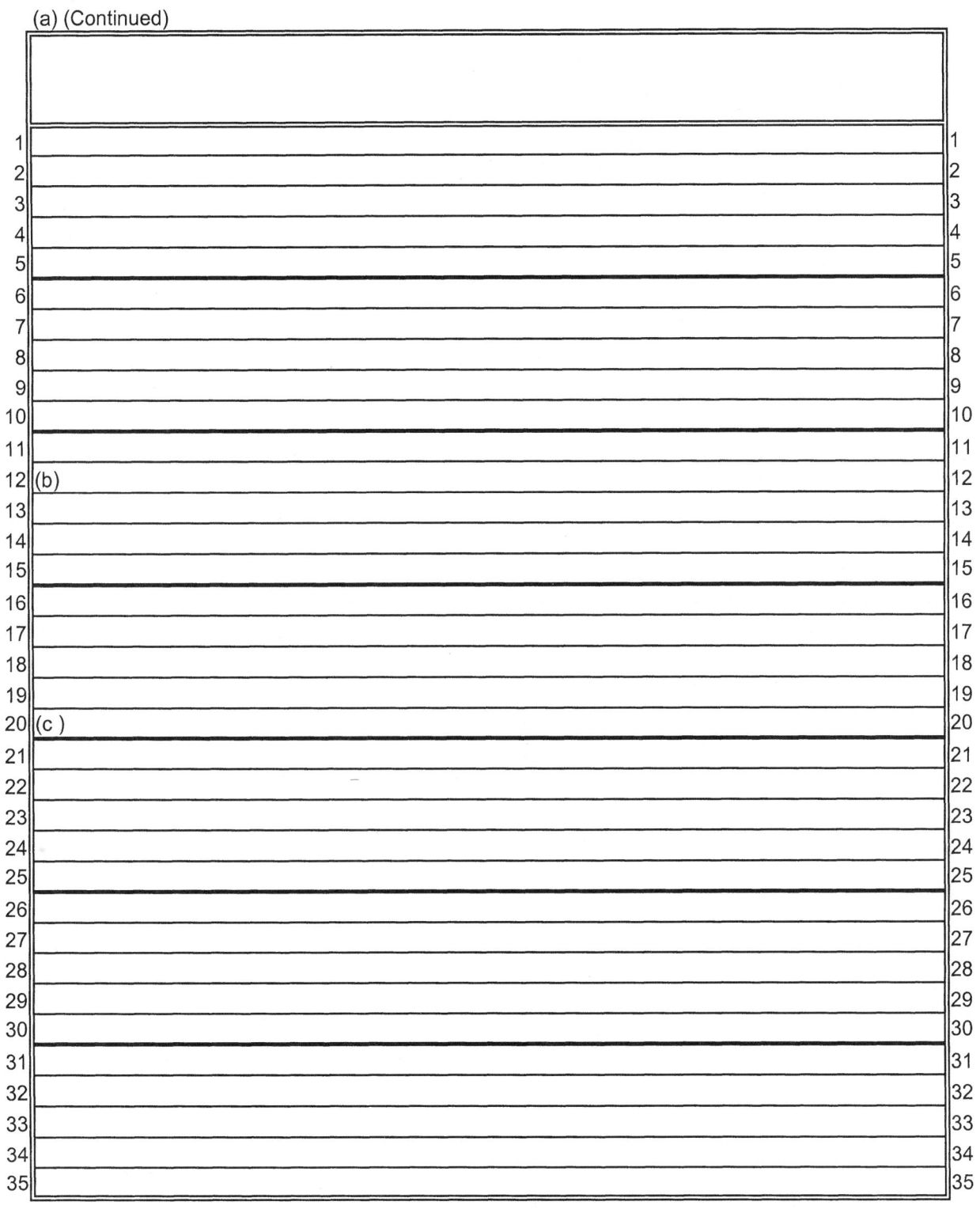

(b)

(c)

(a)	2005	2004	2003
1 Net credit sales			
2			
3 Credit and collection expenses			
4 Collection agency fees			
5 Salary of accounts receivable clerk			
6 Uncollectible accounts			
7 Billing and mailing costs			
8 Credit investigation fees			
9			
10 Total			
11			
12			
13 Total expenses as a percentage			
14 of net credit sales			
15			
16 (b) Average accounts receivable			
17			
18 Investment earnings			
19			
20 Total credit and collection			
21 expenses per above			
22 Add: Investment earnings			
23 Net credit and collection			
24 expenses			
25			
26 Net expenses as a percentage			
27 of net credit sales			
28			
29 (c)			
30			
31			
32			
33			
34			
35			
36			
37			
38			
39			
40			

Name

Section

Date

1	1
2	2
3	3
4	4
5	5
6	6
7	7
8	8
9	9
10	10
11	11
12	12
13	13
14	14
15	15
16	16
17	17
18	18
19	19
20	20
21	21
22	22
23	23
24	24
25	25
26	26
27	27
28	28
29	29
30	30
31	31
32	32
33	33
34	34
35	35
36	36
37	37
38	38
39	39
40	40

1	(a)	1
2		2
3		3
4		4
5		5
6	(b)	6
7		7
8		8
9		9
10		10
11		11
12		12
13		13
14		14
15		15
16	(c)	16
17		17
18		18
19		19
20		20
21		21
22		22
23		23
24		24
25		25
26		26
27		27
28		28
29		29
30		30
31		31
32		32
33		33
34		34
35		35
36		36
37		37
38		38
39		39
40		40

#1

#2

#3

#4

#5

	Year		Book Value	X	Rate	=	Depreciation
	1						
	2						

#6

Depreciation cost per unit:

	Year				
	1				
	2				

#7

	1	2	3	4	5

#8

	Account Titles	Debit	Credit	
(a)				
(b)				

Calculations:

#9

	Account Titles	Debit	Credit	
(a)				
(b)				

Calculations:

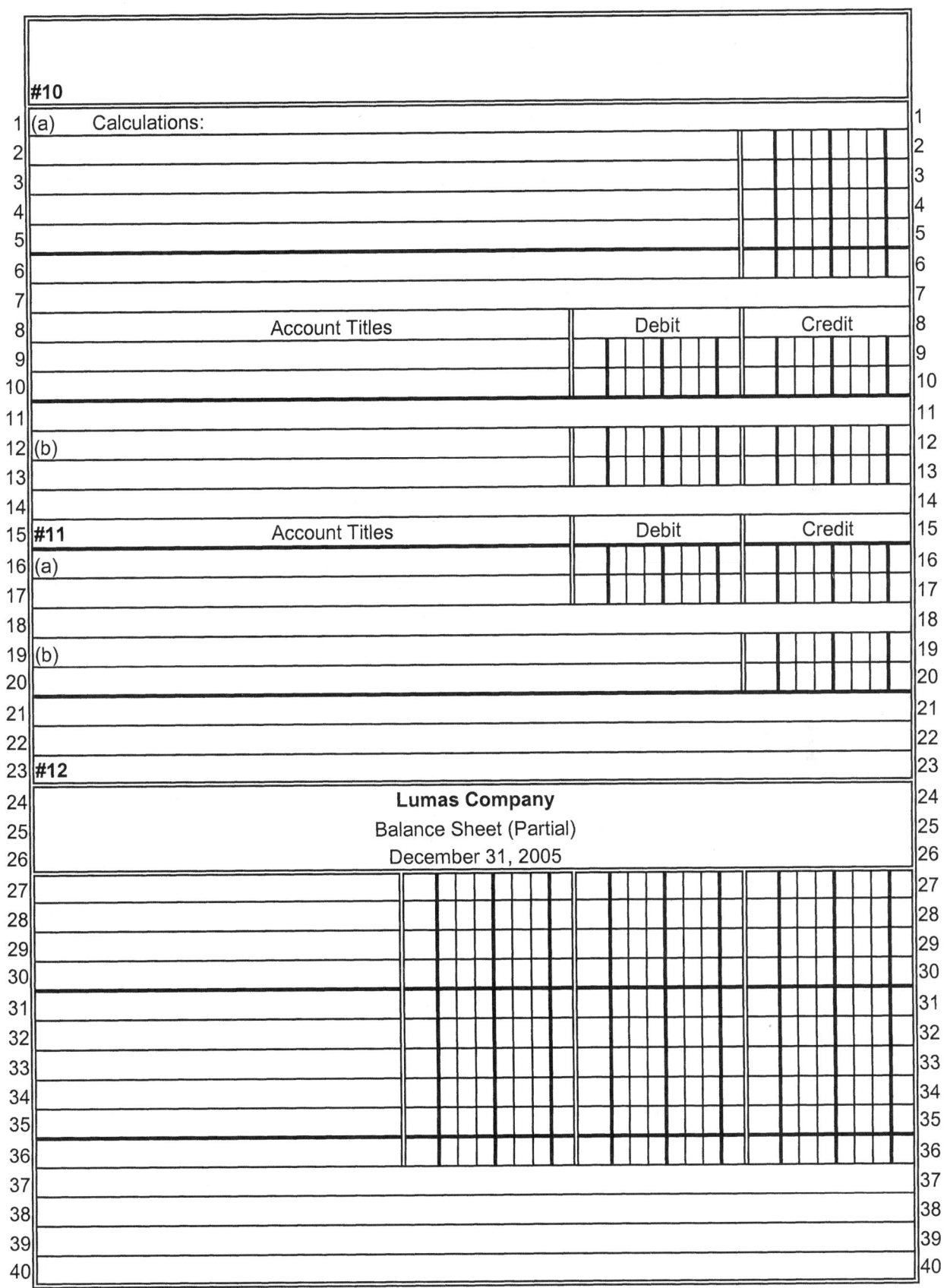

#10

(a)   Calculations:

Account Titles	Debit	Credit

(b)

#11

Account Titles	Debit	Credit

(a)

(b)

#12

Lumas Company

Balance Sheet (Partial)

December 31, 2005

#13

	#14	Account Titles	Debit	Credit	
6					6
7					7
8					8
9					9
10					10

Calculations:

	#15	Account Titles	Debit	Credit	
25					25
26					26
27					27
28					28

Calculations:

#1

1 (a)

2

3

4

5

6

7 (b)

8   1.

9   2.

10   3.

11   4.

12   5.

13   6.

14   7.

15   8.

16

17

18

19

20 **#2**

21 (a)

22

23

24

25

26

27

28 (b)

29

30

31

32

33

34

35

36

37

38

39

40

#3

(a)

	(b) Year	Computation					Annual Depreciation Expense	End of Year	
		Units of Activity	X	Depreciation Cost/Unit	=			Accumulated Depreciation	Book Value
	2005								
	2006								
	2007								
	2008								

#4

(a)   Straight-line method:

(b)   Units-of-activity method:

(c)   Declining-balance method:

#5	Type of Asset	Building	Warehouse	
1	(a)			1
2				2
3				3
4				4
5				5
6				6
7				7
8				8
9				9
10	(b)			10

	Date	Account Titles	Debit	Credit	
11					11
12	Dec. 31				12
13					13
14					14
15					15

#6					16

	Date	Account Titles	Debit	Credit	
17					17
18	Jan. 1				18
19					19
20					20
21	June 30				21
22					22
23					23
24	30				24
25					25
26					26
27					27
28					28
29	Dec. 31				29
30					30
31					31
32	31				32
33					33
34					34
35					35
36					36
37					37
38					38
39					39
40					40

#7

	Date	Account Titles	Debit	Credit	
1	(a)				1
2	Dec. 31				2
3					3
4					4
5	Calculations				5
6					6
7					7
8					8
9					9
10	(b)				10
11					11
12					12

#8

	Date	Account Titles	Debit	Credit	
13					13
14	Date	Account Titles	Debit	Credit	14
15	Dec. 31				15
16					16
17					17

#9

	Date	Account Titles	Debit	Credit	
18					18
19	Date	Account Titles	Debit	Credit	19
20	1/2/05				20
21					21
22					22
23	4/1/05				23
24					24
25					25
26	7/1/05				26
27					27
28					28
29	9/1/05				29
30					30
31					31
32	12/31/05				32
33					33
34					34
35					35
36					36
37	Ending balances:				37
38	Patent				38
39	Goodwill				39
40	Franchise				40
41	R&D expense				41

#10

1			1
2	Asset turnover ratio		2
3			3
4			4

#11

	Account Titles	Debit	Credit	
7	(a)			7
8				8
9				9
10				10
11				11
12				12
13	Calculations:			13
14				14
15				15
16				16
17				17
18				18
19				19
20				20
21				21
22				22
23				23
24	(b)			24
25				25
26				26
27				27
28				28
29	Calculations:			29
30				30
31				31
32				32
33				33
34				34
35				35
36				36
37				37
38				38
39				39
40				40

	Date	Account Titles	Debit	Credit	
1		Astro Company:			1
2					2
3					3
4					4
5					5
6					6
7		Cost of equipment:			7
8					8
9					9
10					10
11					11
12					12
13					13
14					14
15					15
16					16
17		Jay Company:			17
18					18
19					19
20					20
21					21
22					22
23					23
24		Computation of loss:			24
25					25
26					26
27					27
28					28
29		Cost of equipment:			29
30					30
31					31
32					32
33					33
34					34
35					35
36					36
37					37
38					38
39					39
40					40

	Date	Account Titles	Debit	Credit	
1	(a)				1
2					2
3					3
4					4
5					5
6					6
7	Calculations:				7
8					8
9					9
10					10
11					11
12					12
13					13
14	(b)				14
15					15
16					16
17					17
18					18
19	Calculations:				19
20					20
21					21
22					22
23					23
24					24
25					25
26					26
27					27
28					28
29					29
30					30
31					31
32					32
33					33
34					34
35					35
36					36
37					37
38					38
39					39
40					40

	Item	Land	Building	Other Accounts	
				Amount	Account Titles
1					
2	1.				
3					
4	2.				
5					
6	3.				
7					
8	4.				
9					
10	5.				
11					
12	6.				
13					
14	7.				
15					
16	8.				
17					
18	9.				
19					
20	10.				
21					
22					
23					
24					
25					

	Year	Computation	Cumulative, 12/31	
1 (a)		MACHINE 1		1
2				2
3	2002			3
4				4
5	2003			5
6				6
7	2004			7
8				8
9	2005			9
10				10
11				11
12		MACHINE 2		12
13				13
14	2003			14
15				15
16	2004			16
17				17
18	2005			18
19				19
20				20
21		MACHINE 3		21
22				22
23	2005			23
24				24
25				25
26				26
27				27
28				28
29				29
30 (b)	Year	Depreciation Computation	Expense	30
31		MACHINE 2		31
32	(1) 2003			32
33				33
34	(2) 2004			34
35				35
36				36
37				37
38				38
39				39
40				40

Total cost of machinery:

(a) (1)

Account Titles	Debit	Credit

Annual depreciation:

(2)

Account Titles	Debit	Credit

(b) (1)

(2)

Year	Book Value at Beginning of Year	DDB Rate	Annual Depreciation Expense	Accumulated Depreciation
2005				
2006				
2007				
2008				

(b) (Continued) and (c)

	(b) (3) Depreciation cost per unit:		
	Year	Computation	Depreciation Expense
	2005		
	2006		
	2007		
	2008		

(c)

	Year		Depreciation Expense	Accumulated Depreciation	
1	2003				1
2	2004				2
3	2005				3
4	2006				4
5	2007				5
6	2008				6
7	2009				7
8					8
9					9
10					10
11					11
12					12
13					13
14					14
15					15
16					16
17					17
18					18
19					19
20					20
21					21
22					22
23					23
24					24
25					25
26					26
27					27
28					28
29					29
30					30
31					31
32					32
33					33
34					34
35					35
36					36
37					37
38					38
39					39
40					40

(a)   General Journal

	Date	Account Titles and Explanation	Debit	Credit	
1	Apr. 1				1
2					2
3					3
4	May 1				4
5					5
6					6
7	1				7
8					8
9					9
10					10
11					11
12	Calculations:				12
13					13
14					14
15					15
16					16
17					17
18					18
19	June 1				19
20					20
21					21
22					22
23	July 1				23
24					24
25					25
26	Dec. 31				26
27					27
28					28
29	31				29
30					30
31					31
32	Calculations:				32
33					33
34					34
35					35
36					36
37					37
38					38
39					39
40					40

(b)   General Journal

	Date	Account Titles and Explanation	Debit	Credit	
1	Dec. 31				1
2					2
3					3
4	Dec. 31				4
5					5
6					6
7					7
8	Calculations:				8
9					9
10					10
11					11
12					12
13					13
14					14
15					15

(c)

Walton Company
Partial Balance Sheet
December 31, 2006

1			1
2			2
3			3
4			4
5			5
6			6
7			7
8			8
9			9
10			10
11			11
12			12
13			13
14			14
15			15
16			16
17			17
18			18
19			19
20			20

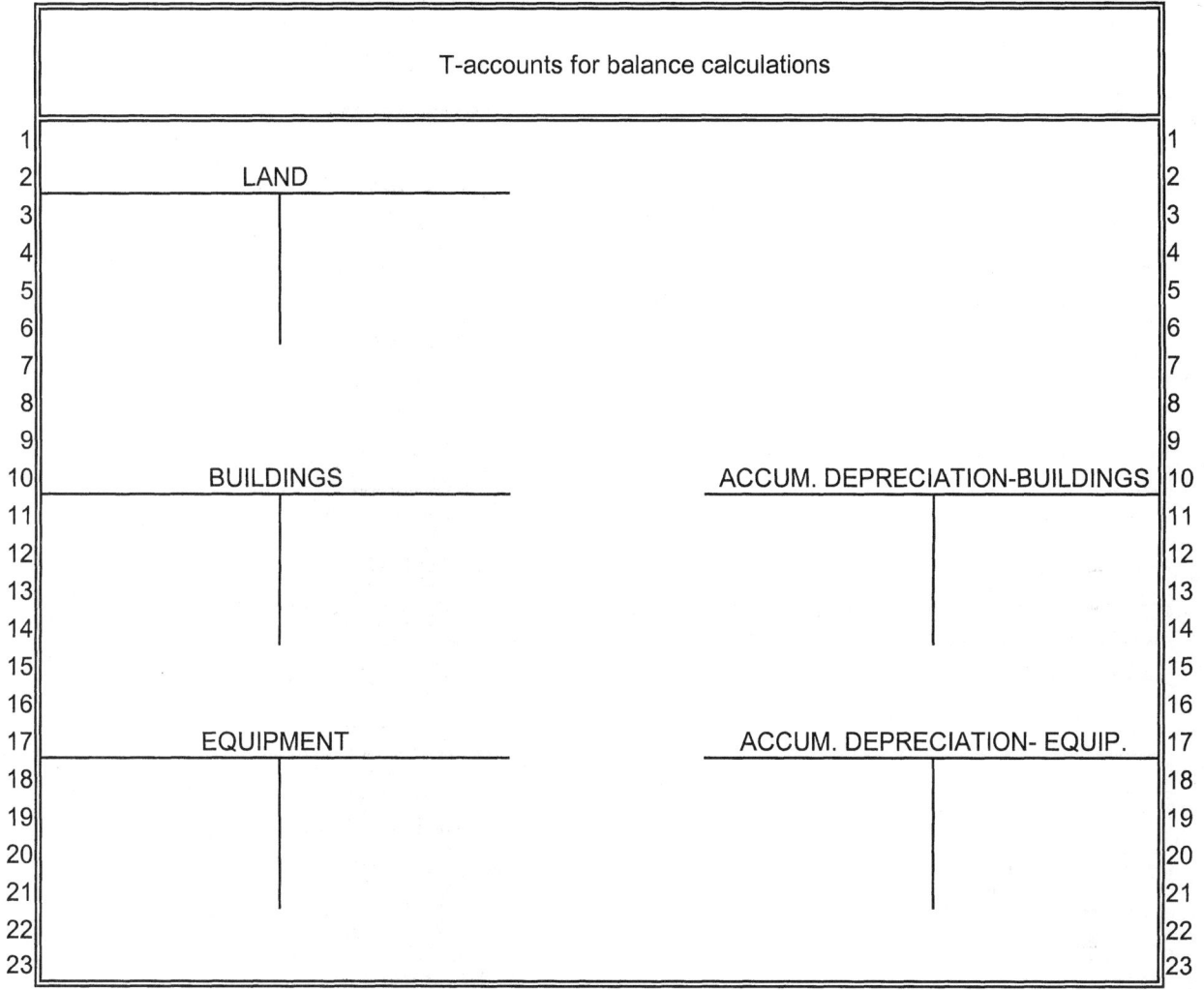

T-accounts for balance calculations

LAND

BUILDINGS

ACCUM. DEPRECIATION-BUILDINGS

EQUIPMENT

ACCUM. DEPRECIATION- EQUIP.

	Account Titles	Debit	Credit	
1	(a)			1
2				2
3				3
4				4
5				5
6				6
7				7
8	(b)			8
9				9
10				10
11				11
12				12
13				13
14				14
15				15
16	(c)			16
17				17
18				18
19				19
20				20
21				21
22				22
23				23
24				24
25				25
26				26
27				27
28				28
29				29
30				30
31				31
32				32
33				33
34				34
35				35
36				36
37				37
38				38
39				39
40				40

Section

Date   Glover Company

General Journal

	Date	Account Titles and Explanation	Debit	Credit	
1	(a)				1
2	Jan. 2				2
3					3
4					4
5	Jan. -				5
6	June				6
7					7
8					8
9	Sept. 1				9
10					10
11					11
12					12
13	Oct. 1				13
14					14
15					15
16	(b)				16
17	Dec. 31				17
18					18
19					19
20	31				20
21					21
22					22
23	(c)				23
24					24
25					25
26					26
27					27
28					28
29					29
30					30
31	(d)				31
32					32
33					33
34					34
35					35
36					36
37					37
38					38
39					39
40					40

General Journal

		Account Titles and Explanation	Debit	Credit	
1	1.				1
2					2
3					3
4					4
5					5
6					6
7					7
8					8
9					9
10	2				10
11					11
12					12
13					13
14					14
15					15
16					16
17					17
18					18
19					19
20					20
21					21
22					22
23					23
24					24
25					25
26					26
27					27
28					28
29					29
30					30

(a)	Dirks Corp	Hewes Corp.
(1) Asset turnover ratio		
(2) Return on assets ratio		

(b)

Item	Land	Building	Other Accounts	
			Amount	Account Titles
1.				
2.				
3.				
4.				
5.				
6.				
7.				
8.				
9.				
10.				

	Year	Computation	Cumulative, 12/31
(a)		BUS 1	
	2003		
	2004		
	2005		
		BUS 2	
	2003		
	2004		
	2005		
		BUS 3	
	2004		
	2005		

	Year	Depreciation Computation	Expense
(b)		BUS 2	
	(1) 2003		
	(2) 2004		

Total cost of machinery:		

(a) (1)

Account Titles	Debit	Credit

Annual depreciation:

(2)

Account Titles	Debit	Credit

(b) (1)

	Debit	Credit

(2)

Year	Book Value at Beginning of Year	DDB Rate	Annual Depreciation Expense	Accumulated Depreciation
2005				
2006				
2007				
2008				

(b) (Continued) and (c)

	Year	Computation	Depreciation Expense
(b) (3) Depreciation cost per unit:			
	2005		
	2006		
	2007		
	2008		

(c)

	Year		Depreciation Expense	Accumulated Depreciation	
1	2003				1
2	2004				2
3	2005				3
4	2006				4
5	2007				5
6	2008				6
7	2009				7
8					8
9					9
10					10
11					11
12					12
13					13
14					14
15					15
16					16
17					17
18					18
19					19
20					20
21					21
22					22
23					23
24					24
25					25
26					26
27					27
28					28
29					29
30					30
31					31
32					32
33					33
34					34
35					35
36					36
37					37
38					38
39					39
40					40

(a)   General Journal

	Date	Account Titles and Explanation	Debit	Credit	
1	Apr. 1				1
2					2
3					3
4	May 1				4
5					5
6					6
7	1				7
8					8
9					9
10					10
11					11
12	Calculations:				12
13					13
14					14
15					15
16					16
17					17
18					18
19	June 1				19
20					20
21					21
22					22
23	July 1				23
24					24
25					25
26	Dec 31				26
27					27
28					28
29	31				29
30					30
31					31
32	Calculations:				32
33					33
34					34
35					35
36					36
37					37
38					38
39					39
40					40

(b)   General Journal

	Date	Account Titles and Explanation	Debit	Credit	
1	Dec. 31				1
2					2
3					3
4	31				4
5					5
6					6
7					7
8	Calculations:				8
9					9
10					10
11					11
12					12
13					13
14					14
15					15

(c)

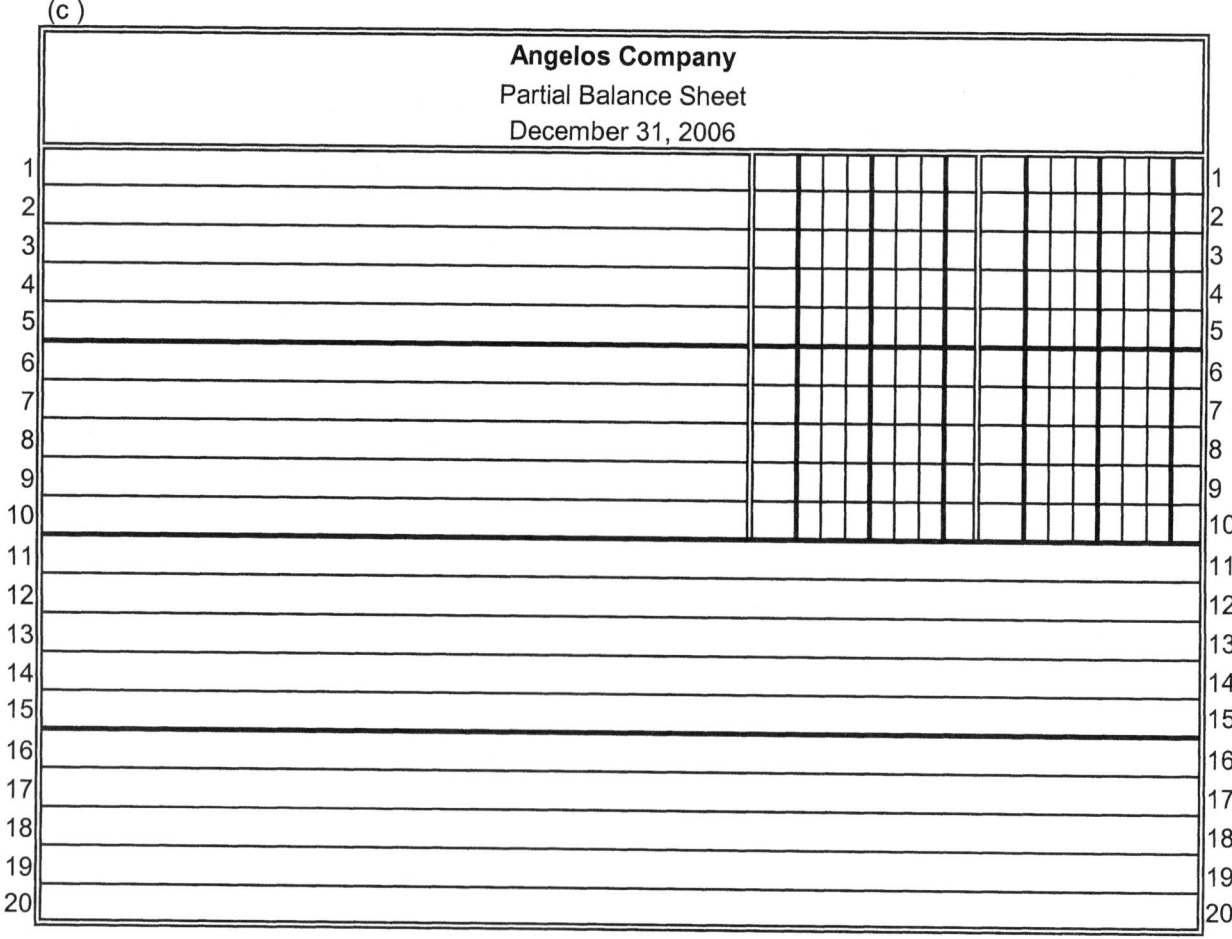

Angelos Company

Partial Balance Sheet

December 31, 2006

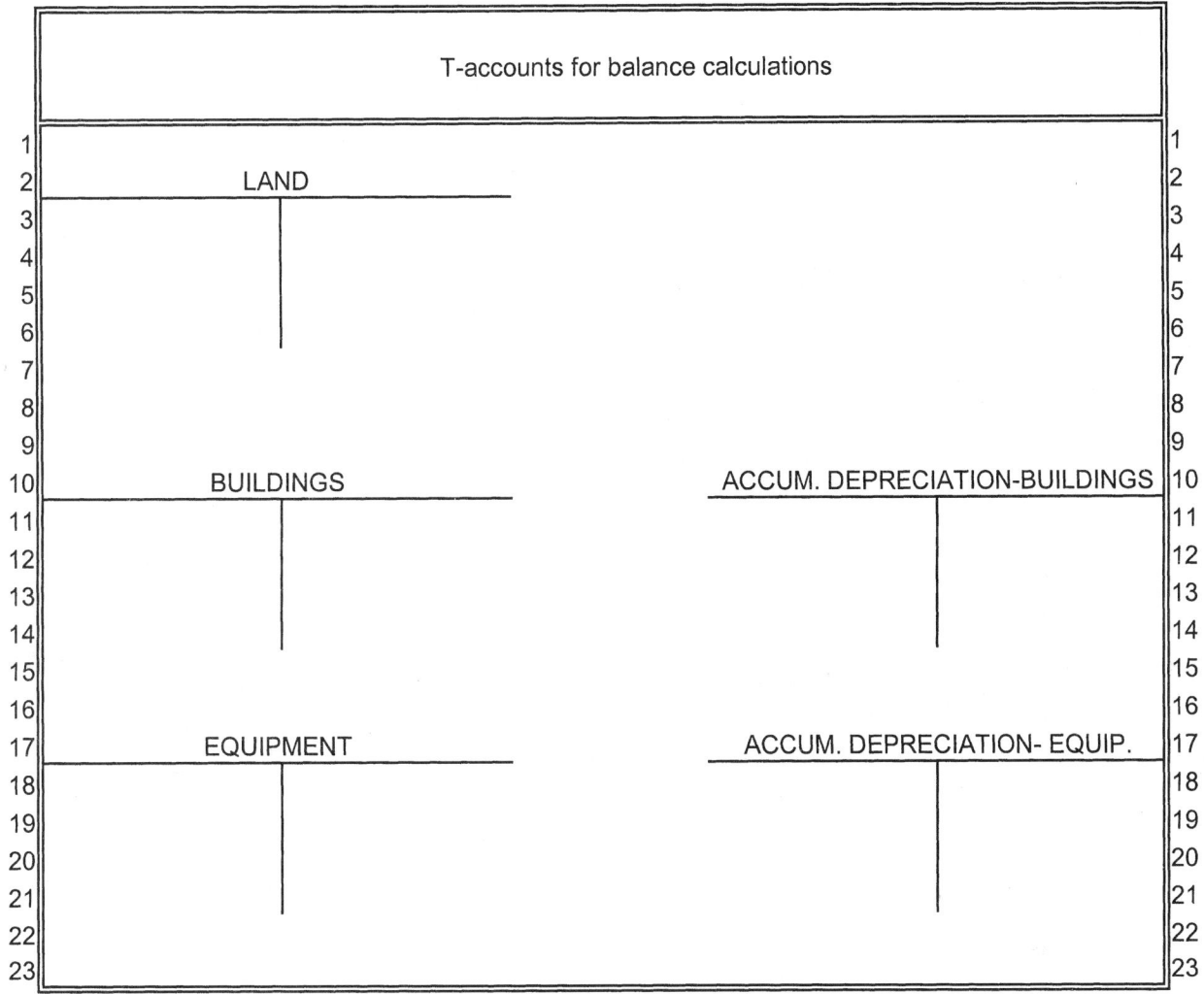

T-accounts for balance calculations

LAND

BUILDINGS

ACCUM. DEPRECIATION-BUILDINGS

EQUIPMENT

ACCUM. DEPRECIATION- EQUIP.

	Account Titles	Debit	Credit
1	(a)		
2			
3			
4			
5			
6			
7			
8	(b)		
9			
10			
11			
12			
13			
14			
15			
16	(c)		
17			
18			
19			
20			
21			
22			
23			
24			
25			
26			
27			
28			
29			
30			
31			
32			
33			
34			
35			
36			
37			
38			
39			
40			

General Journal

	Date	Account Titles and Explanation	Debit	Credit	
1	(a)				1
2	Jan. 2				2
3					3
4					4
5	Jan. -				5
6	June				6
7					7
8					8
9	Sept. 1				9
10					10
11					11
12	Oct. 1				12
13					13
14					14
15					15
16	(b)				16
17	Dec. 31				17
18					18
19	31				19
20					20
21					21
22					22
23	(c)				23
24					24
25					25
26					26
27					27
28					28
29					29
30					30
31					31
32					32
33					33
34					34
35					35
36					36
37					37
38					38
39					39
40					40

Section _____

Date _____ Goslin Company

General Journal

	Account Titles and Explanation	Debit	Credit	
1	1.			1
2				2
3				3
4				4
5				5
6				6
7				7
8				8
9				9
10	2.			10
11				11
12				12
13				13
14				14
15				15
16				16
17				17
18				18
19				19
20				20
21				21
22				22
23				23
24				24
25				25
26				26
27				27
28				28
29				29
30				30

(a)	Nina Company	Vernon Corporation
(1) Asset turnover ratio		
(2) Return on assets ratio		

(b)

Trans.	Account Titles	Debit	Credit
a.1.			
a.2.			
a.3.			
a.4.			
a.5.			
a.6.			
a.7.			
a.8.			
a.9.			
a.10.			

(a) (Continued)

		Account Titles	Debit	Credit	
1	a.11.				1
2					2
3					3
4	a.12.				4
5					5
6					6
7	a.13				7
8					8
9					9
10					10
11					11
12					12
13					13
14					14
15					15
16					16
17					17
18					18
19					19
20					20
21					21
22					22
23					23
24					24
25					25
26					26
27					27
28					28
29					29
30					30
31					31
32					32
33					33
34					34
35					35
36					36
37					37
38					38
39					39
40					40

(b)

	Squarepants Corporation Trial Balance 12/31/2004				
1	Cash				1
2	Accounts Receivable				2
3	Notes Receivable				3
4	Interest Receivable				4
5	Merchandise Inventory				5
6	Prepaid Insurance				6
7	Land				7
8	Building				8
9	Equipment				9
10	Patent				10
11	Allowance for Doubtful Accounts				11
12	Accumulated Depreciation - Building				12
13	Accumulated Depreciation - Equipment				13
14	Accounts Payable				14
15	Salaries Payable				15
16	Unearned Rent				16
17	Notes Payable (short-term)				17
18	Interest Payable				18
19	Notes Payable (long-term)				19
20	Common Stock				20
21	Retained Earnings				21
22	Dividends				22
23	Sales				23
24	Interest Revenue				24
25	Rent Revenue				25
26	Gain on Disposal				26
27	Bad Debts Expense				27
28	Cost of Goods Sold				28
29	Depreciation Expense - Building				29
30	Depreciation Expense - Equipment				30
31	Insurance Expense				31
32	Interest Expense				32
33	Other Operating Expense				33
34	Amortization Expense - Patents				34
35	Salaries Expense				35
36	Totals				36
37					37
38					38
39					39
40					40

(c)

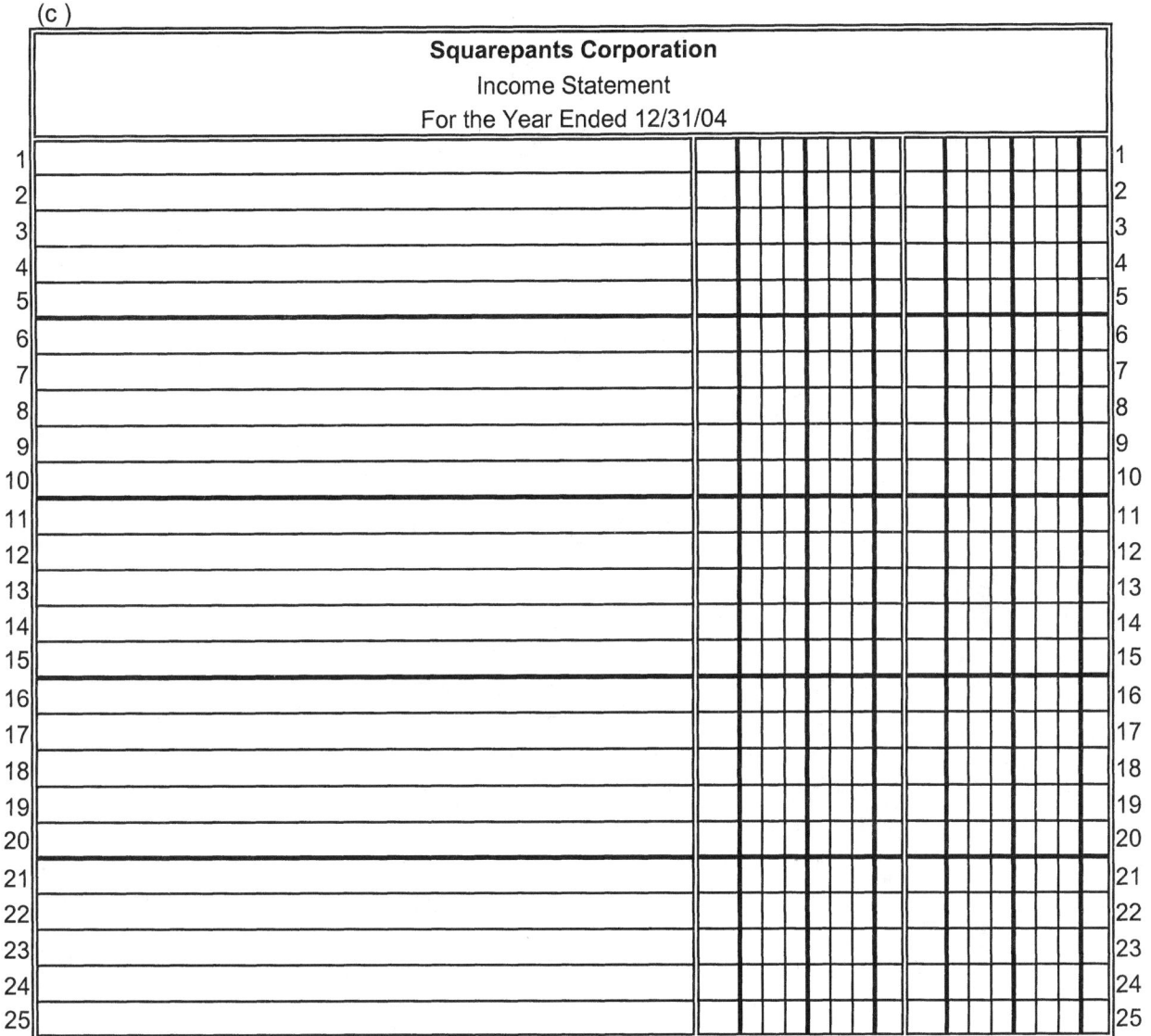

Squarepants Corporation															
Income Statement															
For the Year Ended 12/31/04															
1															1
2															2
3															3
4															4
5															5
6															6
7															7
8															8
9															9
10															10
11															11
12															12
13															13
14															14
15															15
16															16
17															17
18															18
19															19
20															20
21															21
22															22
23															23
24															24
25															25

(d)

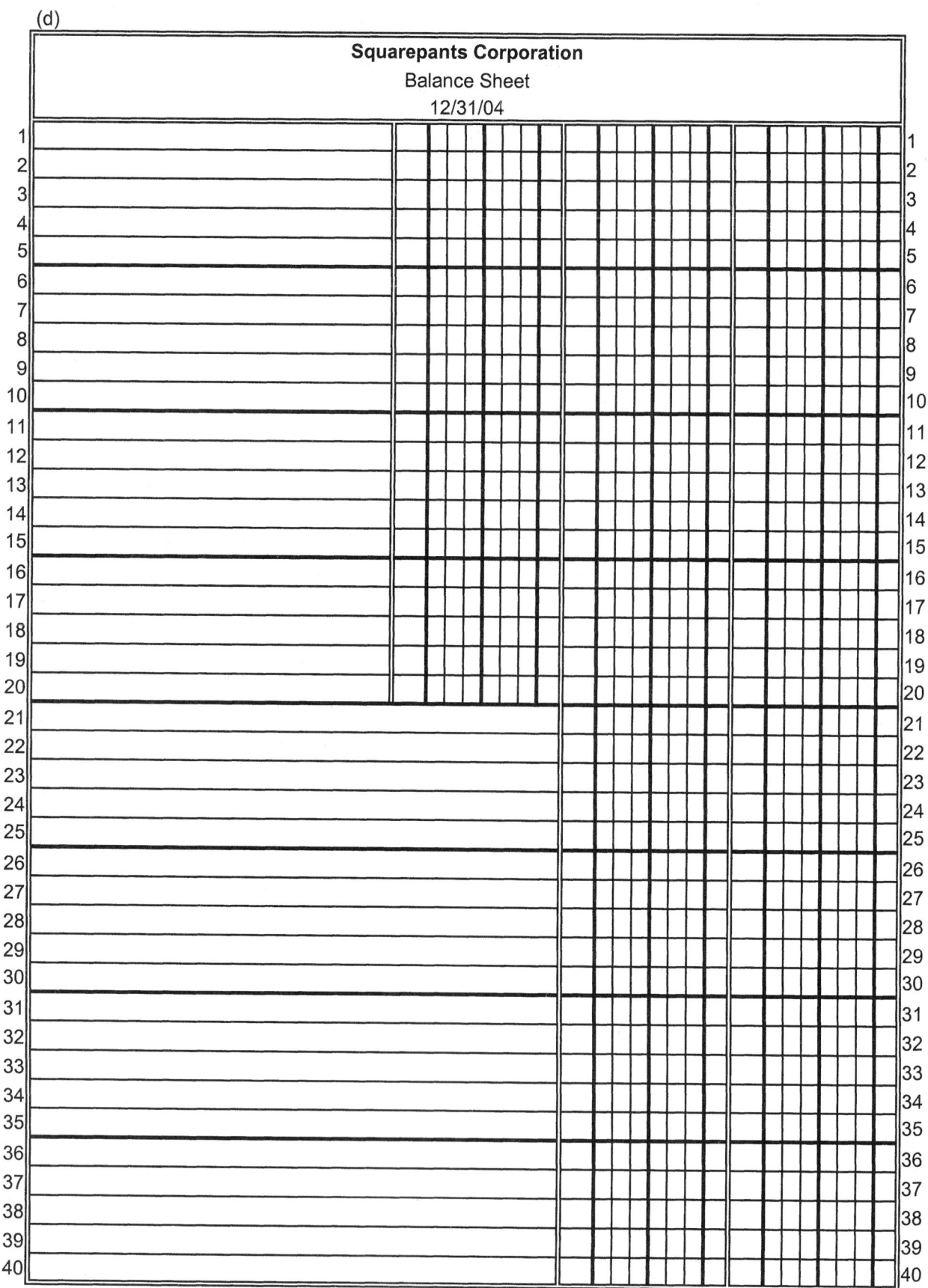

Squarepants Corporation

Balance Sheet

12/31/04

1   (a)

2

3

4

5

6   (b)

7

8

9

10

11   (c)   Depreciation expense was: (all amounts in millions)

12   2002

13   2001

14   2000

15

16   Amortization expense was:

17   2002

18   2001

19   2000

20

21   (d)   PepsiCo's capital spending was:

22   2002

23   2001

24

25

26   (e)

27

28

29

30

31

32

33

34

35

36

37

38

39

40

(a)	PepsiCo	Coca-Cola
Asset Turnover Ratio		

(b)

(a)

(b)

(c)

(d)

1		1
2		2
3		3
4		4
5		5
6		6
7		7
8		8
9		9
10		10
11		11
12		12
13		13
14		14
15		15
16		16
17		17
18		18
19		19
20		20
21		21
22		22
23		23
24		24
25		25
26		26
27		27
28		28
29		29
30		30
31		31
32		32
33		33
34		34
35		35
36		36
37		37
38		38
39		39
40		40

1	(a)	Givens Company- Straight-line method			1
2					2
3					3
4					4
5					5
6					6
7					7
8					8

	Runge Company- Double-declining-balance method			Annual Depreciation	Accumulated Depreciation	
Year	Asset	Computation				
2003	Building					
	Equipment					
2004	Building					
	Equipment					
2005	Building					
	Equipment					

(b)	Givens Co. Net Income	Runge Co. Net Inc. as Adjusted	Computations for Runge Company
Year			
2003			
2004			
2005			
Total			

(c)

1	1
2	2
3	3
4	4
5	5
6	6
7	7
8	8
9	9
10	10
11	11
12	12
13	13
14	14
15	15
16	16
17	17
18	18
19	19
20	20
21	21
22	22
23	23
24	24
25	25
26	26
27	27
28	28
29	29
30	30

		(a)					

(a)

(b)

(c)

	Old Estimates					

	Revised Estimates					

#1

(a)

(b)

(c)

(d)

#2

Date	Account Titles	Debit	Credit

#3

Date	Account Titles	Debit	Credit

#4

	Date	Account Titles	Debit	Credit	
1					1
2					2
3					3
4					4
5					5
6					6
7					7
8					8
9					9

#5

10		10
11	(a)	11
12		12
13	(b)	13
14		14
15		15

#6

	Date	Account Titles	Debit	Credit	
16					16
17					17
18					18
19					19
20					20
21					21

#7

22		22
23	(a)	23
24	(b)	24
25	(c)	25
26	(d)	26
27		27

#8

28				28
29				29
30				30
31				31
32				32
33				33
34				34
35				35
36				36
37				37
38				38
39				39
40				40

#9

Date	Account Titles	Debit	Credit

#10

Date	Account Titles	Debit	Credit

#11

Date	Account Titles	Debit	Credit

#1

	Date	Account Titles	Debit	Credit	
1	(a)				1
2					2
3					3
4					4
5	(b)				5
6					6
7					7
8					8
9	(c)				9
10					10
11					11
12					12
13					13
14	(d)				14
15					15
16					16
17	**#2**				17
18	Date	Account Titles	Debit	Credit	18
19		**Sue Jackson Company**			19
20					20
21					21
22					22
23					23
24		**Person Company**			24
25					25
26					26
27					27
28					28
29					29
30					30
31					31
32					32
33					33
34					34
35					35
36					36
37					37
38					38
39					39
40					40

#3

	Date	Account Titles	Debit	Credit	
1	(a)				1
2					2
3					3
4					4
5	(b)				5
6					6
7					7
8					8
9	(c)				9
10					10
11					11
12					12

#4

		Month	Estimate	Units Defective	Outstanding	
13						13
14	(a) Estimated warrranties outstanding:					14
15						15
16						16
17						17
18						18
19						19
20						20
21						21
22						22

	Date	Account Titles	Debit	Credit	
23					23
24	(b)				24
25					25
26					26
27					27
28					28
29					29
30					30
31	(c)				31
32					32
33					33
34					34
35					35
36					36
37					37
38					38
39					39
40					40

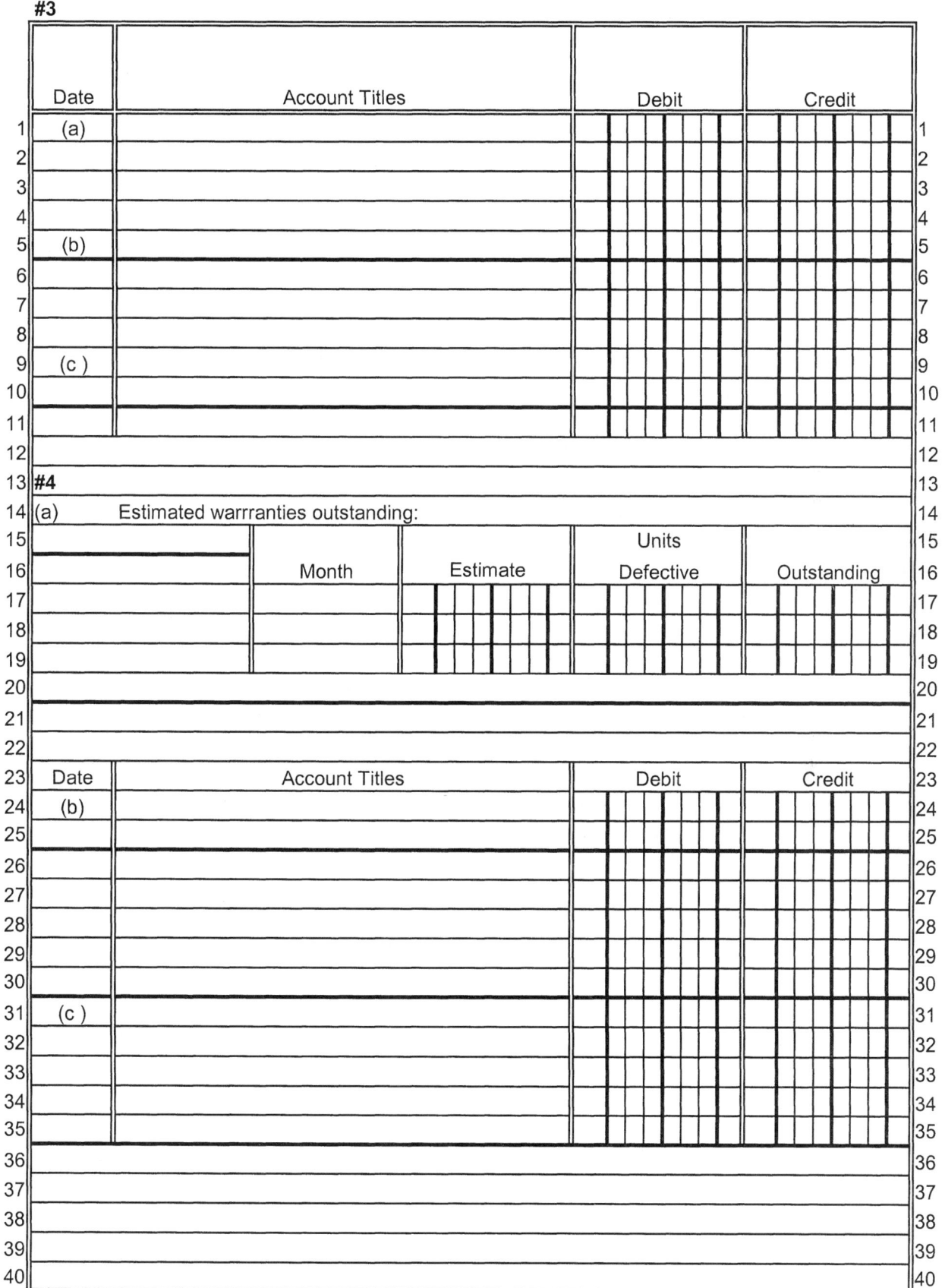

#5 (a)

	Larkin Online Company					
	Partial Balance Sheet					
1						1
2						2
3						3
4						4
5						5
6						6
7						7
8						8
9						9
10						10
11	(b)					11
12						12
13						13
14						14
15						15
16	**#6**					16
17	(a)					17
18						18
19	(b)					19
20						20
21	**#7**					21
22	(a) Current ratio:					22
23	2000					23
24						24
25	2001					25
26						26
27	Working capital:					27
28	2000					28
29						29
30	2001					30
31						31
32	(b) Current ratio:					32
33						33
34						34
35	Working capital:					35
36						36
37						37
38						38
39						39
40						40

#8

(a)

1	(1)	Reular			1
2		Overtime			2
3		Gross earnings			3
4	(2)	FICA taxes			4
5	(3)	Federal income taxes			5
6	(4)	State income taxes			6
7	(5)	Net pay			7
8					8
9					9
10	(b)				10

	Date	Account Titles	Debit	Credit	
11					11
12					12
13					13
14					14
15					15
16					16
17					17
18					18
19					19

20	**#9**	20
21	C. Mays	21
22		22
23		23
24		24
25		25
26	D. Delgado	26
27		27
28		28
29		29
30		30
31	L. Jeter	31
32		32
33		33
34		34
35		35
36	T. Rolen	36
37		37
38		38
39		39
40		40

(a)

Canseco Company Payroll Register For the Week Ending January 31					
Employee	Total Hours	Earnings			
		Regular	Overtime	Gross Pay	
1 M. Hindi					1
2					2
3 E. Benson					3
4					4
5 K. Estes					5
6 Totals					6

(a) Continued

Canseco Company Payroll Register (continued) For the Week Ending January 31					
	Deductions				Net Pay
	FICA Taxes	Federal Income Taxes	Health Insurance	Total	
1 Hindi					1
2					2
3 Benson					3
4					4
5 Estes					5
6 Totals					6

(b)

	Date	Account Titles	Debit	Credit	
1	Jan 31				1
2					2
3					3
4					4
5					5
6					6
7	31				7
8					8
9					9
10					10
11					11
12					12

#11

(a)

Gross earnings:				State income taxes			
Regular		8900		Union dues		100	
Overtime				Total deductions			
Total				Net pay		7215	
Deductions:				Accounts debited:			
FICA taxes		760		Warehouse wages			
Federal income taxes		1140		Store wages		4000	

(b)

	Date	Account Titles	Debit	Credit	
11	Feb 28				11
12					12
13					13
14					14
15					15
16					16
17					17
18					18
19	28				19
20					20

#12

(a)

(b)

Date	Account Titles	Debit	Credit

#13

Date	Account Titles	Debit	Credit
Mar 31			
Mar 31			

General Journal

	Date	Account Titles	Debit	Credit	
1	(a)				1
2	Jan 1				2
3					3
4					4
5	5				5
6					6
7					7
8					8
9	12				9
10					10
11					11
12	14				12
13					13
14					14
15	20				15
16					16
17					17
18					18
19	25				19
20					20
21					21
22					22
23	(b) (1)				23
24	Jan 31				24
25					25
26					26
27					27
28	(2)				28
29	31				29
30					30
31					31
32					32
33					33
34					34
35					35
36					36
37					37

(c)

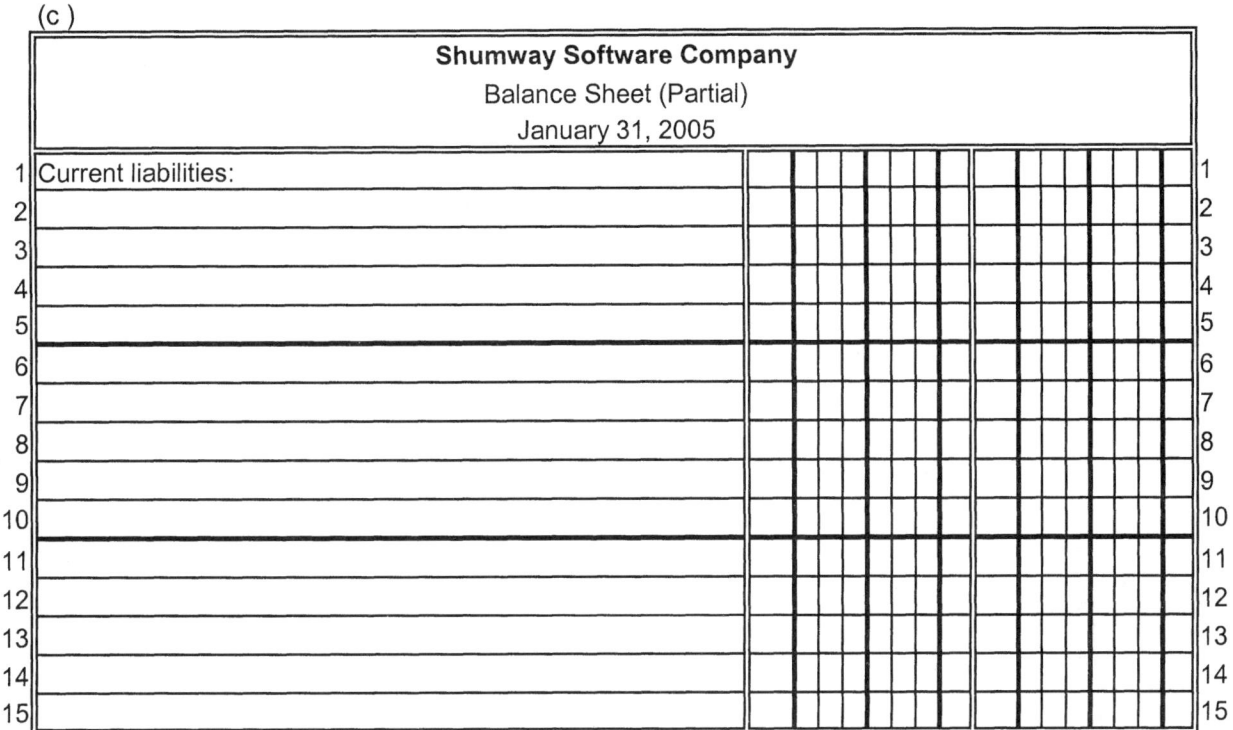

	Shumway Software Company						
	Balance Sheet (Partial)						
	January 31, 2005						
1	Current liabilities:						1
2							2
3							3
4							4
5							5
6							6
7							7
8							8
9							9
10							10
11							11
12							12
13							13
14							14
15							15

(a)

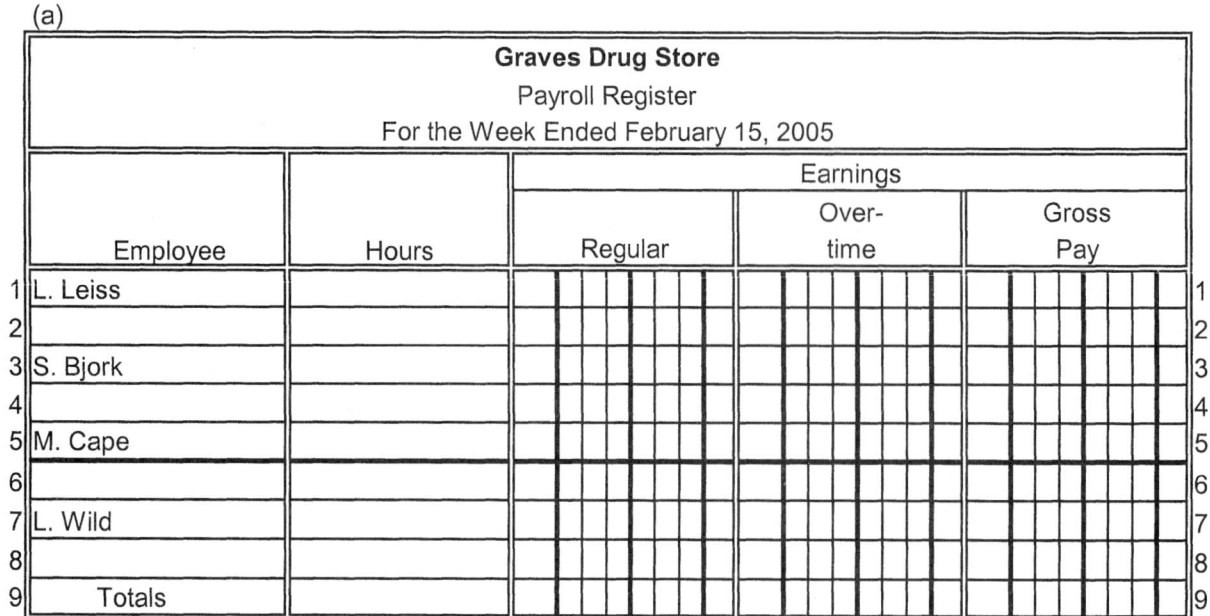

	Graves Drug Store					
	Payroll Register					
	For the Week Ended February 15, 2005					
			Earnings			
Employee	Hours	Regular	Over-time	Gross Pay		
1 L. Leiss						1
2						2
3 S. Bjork						3
4						4
5 M. Cape						5
6						6
7 L. Wild						7
8						8
9 Totals						9

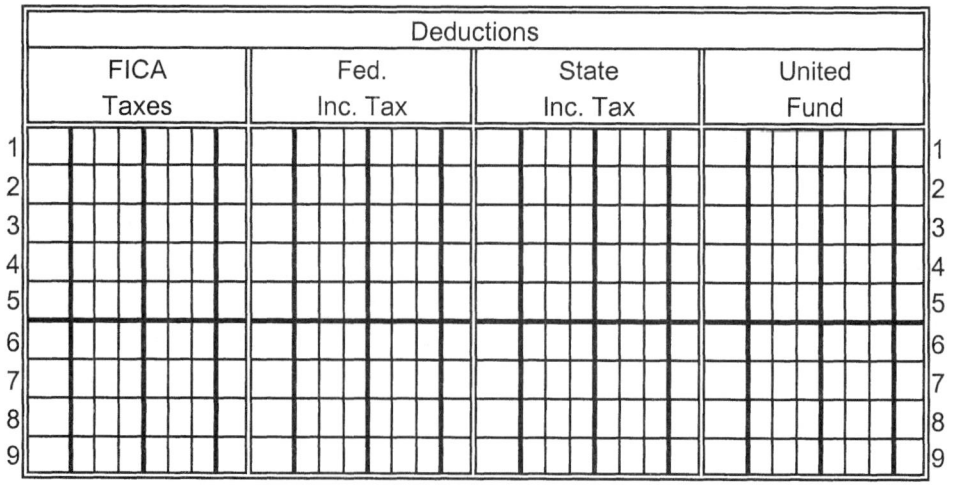

	Deductions			
	FICA Taxes	Fed. Inc. Tax	State Inc. Tax	United Fund
1				
2				
3				
4				
5				
6				
7				
8				
9				

	Deductions Total	Net Pay	Store Wages Exp.	Office Wages Exp.
1				
2				
3				
4				
5				
6				
7				
8				
9				

	Date	Account Titles	Debit	Credit	
1	(b)				1
2	Feb 15				2
3					3
4					4
5					5
6					6
7					7
8					8
9					9
10					10
11	15				11
12					12
13					13
14					14
15					15
16					16
17					17
18					18
19					19
20					20
21	(c)				21
22	Feb 16				22
23					23
24					24
25					25
26					26
27					27
28					28
29					29
30					30
31	(d)				31
32	Feb 28				32
33					33
34					34
35					35
36					36
37					37
38					38
39					39
40					40

	(a) Weaknesses	(b) Recommended Procedures	
1	1.		1
2			2
3			3
4			4
5			5
6			6
7			7
8			8
9			9
10			10
11			11
12			12
13			13
14			14
15			15
16			16
17			17
18			18
19	2.		19
20			20
21			21
22			22
23			23
24			24
25			25
26			26
27			27
28			28
29	3.		29
30			30
31			31
32			32
33			33
34			34
35			35
36			36
37			37
38			38
39			39
40			40

	Date	Account Titles	Debit	Credit	
1	(a)				1
2	Jan 10				2
3					3
4					4
5	12				5
6					6
7					7
8					8
9	15				9
10					10
11					11
12	17				12
13					13
14					14
15	20				15
16					16
17					17
18					18
19	31				19
20					20
21					21
22					22
23					23
24					24
25					25
26					26
27					27
28	31				28
29					29
30					30
31	(b) 1.				31
32	Jan 31				32
33					33
34					34
35					35
36					36
37	2.				37
38	31				38
39					39
40					40

	Date		Debit	Credit	
1	(a)				1
2					2
3					3
4					4
5					5
6					6
7					7
8					8
9					9
10					10
11					11
12					12
13	(b)				13
14					14
15					15
16					16
17					17
18					18
19					19
20					20
21					21
22					22
23					23
24					24
25					25

(c)

	Employee	Wages, Tips, Other Compensation	Federal Income Tax Withheld	State Income Tax Withheld	FICA Wages	FICA Tax Withheld	
1							1
2	R. Lopez	6 0 0 0 0	2 7 5 0 0				2
3							3
4	K. Kirk	2 7 0 0 0	1 1 0 0 0				4
5							5
6							6
7							7
8							8
9							9
10							10

(a)   General Journal

	Date	Account Titles	Debit	Credit	
1	Jan 2				1
2					2
3					3
4	Feb 1				4
5					5
6					6
7	Mar 31				7
8					8
9					9
10	Apr 1				10
11					11
12					12
13					13
14	July 1				14
15					15
16					16
17					17
18	Sept 30				18
19					19
20					20
21	Oct 1				21
22					22
23					23
24					24
25	Dec 1				25
26					26
27					27
28	Dec 31				28
29					29
30					30

(c)

Talley Company
Balance Sheet (Partial)
December 31, 2004

1	Current liabilities:		1
2			2
3			3
4			4
5			5

(b)

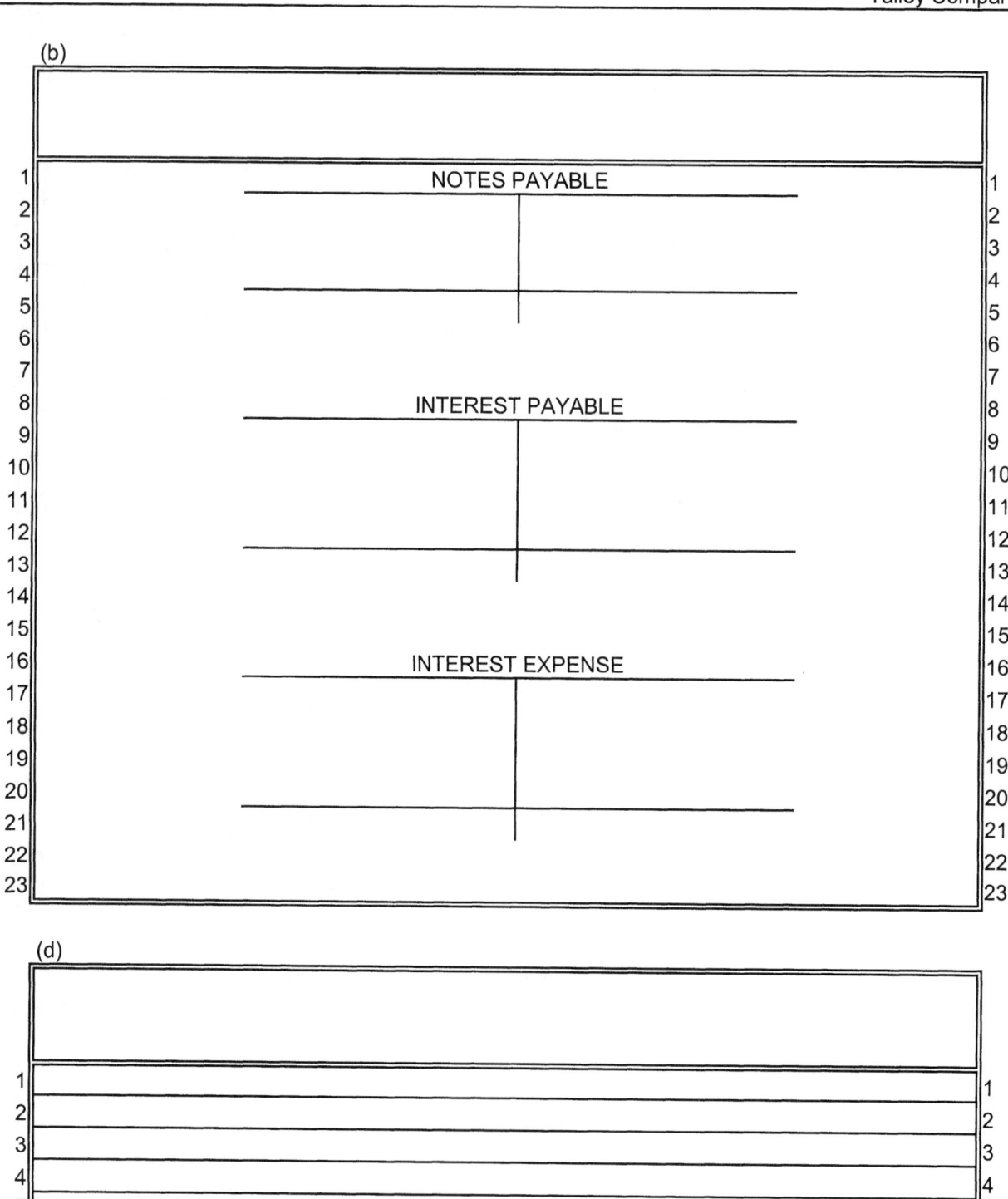

NOTES PAYABLE

INTEREST PAYABLE

INTEREST EXPENSE

(d)

General Journal

	Date	Account Titles	Debit	Credit	
1	(a)				1
2	Jan 5				2
3					3
4					4
5					5
6	12				6
7					7
8					8
9	14				9
10					10
11					11
12	20				12
13					13
14					14
15					15
16	21				16
17					17
18					18
19	25				19
20					20
21					21
22					22
23	(b) (1)				23
24	Jan 31				24
25					25
26					26
27					27
28	(2)				28
29	31				29
30					30
31					31
32					32
33					33
34					34
35					35
36					36
37					37

(c)

Zaur Company		
Balance Sheet (Partial)		
January 31, 2005		
Current liabilities:		

(a)

Lee Hardware Payroll Register For the Week Ended March 15, 2005				
		Earnings		
Employee	Hours	Regular	Over-time	Gross Pay
1 Joe Coomer				
2				
3 Mary Walker				
4				
5 Andy Dye				
6				
7 Kim Shen				
8				
9 Totals				

Deductions			
FICA Taxes	Fed. Inc. Tax	State Inc. Tax	United Fund
1			
2			
3			
4			
5			
6			
7			
8			
9			

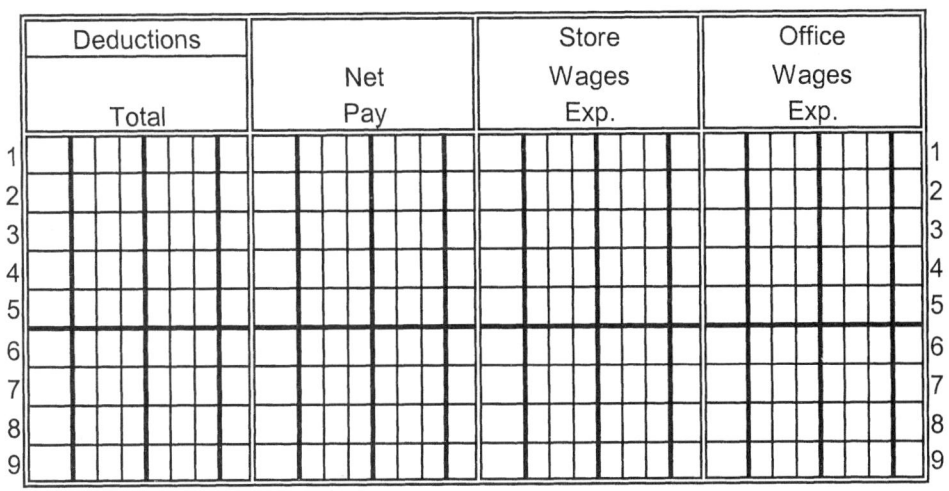

Deductions Total	Net Pay	Store Wages Exp.	Office Wages Exp.
1			
2			
3			
4			
5			
6			
7			
8			
9			

	Date	Account Titles	Debit	Credit	
1	(b)				1
2	Mar 15				2
3					3
4					4
5					5
6					6
7					7
8					8
9					9
10					10
11	15				11
12					12
13					13
14					14
15					15
16					16
17					17
18					18
19					19
20					20
21	(c)				21
22	Mar 16				22
23					23
24					24
25					25
26					26
27					27
28					28
29					29
30					30
31	(d)				31
32	Mar 31				32
33					33
34					34
35					35
36					36
37					37
38					38
39					39
40					40

	(a) Weaknesses	(b) Recommended Procedures	
1	1.		1
2			2
3			3
4			4
5			5
6			6
7			7
8			8
9			9
10			10
11			11
12			12
13			13
14			14
15			15
16			16
17			17
18			18
19	2.		19
20			20
21			21
22			22
23			23
24			24
25			25
26			26
27			27
28			28
29	3.		29
30			30
31			31
32			32
33			33
34			34
35			35
36			36
37			37
38			38
39			39
40			40

	Date	Account Titles	Debit	Credit	
1	(a)				1
2	Jan 10				2
3					3
4					4
5	12				5
6					6
7					7
8					8
9	15				9
10					10
11					11
12	17				12
13					13
14					14
15	20				15
16					16
17					17
18					18
19	31				19
20					20
21					21
22					22
23					23
24					24
25					25
26					26
27					27
28	31				28
29					29
30					30
31	(b) 1.				31
32	Jan 31				32
33					33
34					34
35					35
36					36
37	2.				37
38	31				38
39					39
40					40

Niehaus Electrical Repair Company

	Date		Debit	Credit	
1	(a)				1
2					2
3					3
4					4
5					5
6					6
7					7
8					8
9					9
10					10
11					11
12					12
13	(b)				13
14					14
15					15
16					16
17					17
18					18
19					19
20					20
21					21
22					22
23					23
24					24
25					25

(c)

	Employee	Wages, Tips, Other Compensation	Federal Income Tax Withheld	State Income Tax Withheld	FICA Wages	FICA Tax Withheld	
1							1
2	A. Hashmi	5 9 0 0 0	2 8 5 0 0				2
3							3
4	S. Bishop	2 6 0 0 0	1 0 2 0 0				4
5							5
6							6
7							7
8							8
9							9
10							10

(a)

(b)

(c)

(a)

(b)	PepsiCo	Coca-Cola
(1)　　Working capital		
(2)　　Current ratio		

(c)

(a)

(b)

(c)

(d)

1 (a)	1
2	2
3	3
4	4
5	5
6	6
7	7
8	8
9	9
10	10
11	11
12	12
13	13
14	14
15	15
16 (b)	16
17	17
18	18
19	19
20	20
21	21
22	22
23	23
24 (c)	24
25	25
26	26
27 (d)	27
28	28
29	29
30	30
31	31
32	32
33	33
34	34
35 (e)	35
36	36
37	37
38	38
39	39
40	40

(a)

Davidson Services Inc.

Month	Number of Employees	Days Worked	Daily Rate		Cost	
January - March						
April - May						
June - October						
November - December						
Total Cost						

Permanent Employees

(b)

(1)

(2)

(3)

(4)

Name

Section

Date

Blue Sky Company

1	1
2	2
3	3
4	4
5	5
6	6
7	7
8	8
9	9
10	10
11	11
12	12
13	13
14	14
15	15
16	16
17	17
18	18
19	19
20	20
21	21
22	22
23	23
24	24
25	25
26	26
27	27
28	28
29	29
30	30
31	31
32	32
33	33
34	34
35	35
36	36
37	37
38	38
39	39
40	40

1	(a)
2	
3	
4	
5	
6	
7	(b)
8	
9	
10	
11	
12	(c)
13	
14	
15	
16	
17	
18	
19	
20	(d)
21	
22	
23	
24	
25	
26	
27	
28	
29	
30	
31	
32	
33	
34	
35	
36	
37	
38	
39	
40	

	#1	
1	(a)	1
2	(b)	2
3	(c)	3
4		4
5	**#2**	5
6	(a)	6
7	(b)	7
8	(c)	8
9		9
10	**#3**	10
11	(a)	11
12	(b)	12
13	(c)	13
14		14
15	**#4**	15
16	(a)	16
17	(b)	17
18	(c)	18
19	(d)	19
20	(e)	20
21		21
22	**#5**	22
23	(a)	23
24	(b)	24
25	(c)	25
26		26
27	**#6**	27
28	(a)	28
29	(b)	29
30	(c)	30
31	(d)	31
32		32
33	**#7**	33
34	(a)	34
35	(b)	35
36	(c)	36
37	(d)	37
38		38
39		39
40		40

#8

	Year	Costs Incurred	Total Estimated Cost	Percent Complete	
1	2004				
2	2005				
3	2006				
4					
5					

	Percent Complete	Total Revenue	Revenue Recognized	
6				
7				
8				
9				
10				
11				

#9

Gross profit percentage:

	Year	Cash Collected	Gross Profit Percentage	Gross Profit Recognized	

#10

(a)

(b)

(c)

(d)

#1

1	1.
2	2.
3	3.
4	4.
5	5.
6	6.
7	7.
8	
9	

#2

11	1.
12	
13	2.
14	
15	
16	
17	
18	
19	
20	
21	3.
22	
23	
24	
25	
26	
27	
28	

Account Titles	Debit	Credit

4.

Account Titles	Debit	Credit

#2 (Continued)

1	5.
2	
3	
4	
5	**#3**
6	(a)
7	(b)
8	(c)
9	(d)
10	(e)
11	(f)
12	(g)
13	(h)
14	
15	**#4**
16	1.
17	
18	
19	
20	
21	2.
22	
23	
24	3.
25	
26	
27	
28	4.
29	
30	
31	
32	
33	5.
34	
35	
36	
37	
38	
39	
40	

#5

		Year	Costs Incurred (Current Period)	Total Estimated Cost	Percent Complete (Current Period)	
1		1				
2		2				
3						

		Year	Percent Complete (Current Period)	Total Revenue	Revenue Recognized (Current Period)	
4						
5						
6						
7		1				
8		2				
9						

		Year	Revenue Recognized (Current Period)	Actual Cost Incurred (Current Period)	Gross Profit Recognized (Current Period)	
10						
11						
12						
13		1				
14		2				
15						
16						

#6

		Year	Cash Collected	Gross Profit Percentage	Gross Profit Recognized	
17						
18	(a)					
19		Year				
20		2004				
21		2005				
22		2006				
23						
24						
25	(b)	2004				
26		2005				
27		2006				
28						
29						
30						
31						
32						
33						
34						
35						
36						
37						
38						
39						
40						

	Account Titles	Debit	Credit	
1	1.			1
2				2
3				3
4				4
5				5
6	2.			6
7				7
8				8
9				9
10				10
11				11
12	Account Titles	Debit	Credit	12
13				13
14				14
15				15
16	3.			16
17				17
18				18
19				19
20	Account Titles	Debit	Credit	20
21				21
22				22
23				23
24	4.			24
25				25
26				26
27				27
28	5.			28
29				29
30				30
31				31
32				32
33				33
34	Account Titles	Debit	Credit	34
35				35
36				36
37				37
38				38
39				39
40				40

1	1.
2	
3	
4	
5	
6	
7	
8	
9	
10	2.
11	
12	
13	
14	
15	
16	
17	
18	
19	3.
20	
21	
22	
23	
24	4.
25	
26	
27	
28	
29	
30	
31	
32	
33	5.
34	
35	
36	
37	
38	
39	
40	

		Year	Costs Incurred (Current Period)	Total Estimated Cost	Percent Complete (Current Period)		
1		2004					1
2		2005					2
3		2006					3
4		2007					4
5		Total					5

| 6 | | | | | | | 6 |
| 7 | | | | | | | 7 |

		Year	Percent Complete (Current Period)	Total Revenue	Revenue Recognized (Current Period)		
8							8
9							9
10		Year					10
11		2004					11
12		2005					12
13		2006					13
14		2007					14
15		Total					15

| 16 | | | | | | | 16 |
| 17 | | | | | | | 17 |

		Year	Revenue Recognized (Current Period)	Actual Cost Incurred (Current Period)	Gross Profit Recognized (Current Period)		
18							18
19							19
20		Year					20
21		2004					21
22		2005					22
23		2006					23
24		2007					24
25		Totals					25

26							26
27							27
28							28
29							29
30							30
31							31
32							32
33							33
34							34
35							35
36							36
37							37
38							38
39							39
40							40

Section

Date   Westphal Construction

(a)

	Year	Cash Collected	Gross Profit Percentage	Gross Profit Recognized	
1	2004				
2	2005				
3	2006				
4	Total				

(b)

	Year	Cash Collected	Gross profit Percentage	Gross Profit Recognized	
9	2004				
10	2005				
11	2006				
12	Total				

(a)

(b)

(c)

(d)

(e)

(f)

(g)

(h)

	Account Titles	Debit	Credit	
1	1.			1
2				2
3				3
5				5
6	2.			6
7				7
8				8
9				9
10				10
11				11
12	Account Titles	Debit	Credit	12
13				13
14				14
15				15
16	3.			16
17				17
18				18
19				19
20	Account Titles	Debit	Credit	20
21				21
22				22
23				23
24	4.			24
25				25
26				26
27				27
28				28
29				29
30	Account Titles	Debit	Credit	30
31				31
32				32
33				33
34	5.			34
35				35
36				36
37				37
38				38
39				39
40				40

6.

Account Titles	Debit	Credit

Account Titles	Debit	Credit

1.

2.

3.

4.

5.

Section

Date   Cosky Construction Company

	Year	Costs Incurred (Current Period)	Total Estimated Cost	Percent Complete (Current Period)	
1	2004				
2	2005				
3	2006				
4	2007				
5	Total				

	Year	Percent Complete (Current Period)	Total Revenue	Revenue Recognized (Current Period)	
11	2004				
12	2005				
13	2006				
14	2007				
15	Total				

	Year	Revenue Recognized (Current Period)	Actual Cost Incurred (Current Period)	Gross Profit Recognized (Current Period)	
21	2004				
22	2005				
23	2006				
24	2007				
25	Totals				

(a)

	Year	Cash Collected	Gross Profit Percentage	Gross Profit Recognized	
1	2004				
2	2005				
3	2006				
4	Total				

(b)

	Year	Cash Collected	Gross profit Percentage	Gross Profit Recognized	
2004					
2005					
2006					
Total					

1 (a)	1
2	2
3 (b)	3
4	4
5 (c)	5
6	6
7 (d)	7
8	8
9 (e)	9
10	10
11 (f)	11
12	12
13 (g)	13
14	14
15 (h)	15
16	16
17 (i)	17
18	18
19	19
20	20
21	21
22	22
23	23
24	24
25	25
26	26
27	27
28	28
29	29
30	30
31	31
32	32
33	33
34	34
35	35
36	36
37	37
38	38
39	39
40	40

(a)

	Paris Company	Troyer Company
1. Cash		
2. Accounts Receivable		
3. Allowance for Doubtful Accounts		
4. Merchandise Inventory		
5. Plant and Equipment		
6. Accumulated Depreciation		
7. Total Assets		
8.		
9. Current Liabilities		
10. Long-term Liabilities		
11. Total Liabilities		
12. Owner's Equity		
13. Total Liabilities and Owner's Equity		

(b)

(a)

(b)

(c)

(d)

(e)

(f)

Name

Section

Date

Zane Jones

1	(g)
2	
3	
4	
5	
6	
7	
8	
9	
10	
11	
12	
13	
14	
15	
16	
17	
18	
19	
20	
21	
22	
23	
24	
25	
26	
27	
28	
29	
30	
31	
32	
33	
34	
35	
36	
37	
38	
39	
40	

(a)

(b)

(c)

(a)

1.

2.

3.

(b)

Piper Construction Division

McKenna Securities Division

(a)

(b)

(c)

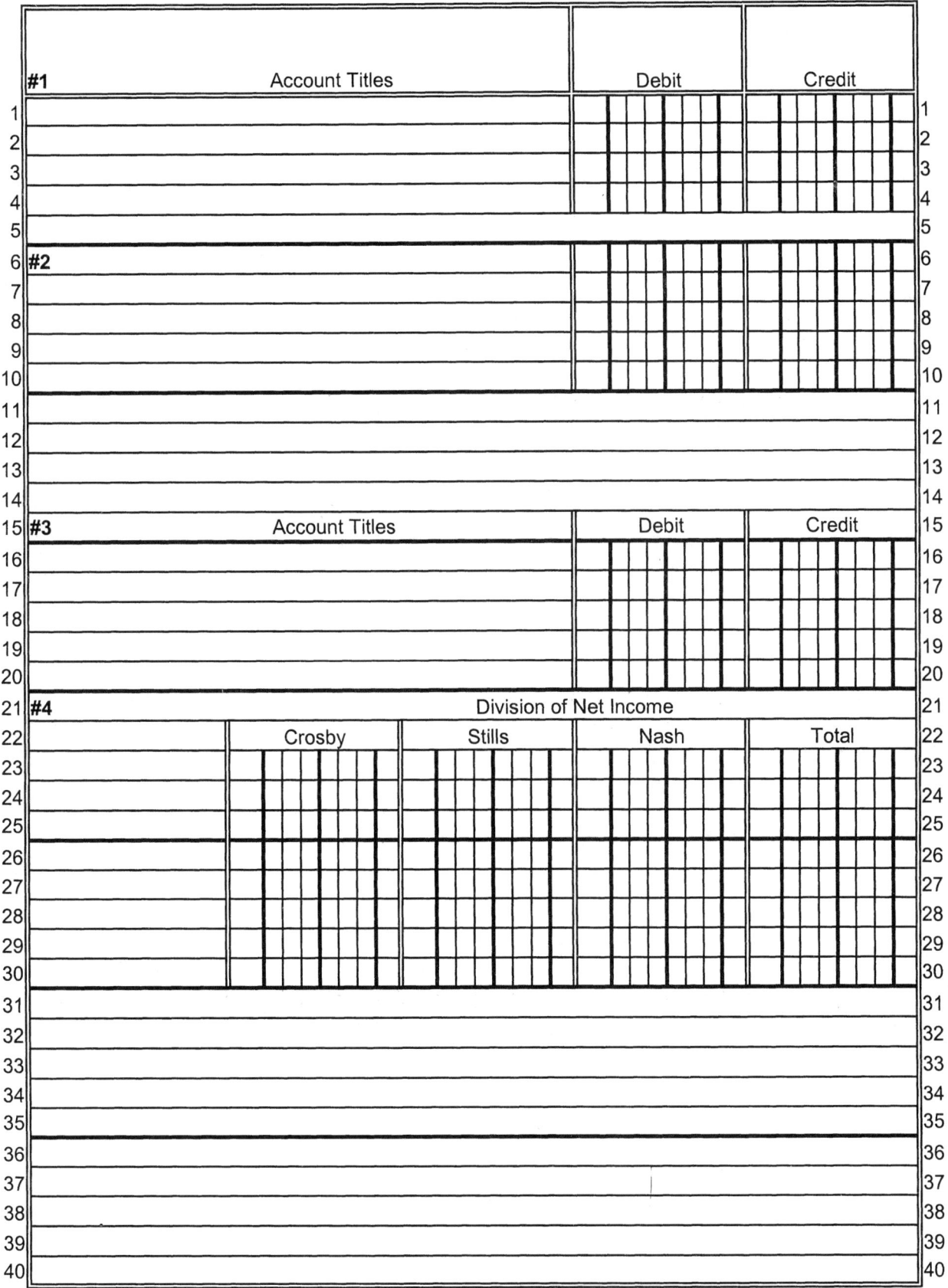

#1	Account Titles	Debit	Credit
1			
2			
3			
4			
5			
#2			
6			
7			
8			
9			
10			
11			
12			
13			
14			

#3	Account Titles	Debit	Credit
15			
16			
17			
18			
19			
20			

#4 Division of Net Income

	Crosby	Stills	Nash	Total
22				
23				
24				
25				
26				
27				
28				
29				
30				

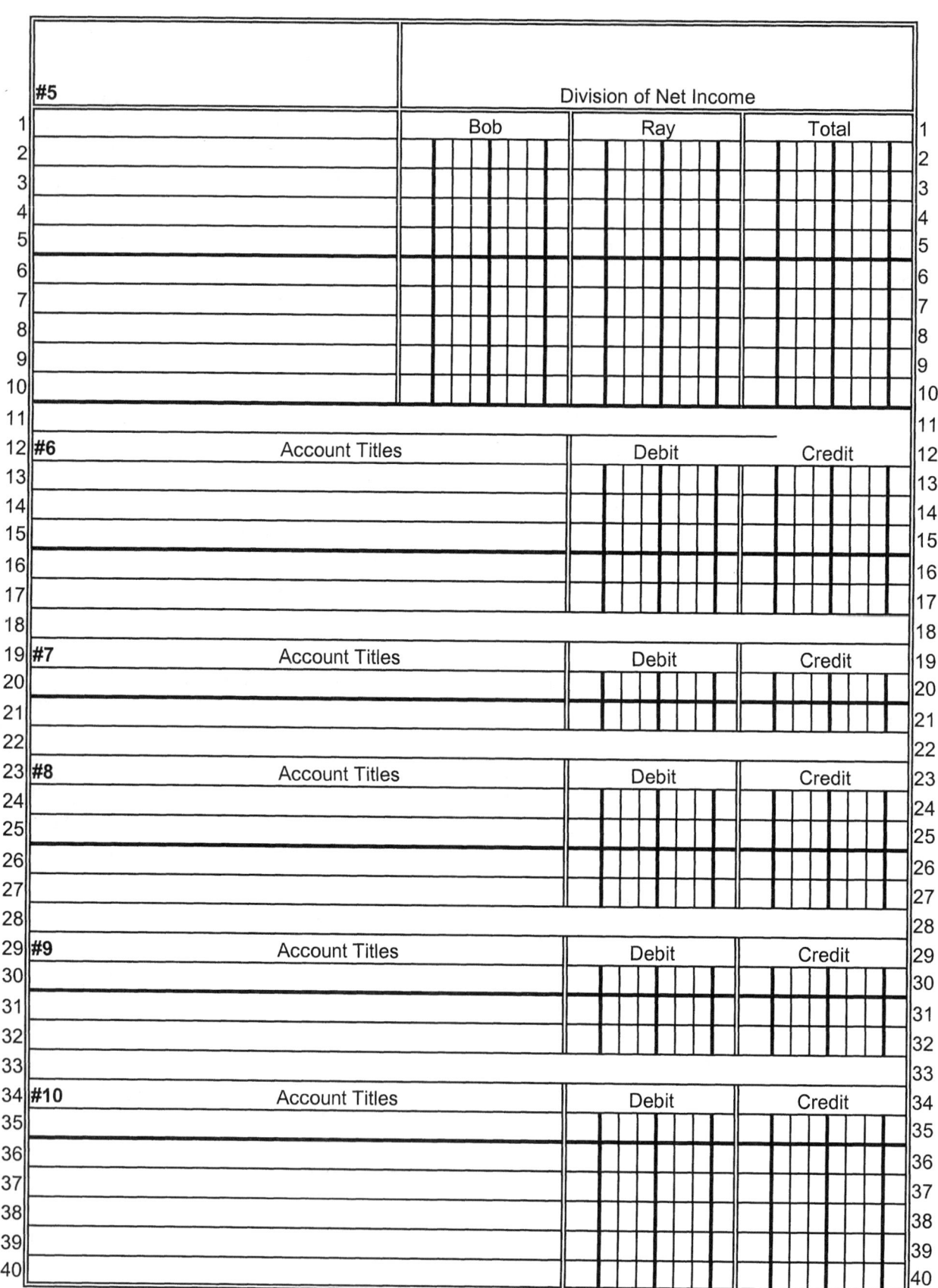

#5	Division of Net Income		
	Bob	Ray	Total

#6 Account Titles	Debit	Credit

#7 Account Titles	Debit	Credit

#8 Account Titles	Debit	Credit

#9 Account Titles	Debit	Credit

#10 Account Titles	Debit	Credit

#1

	Date	Account Titles	Debit	Credit	
1	Jan 1				1
2					2
3					3
4					4
5					5
6					6
7					7

#3 (a)

		D. Rowen	D. Martin	Total	
	Laugh In Co. Partners' Capital Statement For the Year Ended December 31, 2005				
1					1
2					2
3					3
4					4
5					5
6					6
7					7
8					8

(b)

	Laugh In Co. Partial Balance Sheet December 31, 2005			
1	Owner's Equity			1
2				2
3				3
4				4
5				5
6				6

(a)   DIVISION OF NET INCOME

	F. Astaire	G. Rogers	Total
(1) Net income is $55,000:			
(2) Net income is $30,000:			

(b)

Account Titles	Debit	Credit
(1) Net income is $55,000:		
(2) Net income is $30,000:		

The Ares Company
Schedule of Cash Payments

Item	Cash	Non-cash Assets	Liabilities	Cassandra Capital	Penelope Capital
1					
2					
3					
4					
5					
6					
7					
8					
9					
10					
11					
12					
13					
14					
15					
16					
17					
18					
19					
20					

#5

	Date	Account Titles	Debit	Credit	
1	(a)				1
2					2
3					3
4					4
5	(b)				5
6					6
7					7
8					8
9	(c)				9
10					10
11					11
12	(d)				12
13					13
14					14
15					15

#6

	Date	Account Titles	Debit	Credit	
1	(a) (1)				1
2					2
3					3
4					4
5	(2)				5
6					6
7					7
8					8
9	(b) (1)				9
10					10
11					11
12					12
13	(2)				13
14					14
15					15
16					16
17					17
18					18
19					19
20					20

#7

		Account Titles	Debit	Credit	
1	(a)				1
2					2
3					3
4	(b)				4
5					5
6					6
7	(c)				7
8					8
9					9
10					10

#9

		Account Titles	Debit	Credit	
1	1.				1
2					2
3					3
4					4
5					5
6	2.				6
7					7
8					8
9					9
10	3.				10
11					11
12					12
13					13
14					14
15					15

	Account Titles	Debit	Credit	
1	(a)			1
2				2
3				3
4				4
5				5
6				6
7				7
8				8
9				9
10				10
11				11
12				12
13				13
14				14
15				15
16	(b)			16
17				17
18				18
19				19
20				20
21				21
22				22
23				23
24				24
25				25
26				26
27				27
28				28
29				29
30				30
31				31
32				32
33				33
34				34
35				35
36				36
37				37
38				38
39				39
40				40

		Account Titles	Debit	Credit	
1	1.				1
2					2
3					3
4					4
5					5
6					6
7					7
8					8
9					9
10					10
11					11
12					12
13					13
14					14

		Account Titles	Debit	Credit	
15	2.				15
16					16
17					17
18					18
19					19
20					20
21					21
22					22
23					23
24					24
25					25
26					26
27					27
28					28
29					29
30					30
31					31

(a)

	Date	Account Titles	Debit	Credit	
1	Jan 1				1
2					2
3					3
4					4
5					5
6					6
7					7
8					8
9					9
10					10
11	1				11
12					12
13					13
14					14
15					15
16					16
17					17
18					18
19					19
20					20

(b)

	Date	Account Titles	Debit	Credit	
1	Jan 1				1
2					2
3					3
4					4
5					5
6	1				6
7					7
8					8
9					9
10					10

(c)

Blues Brothers Company		
Balance Sheet		
January 1, 2005		

	Assets		
1			
2			
3			
4			
5			
6			
7			
8			
9			
10			
11			
12			
13			
14			
15			
16	Liabilities and Owners' Equity		
17			
18			
19			
20			
21			
22			
23			
24			
25			
26			
27			
28			
29			
30			

(a)

	Date	Account Titles	Debit	Credit	
1	(1)				1
2					2
3					3
4					4
5					5
6					6
7	(2)				7
8					8
9					9
10					10
11					11
12					12
13					13
14					14
15					15
16					16
17					17
18					18
19					19
20					20
21	(3)				21
22					22
23					23
24					24
25					25
26					26
27					27
28					28
29					29
30					30
31					31
32					32
33					33
34					34
35					35
36					36
37					37
38					38
39					39
40					40

(b)

BBB Company			
Division of Net Income			
	J. Bach	L. Beethovan	J. Brahms	Total

	J. Bach	L. Beethovan	J. Brahms	Total
1				
2				
3				
4				
5				
6				
7				
8				
9				
10				
11				
12				
13				
14				
15				
16				
17				
18				
19				
20				

(c)

BBB Company			
Partners' Capital Statement			
For the Year Ended December 31, 2005			
	J. Bach	L. Beethovan	J. Brahms	Total

	J. Bach	L. Beethovan	J. Brahms	Total
1				
2				
3				
4				
5				
6				
7				
8				
9				
10				

Musical Company

Schedule of Cash Payments

Item	Cash	Non-cash Assets	Liabilities	Rogers Capital	Hammerstein Capital	Hart Capital
1						
2						
3						
4						
5						
6						
7						
8						
9						
10						
11						
12						
13						
14						
15						
16						
17						
18						
19						
20						

(b)

Date	Account Titles and Explanation	Debit	Credit
	(1)		
	(2)		
	(3)		
	(4)		

(b)

Cash				Rogers, Capital	
4/30 Bal 28,000				4/30 Bal 25,000

Hammerstein, Capital				Hart, Capital	
	4/30 Bal 11,200			4/30 Bal 4,800

(a)

	Account Titles	Debit	Credit	
1	(1)			1
2				2
3				3
4	(2)			4
5				5
6				6
7	(3)			7
8				8
9				9
10				10
11				11
12				12
13				13
14				14
15				15
16				16
17				17
18				18
19				19
20				20
21				21
22				22
23				23
24	(4)			24
25				25
26				26
27				27
28				28
29				29
30				30
31				31
32				32
33				33
34				34
35				35
36				36
37				37
38				38
39				39
40				40

1	(b)							1
2								2
3	(1)							3
4								4
5								5
6								6
7								7
8								8
9								9
10	(2)							10
11								11
12								12
13								13
14								14
15								15
16								16
17								17
18								18
19								19
20								20

Section

Date

(a)

		Account Titles	Debit	Credit	
1	(1)				1
2					2
3					3
4					4
5	(2)				5
6					6
7					7
8	(3)				8
9					9
10					10
11					11
12					12
13					13
14					14
15					15
16					16
17	(4)				17
18					18
19					19
20					20
21					21
22					22
23					23
24					24
25					25
26	(b) (1)				26
27					27
28					28
29					29
30					30
31					31
32					32
33					33
34	(2)				34
35					35
36					36
37					37
38					38
39					39
40					40

(a)

	Date	Account Titles	Debit	Credit	
1	Jan 1				1
2					2
3					3
4					4
5					5
6					6
7					7
8					8
9					9
10					10
11	1				11
12					12
13					13
14					14
15					15
16					16
17					17
18					18
19					19
20					20

(b)

	Date	Account Titles	Debit	Credit	
1	Jan 1				1
2					2
3					3
4					4
5					5
6	1				6
7					7
8					8
9					9
10					10

(c)

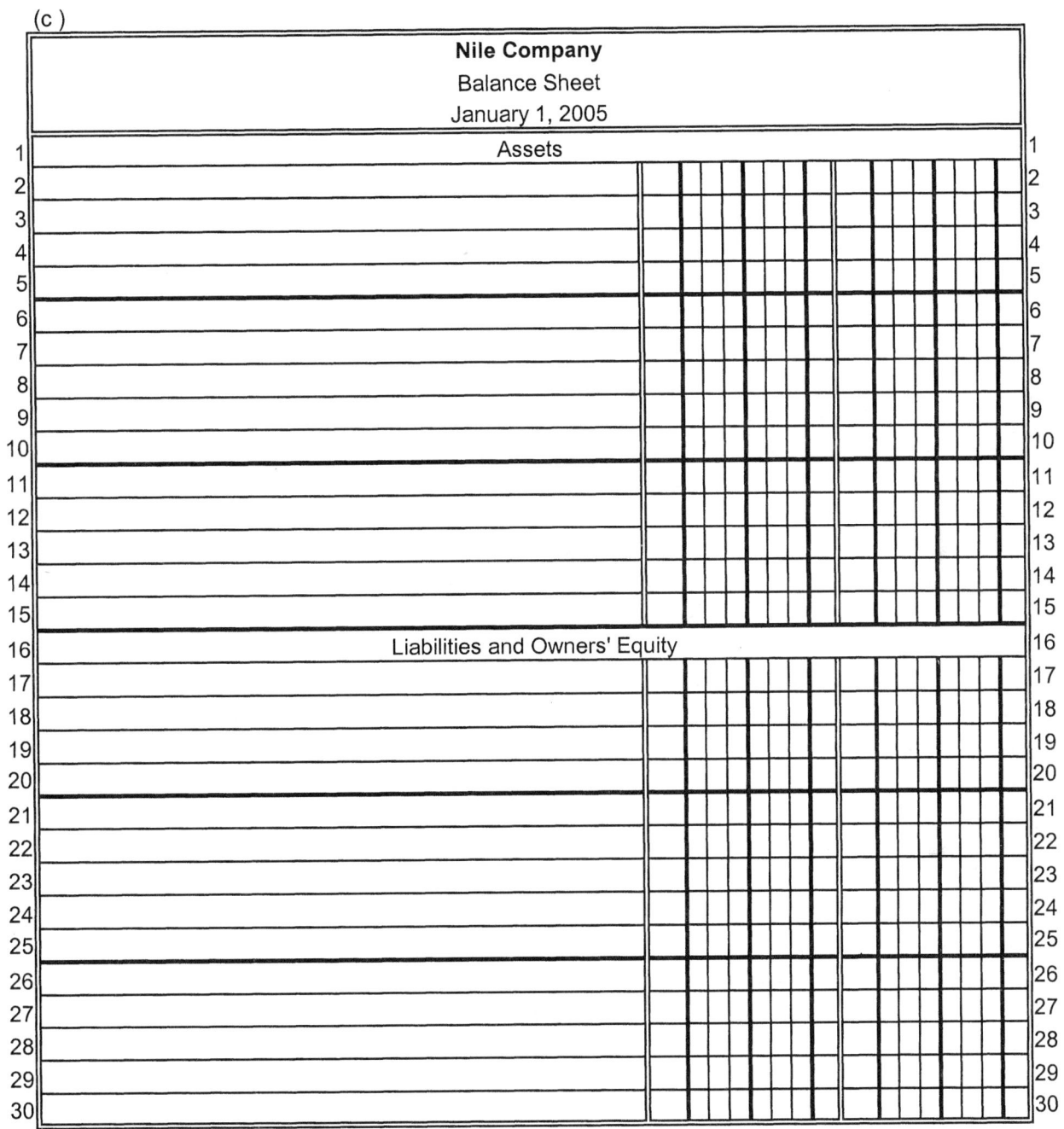

Nile Company

Balance Sheet

January 1, 2005

Assets

Liabilities and Owners' Equity

(a)

Date	Account Titles	Debit	Credit
(1)			
(2)			
(3)			

(b)

Tara Company				
Division of Net Income				
	Rhett Butler	Scarlet O'Hara	Ashley Wilkes	Total
1				
2				
3				
4				
5				
6				
7				
8				
9				
10				
11				
12				
13				
14				
15				
16				
17				
18				
19				
20				

(c)

Tara Company				
Partners' Capital Statement				
For the Year Ended December 31, 2005				
	Rhett Butler	Scarlet O'Hara	Ashley Wilkes	Total
1				
2				
3				
4				
5				
6				
7				
8				
9				
10				

(a)

	Date	Account Titles and Explanation	Debit	Credit	
1		(1)			1
2					2
3					3
4					4
5					5
6					6
7					7
8					8
9					9
10					10
11					11
12					12
13					13
14					14
15		(2)			15
16					16
17					17
18					18
19					19
20					20
21		(3)			21
22					22
23					23
24					24
25					25
26					26
27		(4)			27
28					28
29					29
30					30
31		(5)			31
32					32
33					33
34					34
35					35
36					36
37					37
38					38
39					39
40					40

(b)

CASH				B. CROSBY, CAPITAL		
Bal	27,500				Bal.	33,000

B. HOPE, CAPITAL				D. LAMOUR, CAPITAL		
	Bal	21,000			Bal.	3,200

(c)

	Account Titles	Debit	Credit	
1	(1)			1
2				2
3				3
4				4
5				5
6	(2)			6
7				7
8				8
9				9
10				10
11				11
12				12
13				13
14				14
15				15
16				16
17				17
18				18
19				19

(a)

		Account Titles	Debit	Credit	
1	(1)				1
2					2
3					3
4	(2)				4
5					5
6					6
7	(3)				7
8					8
9					9
10					10
11					11
12					12
13					13
14					14
15					15
16					16
17					17
18					18
19					19
20					20
21					21
22					22
23					23
24	(4)				24
25					25
26					26
27					27
28					28
29					29
30					30
31					31
32					32
33					33
34					34
35					35
36					36
37					37
38					38
39					39
40					40

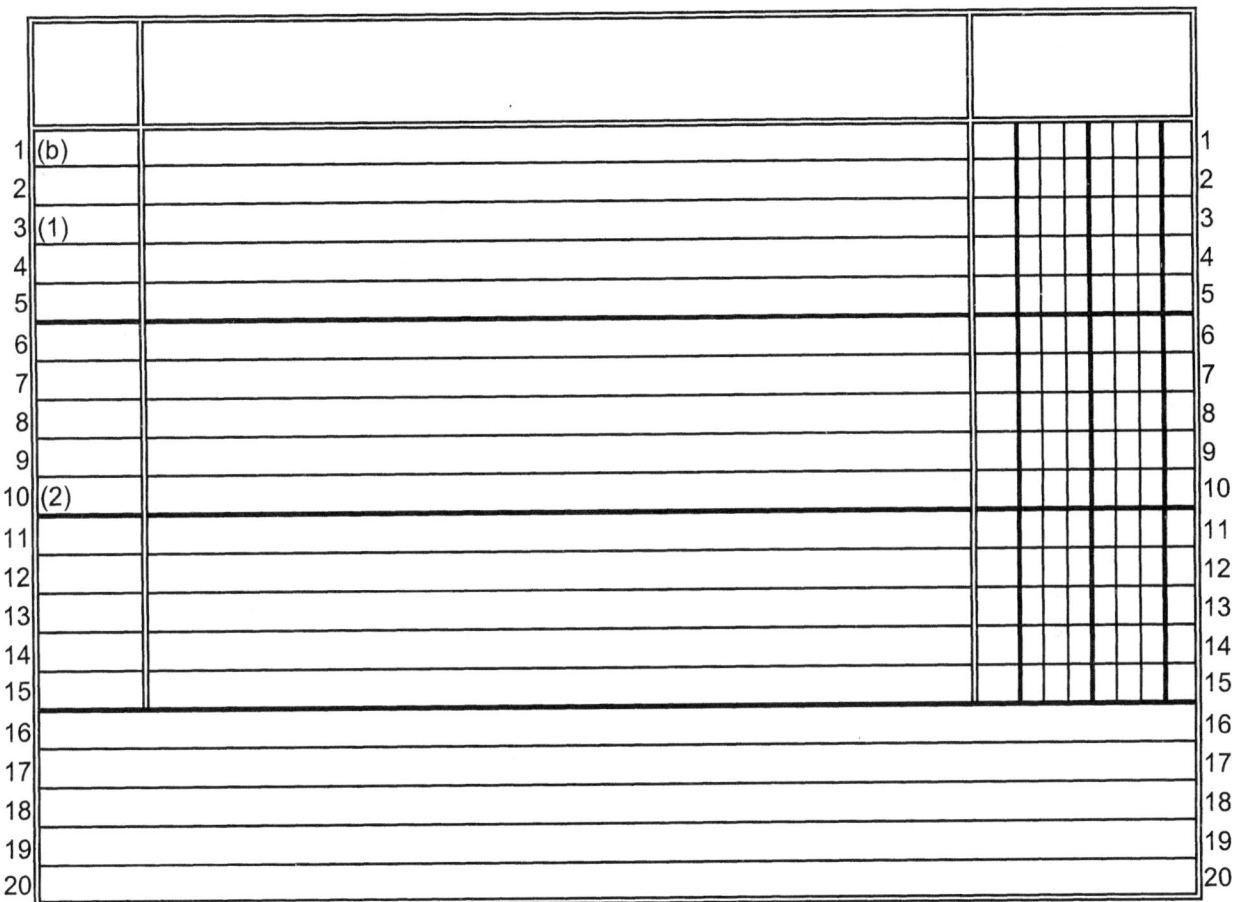

(a)

		Account Titles	Debit	Credit	
1	(1)				1
2					2
3					3
4					4
5	(2)				5
6					6
7					7
8	(3)				8
9					9
10					10
11					11
12					12
13					13
14					14
15					15
16					16
17	(4)				17
18					18
19					19
20					20
21					21
22					22
23					23
24					24
25					25
26	(b) (1)				26
27					27
28					28
29					29
30					30
31					31
32					32
33					33
34	(2)				34
35					35
36					36
37					37
38					38
39					39
40					40

(a)

(b)

(c)

(d)

Name

Section

Date

(e)

	1		1
	2		2
	3		3
	4		4
	5		5
	6		6
	7		7
	8		8
	9		9
	10		10
	11		11
	12		12
	13		13
	14		14
	15		15
	16		16
	17		17
	18		18
	19		19
	20		20
	21		21
	22		22
	23		23
	24		24
	25		25
	26		26
	27		27
	28		28
	29		29
	30		30
	31		31
	32		32
	33		33
	34		34
	35		35
	36		36
	37		37
	38		38
	39		39
	40		40

1	1
2	2
3	3
4	4
5	5
6	6
7	7
8	8
9	9
10	10
11	11
12	12
13	13
14	14
15	15
16	16
17	17
18	18
19	19
20	20
21	21
22	22
23	23
24	24
25	25
26	26
27	27
28	28
29	29
30	30
31	31
32	32
33	33
34	34
35	35
36	36
37	37
38	38
39	39
40	40

(a)

(b)

(c)

NOTES

NOTES

NOTES

NOTES

NOTES

NOTES

NOTES

NOTES

NOTES

NOTES

NOTES

NOTES

NOTES